WOMEN IN THE SOVIET COUNTRYSIDE

WOMEN'S ROLES IN RURAL DEVELOPMENT IN THE SOVIET UNION

SOVIET AND EAST EUROPEAN STUDIES

Editorial Board

The National Association for Soviet and East European Studies exists for the purpose of promoting study and research on the social sciences as they relate to the Soviet Union and the countries of Eastern Europe. The Monograph Series is intended to promote the publication of works presenting substantial and original research in the economics, politics, sociology and modern history of the USSR and Eastern Europe.

SOVIET AND EAST EUROPEAN STUDIES

WOMEN IN THE SOVIET COUNTRYSIDE

Women's roles in rural development in the Soviet Union

SUSAN BRIDGER

*Honorary Research Fellow in Russian Studies,
University of Bradford*

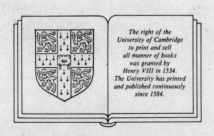

The right of the
University of Cambridge
to print and sell
all manner of books
was granted by
Henry VIII in 1534.
The University has printed
and published continuously
since 1584.

CAMBRIDGE UNIVERSITY PRESS

CAMBRIDGE

NEW YORK   NEW ROCHELLE   MELBOURNE   SYDNEY

Published by the Press Syndicate of the University of Cambridge
The Pitt Building, Trumpington Street, Cambridge CB2 1RP
32 East 57th Street, New York, NY 10022, USA
10 Stamford Road, Oakleigh, Melbourne 3166, Australia

First published 1987

Printed in Great Britain at the University Press, Cambridge

British Library cataloguing in publication data

Bridger, Susan.
Women in the Soviet countryside: women's
roles in rural development in the Soviet Union. –
(Soviet and East European studies)
1. Rural development – Soviet Union
2. Women – Soviet Union – Economic
conditions   3. Soviet Union – Economic conditions
I. Title   II. Series
330.9470854   HC336.25

Library of Congress cataloguing in publication data

Bridger, Susan.
Women in the Soviet countryside.
(Soviet and East European studies)
Bibliography.
Includes index.
1. Women in rural development – Soviet Union.
2. Rural women – Soviet Union.   3. Rural families – Soviet
Union.   4. Soviet Union – Rural conditions.   I. Title.
II. Series.
HQ1240.5.S65B75 1987   305.4'2'0947   87-11723

ISBN 0 521 32862 4

To My Parents

Contents

Figures

Tables

x

Acknowledgements

This book is based on research undertaken for a PhD at the University of Bradford. Over the course of the nine years in which it has slowly and sometimes painfully taken shape many people have combined to make it possible. First of all, my thanks must go to the staff of the Modern Languages Centre at the University of Bradford and especially to Professor James Riordan for his invaluable advice and encouragement which has guided this work from the very beginning. Grateful thanks are also due to Alastair McAuley of the University of Essex for his most constructive and helpful criticism of the PhD thesis. During a research visit to the USSR in 1980–1 I greatly benefited from access to material and meetings with Soviet specialists arranged by Professor Nikolai Grigor'evich Yurkevich and his staff at the Sociological Research Laboratory of the Belorussian State University. I am particularly indebted to my Soviet research supervisor, Vladimir Olegovich Rukavishnikov, and the staff of his department for their tireless efforts on my behalf. Needless to say, the views expressed in this book, together with the inevitable errors and omissions, are entirely my own responsibility.

I owe a special debt of gratitude to four women without whom this book would probably not have been written. Linda McLeod, Maggie Moore, Maggie McAndrew and Terry McKivett have shared with me many of the pleasures and frustrations of Russian studies both in this country and in the USSR. Intermittent conversations with them all over the last seven years have always provided me with a shot in the arm whenever my enthusiasm has flagged. I am especially grateful to Linda and Maggie Moore for their warmth and their unfailing sense of humour through what was, at times, a rather grim Russian winter.

I should like to express my appreciation to Kate Wheeldon who first taught me Russian and shared with me her love of the language and culture. My thanks are also due to Rachel Putz, Jenni Bloom and Alison Ridler for their friendship and good humour through a particularly difficult time.

The final draft of this book was produced with the help of Lee Lane's rapid and efficient typing and Moya Attrill's comments on the introduction. A large measure of personal thanks is due to my closest relatives and friends who have borne with me through what must have seemed an interminable piece of work. Most of all my thanks must go to my husband, Alan, and to my parents, Joyce and Frank Allott, for their constant encouragement, support and unwavering faith in my ability to complete this book. Special thanks are due to my father for re-drawing the cartoons.

Finally, I owe a great deal to the women of Belorussia, who must perforce remain anonymous, who offered me their hospitality and allowed me a brief but fascinating glimpse into their world.

Bradford　　　　　　　　　　　　　　　　　SUE BRIDGER
October 1986

Notes for readers

ASSR   (Avtonomnaya Sovetskaya Sotsialisticheskaya Respublika) Autonomous Republic. Title given to twenty areas of the USSR with significant ethnic minority populations.

delegatka   (Plural: *delegatki*) Woman delegate elected at and responsible to 'delegate meetings' set up by the Zhenotdel in the 1920s as a form of primary political organisation for women.

kalym   Bride price paid by husband to bride's family in Central Asia.

kolkhoz   Collective farm.

Komsomol   (VLKSM) All-Union Leninist Communist Union of Youth. The youth arm of the Communist Party, open to young people aged fourteen to twenty-eight.

RSFSR   (Rossiiskaya Sovetskaya Federativnaya Sotsialisticheskaya Respublika) Russian Soviet Federated Socialist Republic. Largest of the fifteen Union republics of the USSR.

shariat   Islamic law.

sovkhoz   State farm.

Zhenotdel   (*zhenskii otdel*) Women's Department of the Central Committee Secretariat. Party organ leading political work with women 1919–29.

Readers should note that Soviet statistics on rural women are somewhat limited. Data from the early 1970s have been used where, in the author's opinion, they represent the best available information.

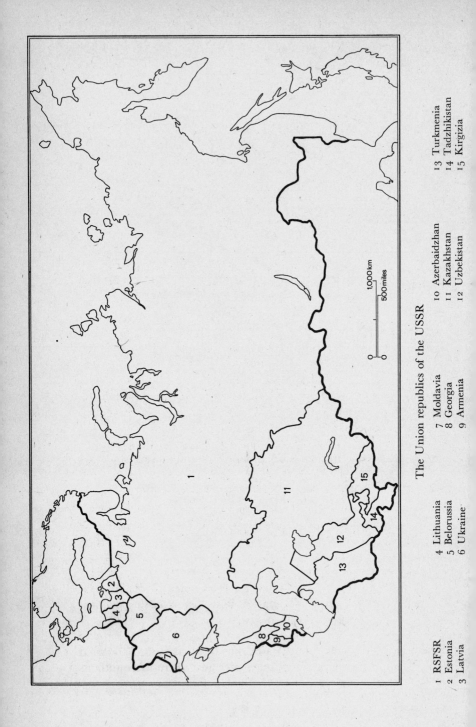

The Union republics of the USSR

1 RSFSR
2 Estonia
3 Latvia

4 Lithuania
5 Belorussia
6 Ukraine

7 Moldavia
8 Georgia
9 Armenia

10 Azerbaidzhan
11 Kazakhstan
12 Uzbekistan

13 Turkmenia
14 Tadzhikistan
15 Kirgizia

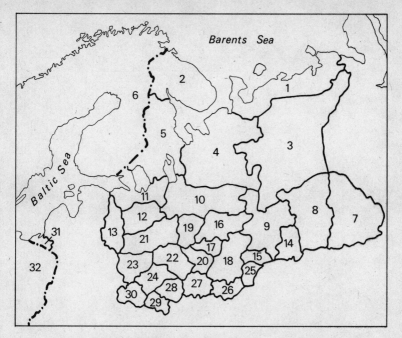

The Non-Black Earth Zone of the RSFSR

1 Nenets Autonomous Area
2 Murmansk
3 Komi ASSR
4 Arkhangel'sk
5 Karélia ASSR
6 Finland
7 Sverdlovsk
8 Perm'
9 Kirov
10 Vologda
11 Leningrad
12 Novgorod
13 Pskov
14 Udmurt ASSR
15 Mari ASSR
16 Kostroma
17 Ivanovo
18 Gorky
19 Yaroslavl'
20 Vladimir
21 Kalinin
22 Moscow
23 Smolensk
24 Kaluga
25 Chuvash ASSR
26 Mordovia ASSR
27 Ryazan'
28 Tula
29 Orel
30 Bryansk
31 Kaliningrad
32 Poland

Introduction

Over the last quarter of a century, issues of development have been consistently brought to world attention, not least by the United Nations' Development Decades. The prime aim of these Decades has been to increase the rate of economic growth of the world's developing countries. This has been accompanied, since 1970, by a greater emphasis on aid from the richer countries to the developing world.

During this period, annual growth rates have indeed accelerated in developing countries. At the same time, however, they have ceased to be self-sufficient in food. As the production of cash crops for export and the development of urban-based industry has become ever more widespread, the production of basic foodstuffs to meet local needs has declined. By the end of the second Decade, 10% of the Third World's total consumption of food grains was imported. In many countries of Africa, Asia and South America the poor now form a greater proportion of the population than they did at the beginning of the sixties.[1]

As the local effects of this pattern of development started to emerge by the beginning of the second Development Decade, women researchers began to point out the particularly distressing consequences for Third World women. Women form the majority of the world's food producers – 60% to 80% of agricultural workers in Africa and Asia[2] – yet their huge contribution, these writers observed, was consistently ignored by development planners. Ester Boserup in her pioneering book, *Women's Role in Economic Development*, demonstrated that, far from directing development programmes towards the women with prime responsibility for food production, planners directed agricultural improvement projects almost entirely towards men.

I

Development planners and government officials alike concentrated on commercial agriculture and the production of cash crops for export using predominantly male wage-labour. The subsistence farming engaged in by women, which fed the rural population, was neglected by development programmes.[3]

The result has often been to make rural women worse off than they were before the development process began. With the emphasis on cash-cropping, commercial cultivation has tended to monopolise the best land. In consequence, women have often been obliged to work smaller plots with poorer soil than before. Where men have been drawn into commercial agriculture, they are less likely to help with subsistence farming in tasks such as clearing land. Women's work may therefore become both harder and less productive. At the same time, men's involvement in commercial agriculture does not automatically confer material benefits on their families. Research has shown not only that agricultural wage rates are often low but also that men may choose to spend their cash income on consumer goods and alcohol. This, together with declining productivity in subsistence farming, may actually cause the nutritional levels within the family to fall.[4]

When agricultural improvement projects and, especially, technology are introduced into rural areas they have often been found to depress rather than enhance female status. Women are rarely given training in the new skills which technological change demands. When mechanisation is introduced to undertake tasks which women previously performed as wage-labourers, they are deprived of an important source of income: 'observers of the development scene are increasingly concerned that where technology frees women from time-consuming, arduous or unproductive tasks there are no viable alternative forms of productive work for them'.[5] The advent of technology, therefore, may contribute to the marginalisation and impoverishment of rural women. Certainly, where women are not recruited into mechanised work, the waged manual labour which remains open to them is likely to have an increasingly diminished status. The tiring and monotonous work which women perform in subsistence farming and domestic labour has not been significantly lightened by new technologies.[6]

Rural women's enormous, unwaged contribution to food production, domestic labour and child care has remained largely unrecognised or undervalued both by their own communities and by development planners. Despite the Development Decades, Zubeida

Ahmad of the International Labour Office, writing in 1980, was still able to describe the majority of rural women in developing countries in the following words:

It has been estimated that rural women's actual daily working hours can be as high as fifteen to sixteen, often considerably more than those of men. They suffer from a double burden of exploitation: along with their menfolk, as part of the rural poor; and, in addition, as members of the female sex. In many parts of the world, from the time they are born, rural women are given a minimum of medical care, less than their fair share of the family's food and an inferior education . . . and have to put up with poor working conditions, including lower wages, for tasks involving hard, physical labour. Finally, women are seldom considered in the planning of rural development projects, with the consequence that modernisation has often had a negative impact on women.[7]

Since the early 1970s, a solution to this state of affairs favoured and promoted by women writers on development issues has been the 'integration of women into development'. The view has become current that if women's needs and interests are taken into account during the process of development, benefits will accrue not only to women as individuals but also to their communities and countries: 'women must be integrated into the process of rural development not only because simple justice demands that it be done, but also because excluding women means under-utilising a high potential resource, and this can eventually have adverse effects on the economic growth rate'.[8]

As a result, governments and agencies which have come to recognise the neglect of women by development planners have added special women's schemes to existing development programmes. Income-generating projects have been set up for women in handicrafts and rural industries as well as in the sphere of agriculture, and women have been recruited into development agencies.

Initiatives of this kind, especially income-generating projects, have, however, been criticised by some writers on women and development for what is seen as their failure to recognise women's key role in the rural economy. By emphasising the generation of cash income, it is argued, the undervaluing of unwaged agricultural work, and especially of domestic labour, is merely reinforced. As Hanna Papanek, writing on development planning in 1977, observed:

A curious ambiguity in the concept of integrating women in the development process hampers the achievement of this goal from the start. For women *are* full participants in all processes of social change, in spite of the fact that they may be affected differently than men. However, these differences often serve to confirm the notion that women are less central to major social processes than men. In turn, this misperception leads many to assume that women are a backward sector of society that need to be 'integrated' in order to be 'modernised'. This false and patronising view is not a good basis for development policies. At the same time, women have, of course, been excluded from the development process in a political and technical sense. They have not participated in the decisions that affect both sexes. Where women must be integrated in development is development planning – the process by which many governments seek to advance the growth and distribution of available resources.[9]

Other feminist writers have taken this argument a stage further. The problem is not simply that policy-makers fail to recognise the current productivity of rural women, or that drawing women into the market economy through home industries may lead to greater exploitation. Nor would the solution simply be greater female involvement in planning, they maintain. The question untouched by much of the literature is seen as far more fundamental and concerns the nature of the development process itself. These writers question whether women really have a great deal to gain from a model of development which involves integrating developing countries into the international market system:

The solution cannot lie in simply 'extending the benefits of modernisation' to women. Modernisation does not benefit the majority of men either, when it is tied to an economic system in which certain countries of the world exploit others, and certain classes within a country profit from the exploitation of both men and women. To be of benefit to women, modernisation would have to be adapted to the needs of women for both production and reproduction, not women to the needs of modernisation, as is usually the case.[10]

There is little evidence, it is argued, that the development of national economies of itself improves the position of women. As women in the developed world predominate in low-skilled, low-paid work, carry the burden of domestic labour and child care and have a subordinate role in their societies, 'this is not a model of development, or of the integration of women into development, that one would care to commend to other countries'.[11]

Genuine development which embraces concepts of equity and justice cannot, in the view of such writers, take place as long as half the world's population is overburdened with work which is undervalued and viewed as marginal to economic development. As Anita Anand has pointed out:

Even to this day, the most ardent proponents of integrating women into development have not realised that neither mainstream nor Marxist models have room for women, as neither group has addressed the problem of patriarchy. Society's acceptance of male domination has pervaded development work. Though much lip service has been paid to the equal participation of women in the male-dominated development circles, this has remained by and large 'integration' without much thought or attempt towards genuine power sharing with women.[12]

As this comment suggests, feminist writers who are critical of the capitalist model of development do not necessarily regard a socialist alternative as desirable for women. The governments of developing countries which espouse socialist doctrine do, however, declare a formal commitment to the principle of sexual equality. Their policies are based largely on the orthodox communist position on women as it was developed by the Communist International after 1917 from the writings of Marx, Engels and Lenin.[13] Developing countries which are closely linked and in varying degrees dependent on the USSR are, however, subject to its influence not simply on the issue of women's emancipation. In their development strategies too, these countries are likely to follow the lead of the USSR. Through their work in the rural economy, women have made an enormous contribution to the modernisation of the Soviet Union. It is the intention of this study to analyse whether the Soviet model of development has been able to promote sexual equality and to avoid the marginalisation of rural women which continues to beset developing countries under capitalism.

RURAL WOMEN IN THE DEVELOPMENT OF THE USSR

As the largest political unit in the world, the Soviet Union covers approximately one sixth of the land surface of the earth. Three-quarters of the USSR lies north of the 50th parallel. This fact, coupled with the predominantly low-lying nature of the country and the great distance of most of its territory from the sea, means that the majority of the Soviet Union is characterised by great extremes of temperature and low rainfall. As a result of both climatic conditions and the predominance of poor quality soils, much of the USSR is highly unfavourable for agriculture. The majority of the areas in which agriculture is concentrated have a short growing season and, hence, acutely seasonal patterns of employment for the rural workforce.

In 1913, the total population of the Russian Empire numbered some 166 million: just under 10% lived in Turkestan and Transcaucasia whilst a further 8% lived in Siberia and provinces which now form part of Kazakhstan.[14] In 1917 the Bolsheviks came to power in a land with an extremely complex ethnic composition. At late as 1970 the Soviet census listed no fewer than 104 national groups resident in the USSR. In addition to their linguistic, cultural and religious differences, the varying historical backgrounds of these nationalities presented the revolutionary government with a population displaying differing, and in many cases pre-capitalist, stages of development. The Russian Empire was an overwhelmingly peasant land. In 1913, 81% of the population lived in rural areas, whilst industry employed a total of less than four million people.[15]

Peasant women in Imperial Russia

In nineteenth-century Russia both rural landowners and peasant communes, the governing institutions of the village, recognised the peasant family as an indivisible unit. Male authority within the family was enshrined in both custom and law which vested in the head of the household almost all property rights and control over inheritance. Tradition continually reinforced women's subordination. 'A crab is not a fish – a woman is not a person', ran the proverb which succinctly summarised peasant attitudes.

Most peasant families adhered to a strict division of labour between the sexes. As a general rule, women had sole charge of the production of vegetables and the care of poultry and dairy cows. The division of labour characteristic of Belorussia in the 1890s is illustrative of the way in which fieldwork was apportioned throughout the year. In this region, men took charge of ploughing, sowing, harrowing, the mowing and carting of hay, threshing in autumn and the care of cattle in winter. The women would till, sow and weed the vegetable garden and also weed flax and potatoes. Later in the year they would pull flax, gather hemp, lift potatoes and harvest grain. In large families this pattern of work would be rigidly adhered to, yet in smaller families where labour was insufficient it was 'not unusual to meet a girl who could mow, thresh and plough really well'.[16]

The agricultural work which women performed was undertaken in addition to their responsibilities in the home. Women alone cooked the family's food, fetched all the water, sewed and washed clothes and converted the fruits of the family's land into cloth and food products. The major domestic responsibility of the men was chopping wood for use as fuel. During the winter months when fieldwork was impossible, women were regularly involved in the domestic production of articles for sale, particularly textiles.

Contemporary observers of the extended peasant family invariably described it as hierarchical, patriarchal and authoritarian. Peasant marriages were usually arranged. As a newcomer to her husband's family, a bride came under the authority of the older women as well as the men. Regular pregnancies were considered an inevitable consequence of marriage and high rates of infant mortality and miscarriage, rather than contraception or abortion, limited family size. Legal divorce was costly and rare amongst the peasantry. Separations, sanctioned by local peasant courts, were more common, though the economic consequences for women without land rights were enough to dissuade most women from taking such a step: 'It is bad with a husband, twice as bad without him', ran a saying current amongst women in the villages.[17]

Such public services as existed in pre-Revolutionary Russia were largely concentrated in the towns. Doctors were so few that villagers usually relied on traditional herbalists for treatment. Primary education was far from universal by the outbreak of the First World War and only one in eight women under the age of fifty could read.[18] For most women in rural Russia, unwaged work in the home and on the family's land was the dominant feature of their lives.

Socialist theory on the woman question

Commitment to sexual equality became a declared policy of Russian Social Democrats in 1903, when, at the Second Congress of the Party, the programme was extended on Lenin's initiative to include demands for equality in education and in civil and political rights.[19] Socialist theory on the woman question, on which these demands were based, had first been expounded by Marx and Engels in the Communist Manifesto of 1848, and subsequently developed by the German Marxist, August Bebel, in his *Woman and Socialism* of 1879, and by Engels himself five years later in *The Origin of the Family, Private Property and the State*. By 1917 further contributions to the debate had been made not only by European Marxists but also by Russian socialist women, notably Nadezhda Krupskaya in her pamphlet *The Woman Worker* of 1901 and Alexandra Kollontai in her 1909 *Social Bases of the Woman Question*.

For all these writers the solution to the problem of sexual inequality lay in the abolition of capitalism. The phenomena of oppression and exploitation were seen as the essential superstructural reflection of the economic base of capitalist society. It was thus inevitable that in a society based on private property women would be oppressed. With the overthrow of capitalism and the establishment of socialist production relationships, human relationships would be unbounded by economic necessity and all exploitation would cease. For Engels, the oppression suffered by women was a function of their exclusion from public production and their confinement to private production and reproduction within the family. Within the context of the bourgeois family, he argued, women were reduced to domestic slaves whilst their husbands held exclusive power conferred by their economically dominant position. 'In the family', he wrote, '[the husband] is the bourgeois, the wife represents the proletariat.'[20] Women's inferior status in society was thus a consequence of their dependence on men within the family. The family itself was seen as a social institution whose relationships were determined not by biology but by economics. Under capitalism the family was the repository of private property 'for the safeguarding and inheritance of which monogamy and male domination were established'.[21]

Under socialism, therefore, as the means of production passed into common ownership, women would gain equal access to economic, social and political activities, private housekeeping would be transformed into a social industry and child care would become a public affair. 'The emancipation of women', Engels stated, 'becomes possible only when women are enabled to take part in production on a large, social scale, and when domestic duties require their attention only to a minor degree.'[22] As property was seen as the exclusive definer of personal relationships, then the absence of private property under socialism would result in a profound change in the quality of relationships between men and women. The domination of women by their husbands, Engels believed, would simply vanish as male economic predominance disappeared. With full economic equality, he argued, there would be no basis for marriage other than 'individual sex love' which, being by nature exclusive, would result in a new and higher form of monogamy. Under socialism, 'monogamy, instead of declining, finally becomes a reality'.[23] This view of sexual relationships expounded by Engels formed the basis of Russian Marxist thought on the question. Yet only Alexandra Kollontai in her much criticised and misunderstood writings of the early twenties was to appreciate how complex were questions of personal relationships and to attempt a more sophisticated analysis of the relationship between love, sex and social change.[24]

The Bolsheviks and the Russian peasantry

The 1917 Decree on Land provided for all land to 'be taken over without compensation and become the property of the whole people, to be used by those who cultivate it'.[25] For the Bolsheviks the Decree marked the first of many attempts to come to terms with the essential paradox of their position. Having seized power with the support of a sector of the relatively tiny urban working class, they were obliged to consolidate their gains in a predominantly peasant country. The troubled relationship between the Bolsheviks and the peasantry in the 1920s was characterised by alternating government attempts at appeasement and coercion

Compulsory requisitioning of grain during the Civil War was replaced in 1921 by a system of progressive taxation under the New Economic Policy. The aim was to feed urban workers and develop industrial production. As the expected world socialist revolution failed to materialise, the Bolsheviks viewed industrial development as a matter of urgency. Instead of the hoped-for international support for socialist construction in Russia, the country faced economic and political isolation. In these circumstances, the capital needed for industrial development had to be found from domestic sources and, initially, this meant from the peasantry.

The period of national emergency during the Civil War caused both economic collapse and enormous social upheaval. In consequence, the Bolsheviks faced immense practical difficulties in attempting to implement Marxist policies on sexual equality. The reintroduction of market forces into the economy in 1921 had an adverse effect on female employment. At the same time, giving priority to industrial development severely limited social welfare programmes. The emancipation of women by the accepted Marxist route of their mass introduction into public production and the socialisation of domestic labour and child care therefore became the subject of much rhetoric but little action. Legislative change and political mobilisation became prime instruments in the revolutionary transformation of female roles and status attempted during the first decade of Soviet rule.

Women were seen by the Bolsheviks as indispensable participants in the social revolution needed to produce the future socialist state. In transforming their own lives, it was believed, women would significantly weaken the influence of traditional authority and provide a means by which new cultural values might be established. The political mobilisation of rural women, therefore, had a twofold aim: to lay the foundation for female emancipation in the countryside and, secondly, but of no less importance, to give the Party a foothold in the hostile peasant world.

The impact of the Revolution 1917–29

In 1919 the Women's Department of the Central Committee Secretariat (Zhenotdel) was established as an official Party organ to direct systematic work amongst women. It founded a network of local women's departments staffed by Party members and volunteers. In order to draw women into public life, the Zhenotdel devised a system of 'delegate meetings' which operated in both town and country throughout the 1920s. Local women's organisers would arrange meetings of working or peasant women at which one of their number would be elected as a delegate (*delegatka*) to the Zhenotdel for between three and six months. The elected *delegatka* would then become an observer or trainee worker in a local Soviet, trade union, school or other public service body from which she would report back before ceding her place to one of her peers. Meetings of delegates were to be held twice a month to allow them to share their experiences and hear lectures on Soviet government, the position of women, hygiene or co-operatives.

Over a million peasant women became *delegatki* during the mid-1920s, yet they represented only a tiny minority of the rural female population. For most peasant women, the role of delegate was alien and demanding and its possible benefits were far from clear. Women who had been keen to become delegates would often give up the work on discovering that it conferred no special privileges. There was an understandable reluctance on the part of village women to add a further thankless task to their already overburdened lives. The lack of comprehension of rural life demonstrated by the leaders of this urban-inspired movement was criticised by rural sociologists of the time: 'It is essential to learn to respect the peasant women's time and consider her position in the family . . . Only then will we avoid such failures as when we deliver her a lecture on "Lenin and the Peasant Woman" and do not see that under our very noses there is not a single girl at school.'[26] Nevertheless, such growth as took place in the participation of peasant women in local Soviets and co-operatives during the 1920s owed much to Zhenotdel influence.

The communes and co-operatives which sprang up after the Revolution were not systematically organised until the late 1920s. Their contribution under the New Economic Policy was insignificant, involving around 1% of peasant households. Even in those which flourished, however, women had little influence. As the household, rather than the individual, was the usual unit of membership, men normally became households' representatives in the collective.[27] The 1922 Land Code provided protection for pregnant women and introduced maternity leave for agricultural labourers. Problems of enforcement, however, meant that few women felt the effects of the new law. Women wage-labourers now preferred to seek work on state farms, where these existed, as pay was better than on individual peasant farms. Yet in government enterprises, as in private farming, the concept of equal pay for equal work remained alien to the rural community.[28]

For most women in the countryside the patterns of work developed during the nineteenth century changed little in the 1920s. The family's home and land continued to be the focus of most women's working lives and as such became for the first time the object of serious analysis by sociologists and economists. Their observations paint a vivid picture, not only of how universal was the burden of domestic work on women, but also of how totally dependent on female labour was the running of the peasant household. Only in fetching water, preparing fuel and home maintenance did peasant men make any significant contribution. As a result, women spent almost six times longer on domestic labour than did their menfolk.[29]

The abolition of the 'bourgeois' family was seen as an essential prerequisite for the construction of socialist society. Soon after the Revolution, civil marriage and free divorce were introduced and abortion was legalised. By the mid-twenties, it had become apparent that certain aspects of the 1918 Code were in need of reform. The ravages of war, epidemic and famine with the accompanying mass movements of population had led to the breakdown of many families. In the cities, if not in the countryside, casual sexual relationships had become common. Women in unregistered relationships were unprotected by existing law and their children often remained without support. At a time of high female unemployment, the abandonment of children by deserted women became increasingly frequent and gave rise to much public concern. The 1926 Family Law recognised 'common law' marriage and, in an attempt to make registered marriage more attractive, simplified divorce still further.

The Family Codes were considered by the Party to represent an enshrinement in law of the socialist belief in sexual equality. Yet, for the mass of the population of this peasant country the new laws appeared inappropriate, their sponsors uncomprehending of rural tradition or the needs of the peasant economy. Whilst the calculation of maintenance on divorce was relatively straightforward when the parties involved were urban wage-earners, in the conditions of subsistence farming by extended family groups the matter became notoriously complex. Rural opinion feared that the payment of maintenance would lead to the impoverishment of small peasant farms.[30] Some criticised the liberality of the divorce laws for their likely impact on rural women. Under the Land Code, an individual was obliged to contribute two years' labour to a household before gaining land rights. For women in short-lived marriages, divorce could therefore be disastrous. As one women activist expressed it, 'life under such conditions is terribly difficult. The result of it all is poverty, and we have too much of that as it is.'[31]

By comparison with the radical changes which took place in the cities, the political campaigns and legislative change of the 1920s had only a marginal impact on the lives of the majority of rural women. Yet the difficulties faced by the new regime in the countryside were such that change of any kind was extraordinarily difficult to effect. In this huge country with its poor communications and scattered communities, the weight of centuries of custom and tradition formed an often impenetrable barrier to attempts at rapid transformation. At the same time, the ideological commitment of the Bolsheviks to urban development and the consequent ambivalence of their policies towards the mass of Russia's population made for an atmosphere of suspicion and resentment in the countryside. Well aware of the scale of the problem, Zhenotdel leaders warned their activists that the old way of life would 'seize by the throat any attempt to fight it'.[32]

By 1928 the period of confrontation between Party and peasants had commenced and, as tension mounted in the countryside, there began a series of developments which were to have profound effects on the lives of rural women. For the peasants engaged in the family law debates of 1926 it could scarcely have been foreseen that within five years the burning issues of divorce and maintenance would lose their significance as the entire foundation of the rural economy was transformed.

Women in the collectives 1930–41

The 1st Five-Year Plan, inaugurated in 1928, provided for a strategy of industrial development on the basis of gradual and voluntary collectivisation of peasant farming. Yet the failure of the peasantry to deliver a sufficient quantity of grain to the towns in 1928 and 1929 threatened to place the entire programme in jeopardy. The alternatives of famine and unrest in the cities or further concessions to capitalist farming precipitated the Soviet government into a course of drastic action: wholesale collectivisation of agriculture and the expropriation of the prosperous peasants.

The immediate consequences of forced collectivisation were catastrophic. The effect on animal husbandry in particular was still in evidence in the mid-1950s; only then did livestock numbers once more reach pre-collectivisation levels.[33] In the longer term, the events of 1929–30 were significant in that they established the pattern of development of the Soviet economy under Stalin. Rapid industrial expansion, with an emphasis on investment in heavy industry, was to be the hallmark of these years. The political control over the peasantry gained through collectivisation allowed the government to procure an extremely large share of agricultural output to feed the urban population, as well as for export and, hence, for capital formation. In this situation, the rural economy continued to demand that rural dwellers provide much of their own subsistence from the private plots permitted them in the new collectives. For the peasants the effects of Stalin's policy were traumatic. Poverty drove millions to the cities, whilst for those who remained on the land the old order was completely shattered as the state extended its control into all areas of rural life.

The level of participation by women in the collective farms (kolkhozes) was highly variable. However, with the rapid expansion of industry during the decade, an estimated 18.5 million migrants, most of them men, moved from village to city. As a result, by 1939, women formed the majority of the agricultural workforce across the USSR; over 20 million women made up 58% of those employed on the land.[34]

Women, however, worked on the kolkhozes fewer days in the year and for shorter hours than men. The reason was to be found in their heavy involvement in subsistence farming and domestic labour which made their total working time considerably longer than that of men. As a result, both the pay and the status acquired by women in the collective farms were severely limited. Their unwaged work in private subsidiary agriculture, as it was known, which produced the equivalent of almost half the average kolkhoz family's income, had little recognition or prestige.[35] The production of vegetables and care of domestic livestock had always been viewed by the peasantry as an extension of women's housework. Such a view was unlikely to be challenged in a socialised system of agriculture where the continuation of private subsistence farming was regarded as a necessary evil.

The continuing responsibility of women for subsistence agriculture restricted their access to skilled work or managerial posts on the collective farms. Less than 3% of farm managers or leaders of field brigades were women.[36] With the widespread introduction of tractors and combines into Soviet agriculture during the decade the woman tractor driver, epitomised by the leader of their movement, Pasha Angelina, was promoted as a symbol of economic progress and sexual equality under socialism. Yet, in reality, only 8% of tractor and combine drivers were women, a minute proportion of the female agricultural workforce. Where technology was introduced it was placed firmly into the hands of men. Training women to operate machines was, from the first, justified as a 'strengthening of the home front' in the event of war. The early years of collectivisation did little to challenge the traditional division of labour on the land and, indeed, where technology was introduced, served largely to reinforce it. 'Female labour predominates', one observer remarked, 'in all types of manual work and work involving the old peasant implements.'[37]

In 1929 the Zhenotdel was abolished. Campaigns and political structures run by and for women came to be less concerned with specifically female interests. Instead, women were organised to meet the economic goals set for the nation by the Party. The mass entry of women into the socialised labour force became synonymous with female emancipation. The absence of a simultaneous socialisation of the domestic economy did not prevent the Soviet leadership from officially considering the woman question resolved. The delegate meetings of the 1920s were replaced by women's production conferences where rural women were mobilised for the major agricultural campaigns. In Central Asia, where women active in the campaign against female seclusion in the 1920s had been met with savage reprisals, the system of delegate meetings was continued. Yet here too the function of these bodies became predominantly economic.[38]

Despite increasing participation in village Soviets, very few women in the Soviet countryside of the 1930s held positions of political influence. As central control tightened, such women as were prominent in political activity were concerned exclusively with transmitting Party directives to the people of their locality and with translating into action the plans of the leadership. As the influence of the Party and Komsomol in the village grew, women were drawn into literacy, hygiene and anti-religious campaigns. By the end of the decade, the improvement in female education was impressive. Almost four-fifths of rural women under the age of fifty in the Russian Republic were literate by 1939. Four-year primary education became compulsory in 1931, the proportion of girls amongst rural pupils rising to 47% by 1935. In Central Asia, the increase in female education was spectacular. Over an eight-year period to 1935, the proportion of girls at school rose from 10% to 38%. Less than 4% of Soviet rural women had received secondary education by 1939.[39]

From the early 1930s, the Soviet media began to reflect the disapproving attitudes of many in the Party towards the irresponsibility which they felt had become the hallmark of personal relationships in the previous decade. In June 1936, family law was amended with the aim of 'combating light-minded attitudes towards the family and family obligations'.[40] The new law prohibited abortion except on the most serious medical grounds. At the same time, it offered increased child allowances, grants and improved employment protection to mothers. A scale of charges was introduced for divorce. The new law was accompanied by hymns of praise in the press to the joys of motherhood, yet it aimed at far more than boosting the birthrate and discouraging the sexual exploitation of women and abandonment of children. In reinstating the family as a fundamental institution of the Soviet state, the Party leadership sought to end what it saw as the nation's preoccupation with sexual adventures and develop a responsible society more fitted for the tasks of industrialisation.

For rural women, however, the main effect of the law was to increase illegal abortions.[41] The sexual revolution which had taken place in Soviet cities in the 1920s had had little effect on behaviour in the villages, even in European areas of the country. The reactionary policies of the thirties, therefore, applied a brake to the slow process of change within the rural family begun in the previous decade and allowed traditional attitudes towards women to continue unchallenged for many years to come.

War and reconstruction 1941–53

Within two years of the German invasion of the USSR, women formed three-quarters of the country's agricultural workforce. As men were mobilised and childless women directed into industry, construction or forestry, mothers were left with only elderly relatives to help provide for themselves and their children. As family income was cut through the loss of workers it also suffered the effects of wage cuts by the collective farms. Small wonder, then, that women worked so hard on the farms throughout the war, tackling unfamiliar jobs such as sowing, mowing and handling working animals. At the same time, private agriculture was vital for keeping rural families alive.[42]

The outbreak of war brought with it a rash of appeals to women to train as tractor drivers. Short, intensive courses gave thousands of women the basic skills of machine operation. By 1943, well over half the USSR's tractor and combine drivers were women. Replacements also had to be found for thousands of farm managers and specialists. At the height of the war, around half the collectives' brigade leaders, accountants and heads of livestock farms were female. Women still accounted for less than 12% of farm managers across the country, though in the front line regions their proportion rose to around one third. In these same areas and in the occupied territories rural women became involved with the partisans and the resistance whilst a small minority volunteered for active service in the armed forces.[43]

The German occupation brought massacres of Jews and groups of Slavs, the burning of entire villages and the transportation of thousands of civilians to forced labour in Germany. The destruction of many farms and the sheer poverty in the countryside took its toll of the women who bore the brunt of agricultural work during these years. Throughout the country, rural women suffered from low rations, overwork and nervous strain. The enormous losses of the Second World War, estimated at around 20 million, crowned thirty years of intermittent upheavals and destruction for the Soviet population. By 1945 a massive job of reconstruction awaited the country. In the rural areas, the disastrous loss of life would mean that in peacetime, as in war, the burden of work was to fall to women.

At the end of the war women made up more than two-thirds of all able-bodied collective farmers over the entire country. In the former occupied territories and the front line provinces where few young men returned to their native villages, the overwhelming majority of the agricultural workforce was female. During the period of reconstruction, demobilised collective farmers were recruited into the economic priority areas of heavy industry, exacerbating the shortage of male labour on the farms. With effort and investment concentrated in the towns, the meagre returns for work in the socialised sector of agriculture continued to make rural families highly dependent on private farming for subsistence.[44]

The loss of men at the front and to post-war industry severely disrupted patterns of family life. Thousands of rural women were deprived of the chance to marry or re-marry. The state's response to the devastating wartime losses and their inevitable consequences came in the Family Law of 1944. Its aim was to encourage births even though many women would be unable to marry. The law ceased to recognise common law marriage, tightened up divorce procedures and no longer permitted women with unregistered marriages to claim maintenance for their children. At the same time, a scale of allowances was introduced for single mothers as well as a range of honours for women bearing more than five children. The benefits, however, applied only to women giving birth after 1944. Those who were widowed and bore no more children had no entitlement to them.[45]

In the poverty of the post-war countryside the appeal to women to have large families must have seemed to many utterly unrealistic. Following demobilisation the number of women seeking abortions in both town and country rose sharply, far exceeding the number performed in 1939. For thousands of single women, motherhood bore little resemblance to the joyful picture portrayed in the nation's press. For many the post-war years were marked by a solitary and constant battle to feed and clothe their children and themselves. As one Ukrainian farm manager described the results: 'Women suffered from overwork and exhaustion and the number of invalids increased yearly. By the age of thirty-five most women were already old.'[46]

The countryside after Stalin 1953–60

After Stalin's death the rural family appeared in many areas to be in a state of flux. The older generation still clung to the habits of the past yet their success in imposing them on the young was steadily diminishing. The city's influence began to reach into more and more peasant homes as family members found work in factories or attended training courses in the towns. In particular, the growth of education in the villages had a profound effect on the outlook of the post-war generation and presented an effective challenge to traditional wisdom. By 1959, 23% of women and 30% of men in the Soviet countryside had received some form of secondary education. Nevertheless, extended peasant households still operated a common family budget with kolkhozes making payments to the family unit rather than to the individual. It appeared to be almost unknown for women in such families to retain personal control over their own earnings.[47]

Young people in the village were increasingly intolerant of parental interference in their choice of a marriage partner. The functional view of marriage traditionally held by the peasantry had by no means disappeared, however: prolonged courtships were rare, dowries were universally given on marriage and deferential attitudes by women towards their husbands were still said to be common. The law proscribing abortion was repealed in 1955 but many rural women continued to turn to local midwives for illegal abortions.[48]

After 1953, the Soviet government began to turn its attention to the problems of agriculture and, in particular, to improve livestock production and increase the sown area of the USSR. By 1959 almost 3 million women, one in six of all female agricultural workers, were concentrated in livestock farming.[49]

Expanding educational opportunities led to a rapid increase in the number of women agricultural specialists. By 1959, over a third of these workers were women. The improvement in the numbers of women specialists during the 1950s was not, however, matched in the sphere of management. Women's representation amongst brigade leaders rose only marginally, whilst amongst heads of livestock units it actually fell, despite female predominance in dairying, pig and poultry farming. The same was true at the highest management levels on both collective and state farms. The reasons for women's diminishing authority lay primarily in the policy of merging collective farms. As both kolkhozes and livestock units became larger, there was a clear tendency to appoint men to run them. Women were squeezed out of management as the new, enlarged units emerged.[50]

At the end of the war, the number of women machine operators had fallen dramatically as women withdrew into subsistence farming to support their families. Though mechanisation increased steadily during the 1950s, the proportion of women employed in this sphere continued to decline. By 1959, only 17,000 women drove agricultural machines in the USSR, a mere 0.7% of all drivers.[51] The legendary figure of the woman tractor driver had become very firmly an image of the past.

Despite the expansion of livestock production and the rapid rise in the numbers of women specialists, the overwhelming majority of female agricultural workers were employed as before in gang labour in the fields. No less than 81% of the female agricultural workforce had no specialism whatsoever. Women employed in the socialised sector continued to be heavily involved in private subsistence agriculture, with 13% of working-age women still working exclusively in the private sector.[52] By the end of the fifties, the abilities which women had displayed in wartime had been almost completely forgotten; men operated machinery whilst women performed those tasks which machines were as yet unable to tackle. Whilst their country's industrial development astonished the West, the working lives of these women remained quite untouched by technological advance.

The socialist government which came to power in 1917 was the first in the world to proclaim a commitment to sexual equality. Nevertheless, by 1960, neither this stated aim nor the alteration in the relations of production brought about by collectivisation had allowed rural women to reap the benefits of modernisation on a par with men. The nature of the Soviet development process and of the theory which informed Soviet policies on women lay at the root of the problem.

Soviet theory on female emancipation rested heavily on nineteenth-century Marxist writings which focused on women's oppression in the bourgeois family under capitalism. These writings saw women's entry into paid employment as the key to their emancipation. The application of such a theory to a peasant society in which women were already heavily involved in subsistence farming did little to increase recognition of women's unwaged work in agricultural production. Indeed, the antipathy of the Soviet government towards private farming compounded the low status of women's contribution to this vital element of the rural economy.

The primacy of urban, industrial development, a course over which rural women had no control, diverted resources away from the countryside under Stalin. As one Party secretary described it, 'year after year, financial, material and technical aid to the farms was cut, and the attempt was made to pump as many resources as possible out of agriculture'.[53] As a result, the socialisation of domestic labour and child care, which had by no means been achieved in the towns, was even further from fulfilment in the rural areas.

By the end of the 1950s, the majority of the Soviet population still lived on the land. Twenty years later, Soviet agriculture remained underdeveloped by comparison with major Western countries. Approximately 20% of the Soviet workforce in 1979 was engaged in agriculture, compared with less than 4% in the United States and 3% in Britain. In 1974, Moshe Lewin described the situation in the following words:

Soviet agriculture has not yet managed to effect a real technological revolution similar to the one which took place some time ago in other developed countries. Agriculture is still rather primitive and a great problem and there is no doubt that the consequences of the first quarter of a century of kolkhoz history still weigh heavily and are far from being overcome.[54]

It is the aim of the chapters which follow to analyse the results of the Soviet development process for women in the contemporary country-side. Women's roles in the workforce, the family and in culture are examined in order to assess whether the marginalisation of rural women which had occurred by 1960 has been reversed by greater access to education or, alternatively, intensified as mechanisation has increased.

I

Women in the rural workforce

THE EFFECT OF MIGRATION

In 1960 51% of the Soviet population lived in rural areas. Twenty years later the rural share of the population had fallen to 37%. By the latter half of the 1960s out-migration from the villages had become greater than the natural growth rate of the rural population. As a result, the rural population began to decline in absolute terms. Though the rural birthrate remained higher than that in the towns, the rural population fell from 109 million in 1959 to 98 million in 1980. In the same period the urban population increased from 100 million to 166 million.[1]

Far from being a universal phenomenon, however, the decline in the rural population was experienced only in the most developed regions of the USSR. Between 1959 and 1970 out-migration was at its most intense in the central region of the Non-Black Earth Zone, with Western and parts of Eastern Siberia also experiencing a significant decline in rural population. During the 1970s a high level of out-migration continued to be characteristic of the Non-Black Earth Zone, as Figure 1 illustrates. In this same period, however, rural population decline intensified in Belorussia, the Ukraine and regions of the Volga and Urals areas. In addition, rural population decline was experienced for the first time in Northern Kazakhstan.

In the course of these two decades rural population increased in Central Asia, Kazakhstan and much of the Caucasus. The Central Asian region, in particular, was characterised by a high birthrate and largely static rural population. In consequence, the decline in the proportion of the Soviet population resident in the countryside since 1960 was a product of intense out-migration from the European USSR and Siberia. The resulting distribution of the Soviet rural population is

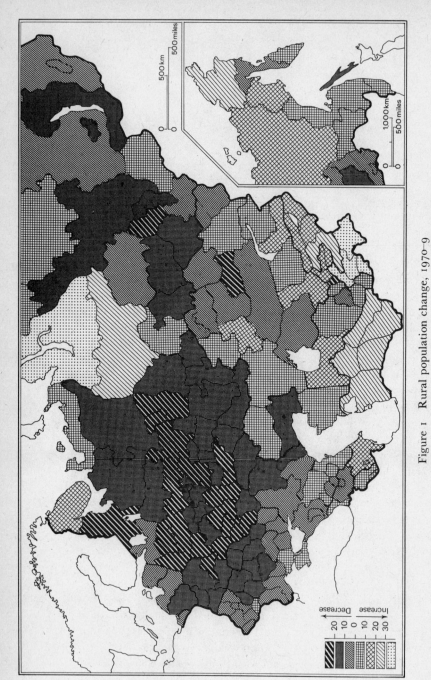

Figure 1 Rural population change, 1970–9

Sources: Itogi vsesoyuznoi perepisi naseleniya 1970 goda, Moscow, 1972–4, Vol. II, Tables 1 and 4; *Vestnik statistiki*, 5, 1979, pp. 69–73. Projection based on John C. Dewdney, *A Geography of the Soviet Union*, Oxford, 1979, p. 144.

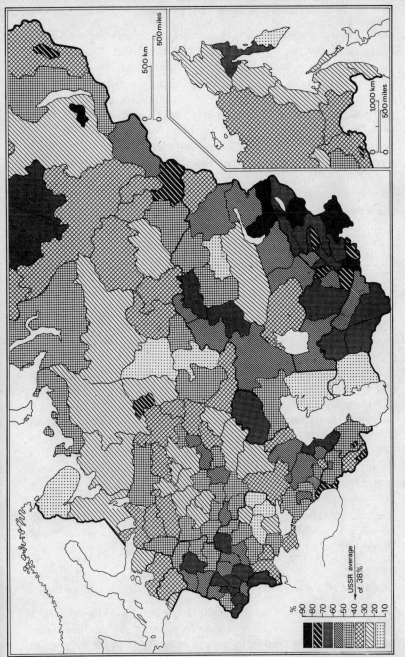

Figure 2 Rural population as percentage of total, 1979

Source: Vestnik statistiki, 5, 1979. Projection based on Dewdney, p. 144.

illustrated in Figure 2. By 1979 rural inhabitants continued to form the majority of the population in much of the North Caucasus and Kazakhstan. In almost all of Central Asia a large majority of the population lived in rural areas; in some regions the proportion of rural inhabitants stood at more than double the national average. Outside these southern areas of the country, very few districts remained predominantly rural by 1979: notable exceptions being Western Belorussia and the Western Ukraine and regions of the RSFSR with large ethnic minorities. In the Non-Black Earth Zone, the Baltic republics and much of the Volga and Urals regions and Siberia the rural population had, by 1979, fallen below the national average.

The overwhelming majority of migrants to the cities were young people in search of educational or employment opportunities which were unavailable to them in the countryside. In certain areas, notably the Non-Black Earth Zone and parts of Siberia, this has created a marked imbalance in the rural population structure. An ageing population, few young families on many farms and, hence, a low birthrate has created anxiety over the future of the labour force in these areas. At the same time, Central Asia has become a region with an expanding and underemployed rural labour force where young people regularly display a reluctance to leave the land.[2]

Figure 3 illustrates the effect of differential rates of both migration and natural growth on the rural female population in the Union republics. By 1970, in the most developed republics, more than a quarter of rural females were over the age of fifty-five. These areas had a correspondingly low proportion of females under nineteen. In Central Asia, Azerbaidzhan and Armenia, however, more than half of the rural females were under nineteen, whilst no more than 13% were over fifty-five. This has produced a situation in which the most developed regions, particularly the Non-Black Earth Zone of the RSFSR, are experiencing difficulty in retaining young women to staff livestock units whilst Central Asian agriculture has a large reserve of labour which is overwhelmingly female.[3]

CHANGES IN THE STRUCTURE OF THE RURAL WORKFORCE

With the decline in the rural population the rural workforce has also decreased significantly since 1960. In 1959, 52% of the Soviet workforce was employed in the countryside. By 1979 the proportion had fallen to 34%. The decline in the rural workforce has thus been

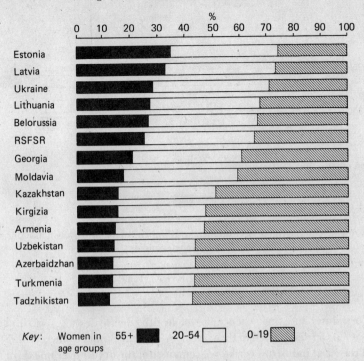

Key: Women in 55+ ■ 20-54 □ 0-19 ▨
age groups

Figure 3 Age structure of the rural female population, by republic, 1970
(republics in descending order by proportion of women over fifty-five)

Source: Itogi ... 1970, Vol. II, Table 3.

sharper than the decline in the rural population. In 1970 rural women
formed 49% of the rural workforce and 38.3% of the female workforce
of the USSR.[4] Figure 4 illustrates the changing pattern of employment
of rural women and men between 1959 and 1970. In the period
between the two censuses the numbers of both men and women
employed in the rural workforce each fell by approximately 4 million.
A striking feature of this decline was the contraction of the female
agricultural labour force. In 1959, 76% of employed rural women but
only 63% of employed rural men worked in agriculture. By 1970
agriculture occupied roughly the same proportion of both the male
and female workforce. More than a third of rural women in 1970 were
employed outside agriculture, the majority of these in the non-
productive sector. The expansion in rural health care and education
accounted for much of this increase. In 1959 only 9.1% of rural women

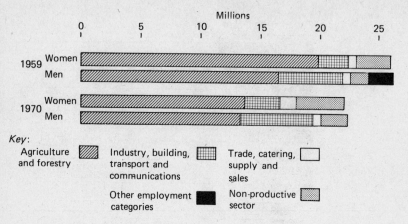

Figure 4   Employment of rural men and women, 1959 and 1970 (in millions, by sector of the economy)

Sources: Itogi ... 1970, Vol. v, Table 12; *Itogi vsesoyuznoi perepisi naseleniya 1959 goda, SSSR (svodnyi tom)*, Moscow 1962, Table 33.

worked in education, science, art or health. By 1970, 15.4% of rural women were employed in these areas. At the same time, women's share of the rural industrial workforce remained static at just over one third of those employed.

As late as 1959 agriculture was still the major employer of Soviet women though it had long since ceased to hold such a position for Soviet men. Eleven years later, however, industrial expansion together with the modernisation of agriculture and the contraction of its workforce had combined to diminish the importance of agriculture as an employer of Soviet women. By 1970 a quarter of all employed Soviet women worked in agriculture.[5]

WOMEN IN AGRICULTURAL EMPLOYMENT

Despite the decline in the workforce outlined above, agriculture, as would be expected, remained the principal employer of women in the countryside: over 62% of employed rural women in 1970 worked in agriculture or forestry. Since the late 1950s a policy of converting collective farms into state farms has been carried out. As a result, an increasing proportion of women working in agriculture has been employed directly by the state. Between 1960 and 1975 the representation of women amongst the state farm workforce rose from 43% to 45% whilst the proportion of women amongst those participating in the socialised sector on collective farms fell from 56% to 51%. By 1974 almost 37% of the female agricultural workforce was employed on state farms.[6]

The significance of this change in agricultural employment for women lies in the improved pay and conditions available to employees of the state sector. Until the mid-sixties, payments to collective farmers continued to take the form of a proportion of the farm's residual income after cash had been allocated for investment and to discharge financial obligations. As a result, rates of pay to collective farmers varied enormously according to the prosperity of individual farms and could be extremely low on farms which were in a difficult economic position. From 1966 guaranteed monthly payments to collective farmers began to be introduced. These were no longer to be made on the basis of a farm's anticipated residual income but at rates similar to those on state farms. Throughout the period since 1960, however, state farms have continued to offer higher rates of pay than collectivised agriculture. Table 1 illustrates pay relativities in industry and the two sectors of socialised agriculture between 1965 and 1975. The disparity between the average pay of state and collective farmers, as well as between collective farmers and industrial workers, narrowed between 1965 and 1970, yet widened between 1970 and 1975. By 1978 average monthly earnings in collectivised agriculture stood at 76% of those on state farms. Huge regional variations are concealed by these figures: in Estonia, for example, the average wage on collective farms in 1976 was reported to be only 1% lower than the average industrial wage. The material benefits of employment by the state have, however, been reaped more readily by men than by women. Women have remained in a minority on state farms, largely as a result of the greater degree of mechanisation in state agriculture and, hence, demand for skilled machine operators: an almost exclusively male profession.[7] Occupational segregation is, therefore, a further important factor in determining male and female earnings, as is the extent of participation in the socialised sector of agriculture.

Table 2 shows that women have consistently participated less in the socialised sector on collective farms than have men, despite forming a majority of the workforce. By 1974 women were working, on average, 20% more days per year than in 1960 and, in consequence, the gap between male and female rates of participation had narrowed con-

Table 1 *Average earnings of agricultural workers, 1965–75 (as % of industrial earnings)*

	1965	1970	1975
Industrial workers	100.0	100.0	100.0
State farm employees	73.3	77.4	79.1
Collective farmers	50.6	57.2	56.9

Source: R. K. Ivanova, *Sblizhenie sotsial'no-ekonomicheskikh uslovii zhizni trud-yashchikhsya goroda i sela,* Moscow, 1980, p. 55.

siderably. Nevertheless, this lower rate of participation by women must inevitably affect their annual earnings from the socialised sector. Collective farms demand differing minimum inputs of labour from their members according to such factors as the availability of workers and the economic strength of individual farms. Fewer days work per year are required of women on almost all farms. On the most prosperous kolkhozes lower minima are set for women with large families and for older women. Nevertheless, these regulations appear not to be rigorously enforced as a small proportion of women continue to be employed exclusively in the private sector. As will be discussed below, private subsidiary agriculture continues to make an important contribution to the income of rural families and to rely heavily on female labour.[8] The extent and significance of occupational segregation in agriculture is examined in subsequent sections of this chapter. Traditional views on appropriate male and female spheres of employment are far from having disappeared in rural areas. A pronounced sexual division of labour together with a reluctance to entrust women with posts of responsibility still contribute to the persistence of sexual inequality in the Soviet countryside.

WOMEN MACHINE OPERATORS

Since 1960 levels of mechanisation in Soviet agriculture have increased significantly. Today, the principal operations of ploughing, sowing and harvesting grain and fodder crops are all fully mechanised. The use of machinery in the major areas of horticulture continues to increase year by year. As a result the machine operator has become a key figure in the Soviet countryside. Between 1960 and 1980 the

Table 2 *Female participation in collectivised agriculture, USSR, 1960–74*

	1960	1965	1970	1974
Women as % of all employed in socialised sector of kolkhozes	56	55	53	51
% total days worked by women	49	48	47	47
Average number of days worked by men	232	222	233	244
Average number of days worked by women	170	170	185	204
Days worked by women as % of days worked by men	74	77	80	84

Source: M. Fedorova, 'Ispol'zovanie zhenskogo truda v sel'skom khozyaistve', *Voprosy ekonomiki*, 12, 1975, p. 55.

number of tractor, combine and lorry drivers employed on the farms rose from 2.5 million to 4.5 million. By 1980, 16% and 18% of employees on collective and state farms respectively are machine operators.[9]

Yet the increase in numbers in these professions has not kept pace with the growing availability of machinery or the demands of agriculture for a more intensive use of existing plant. The introduction of shiftwork for machine operators has received full government backing as a means of raising agricultural productivity. Many areas, however, have found it impossible to implement a two-shift system owing to a lack of skilled workers. Across the country as a whole in 1978, there were only 109 drivers for every 100 tractors, making the universal introduction of shiftwork impossible. This shortage of machine operators has not resulted from an inadequate training programme. During the 9th Five-Year Plan (1971–5), for example, almost 3.5 million machine operators were trained in the USSR, yet in this same period the total number employed on the farms increased by only 361,000. Although almost all the machine operators trained in rural vocational-technical colleges take up work in agriculture, few make farmwork their career. Their rate of turnover is extremely high: between 78% and 96% of all trained tractor and combine drivers left the farms each year during the 9th Five-Year Plan.[10]

A major reason for this huge loss of skilled workers to agriculture can be found in the nature of the machine operator's job on many farms today. In the absence of a shift system hours of work from spring to autumn are frequently extremely long and days off a rarity. The work itself is often unattractive as dust, fumes and vibration from much agricultural machinery are all considerably higher than approved levels. Design faults, even on the newest machines, lead to an excessive amount of time being spent on repairs and maintenance, which inevitably reduces earnings. Add to this an apparently widespread lack of management concern for young and inexperienced workers and it becomes clear why thousands of young men with technical skills leave the farms each year in search of a more ordered working life in industry.[11]

The recruitment of women

The rapid turnover of trained operators and the consequent shortage of skilled workers at peak agricultural periods was already in evidence in the 1960s. By this time the representation of women in the profession was almost negligible. During the period 1966–9 only 0.3% of tractor drivers were women. By 1970 the job which had once represented the pinnacle of achievement for women on the land had disappeared completely from the table of women's employment in the census of that year. Twelve months earlier, however, the government had taken a significant step in drawing women back into the work. The USSR Council of Ministers' Resolution, 'On the wider encouragement of women to take part in skilled work in agriculture', of January 1969, provided for the development of vocational training for women to become machine operators and instructed farm managements to assign women the newest machines and full technical support. In addition, work quotas for women were to be set 10% lower than for men. In March 1975 further benefits were announced for women who made a career in this work. The retirement age was lowered to fifty for women with fifteen years' service as a machine operator and a minimum of twenty years employment in all. At the same time an additional six days paid holiday per year was granted to all women operators.[12]

Yet this initiative to attract women into work on agricultural machinery has been almost universally seen as a means of solving a critical problem for the farms rather than an attempt to ensure equal access to this area of rural employment. From government officials to the women themselves the view is commonly expressed that women form an 'enormous reserve' for improving agricultural productivity. Where women have achieved success in these professions the explanation is frequently offered that their region suffers from a chronic shortage of skilled labour. Conversely, where there are few women involved in the work, local officials often state that there is no staff shortage in their area.[13] The campaigns of the 1970s have had little success in challenging the view that driving agricultural machines becomes a woman's job only when men are unavailable.

The press campaign

The move to recruit women into this sphere of work has, however, suffered neither from a lack of central government support nor of nationwide publicity. The press, led by the national rural women's magazine, *Krest'yanka* (Peasant Woman), has given both a great deal of coverage and direct encouragement to the new movement. Each year thirty women, winners in socialist competition from every Union Republic, are bought to the Moscow offices of *Krest'yanka* to receive the 'Pasha Angelina Prize' from the hands of the Minister of Agriculture. The prizewinners are photographed and interviewed and are made honorary members of *Krest'yanka*'s 'Pasha Angelina Club' for women machine operators. Books containing extensive biographies of each of them have been published and even a song has been composed in their honour. Throughout the year both local and national competitions in which women participate, from events for the newly qualified to the All-Union team ploughing contest, are given prominence in the magazine. Open letters from prizewinners have been featured in *Krest'yanka* urging rural women to follow in their footsteps. 'We appeal to all rural women to master more boldly the machinery which each year becomes more common in every branch of agriculture. There are no machines which women's hands cannot operate', runs a typical extract.[14]

In the many interviews and articles on women machine operators which appear in the women's press the writers are often at pains to stress their own job satisfaction and dispel the image of machine operation as heavy, physical labour. As one women who had trained when her children had grown up described the work:

I know that many women don't go on machine operators' courses because they think that a tractor driver's work is hard. This is a great misconception. When

I worked in a brigade as a manual labourer, dragging animal feed by hand and distributing it, I used to get so tired that I sometimes had to go to bed when I got home. Now I come home from work in good spirits.[15]

Training

To complement the publicity provided by the media, successful women machine operators visit schools and clubs to talk to young people about their work and to urge teenage girls to seek training. Their reports suggest that girls are not entirely impervious to these appeals, yet very few actually receive training. In the rural vocational-technical colleges women have formed no more than 9.5% of trainees in any year since 1953 when these colleges were first introduced. As one woman prizewinner described her annual experience of talking to school leavers, 'The girls listen attentively. You can see from their faces that they have seriously considered what we have said. But what then? The boys in the top class diligently learn to drive a tractor and get a tractor driver's licence together with their certificate of secondary education. But the girls still seem to hold back.'[16] Sociologists have expressed the view that career guidance in rural schools is often at fault in not encouraging girls to consider traditionally male fields of employment. In the words of one rural sociologist, career guidance for girls 'takes little account of the prospects for the industrialisation of agricultural production and, linked to this, any technical orientation in young women is disparaged'.[17] In Belorussia, where only one in every thousand women agricultural workers drives a tractor, the view was expressed to me both by women journalists and by collective farm officials that the fact that so few girls entered this profession was simply 'a matter of taste', and that this reflected a 'natural preference' in young women for non-technical work.[18]

Yet it is clear that a major factor in the failure of girls to train as machine operators is the policy of many rural schools towards vocational training. It is usual for classes in school workshops and production brigades to be rigidly divided by sex. Whilst boys learn mechanics and the skills of tractor driving, girls usually grow vegetables or milk cows. In those schools which expect all pupils to learn tractor driving and maintenance, courses for girls are often shorter and supplemented by classes on animal husbandry.[19] A highly traditional view of appropriate male and female behaviour and occupations which culminates in such a rigid approach to vocational training permeates the curricula of rural schools.

Girls who are interested in a technical career often meet with discouragement from their teachers and opposition from their parents. An upper form pupil in an Orenburg Region village school wrote to the newspaper *Sel'skaya zhizn'*, 'I want to be a combine driver but when I wrote about this in my school essay I was held up to ridicule. Why did it happen? In the papers it says "Girls to the tractors!" but we still haven't got any movement of the sort. At home, girls who wish to become machine operators may well be told, "it's not a woman's job".'[20] Perseverance and resolution appear to be essential prerequisites for girls aspiring to a place on a training course. It has been noted that staff in rural vocational-technical colleges are also affected by the prevailing rural attitudes towards women and technology. A Belorussian researcher discovered that these colleges were often unwilling to admit girls as students and would accept only a tiny proportion of those applying. In 1975 the USSR Council of Ministers instructed that there should be an increase in the admission of young women to rural vocational-technical colleges. No notable increase in female representation had, however, been achieved by 1984.[21]

The scale of women's employment

Where women do receive training and begin work on the farms very few make a career of the work. Successful women machine operators from many regions have observed how often attempts to form women's brigades have rapidly petered out. A prize-winning tractor driver from Mordovia, insisting that in her area many girls receive a tractor driver's licence whilst still at school, recorded how the forty women employed in the region in 1978 had dwindled to twenty by 1981. Similarly, in Gorky Region, the movement flourished in one district in 1977 with forty-four women's teams at work in the fields. By the following summer only fourteen teams were left and these too had lost members. Even with notable success and much local publicity, the isolated groups of women machine operators across the country generally fail to develop into a mass movement. One member of a women's youth team in Saratov Region which had appeared on television and was well known in the area expressed surprise that their example had not been followed, 'On many farms things are completely different! There the girls don't become machine operators, their parents won't let them.'[22]

Despite years of publicity, the results of the campaign to recruit women machine operators have been disappointing. Data on the numbers of women involved are patchy and often conflicting as many writers are inclined to report the numbers of women trained rather than actually at work. However, the most reliable figures indicate that by 1975 there were some 14,000 women tractor and combine drivers in the USSR, 0.3% of the total. By 1978 approximately 24,000 women were working as agricultural machine operators, with a further 1,000 employed by 1982. Women, therefore, still make up less than 1% of all those employed in these professions.[23]

The reasons for the campaign's evident lack of success are regularly debated in the press. In the view of one woman team leader from Orenburg Region, 'there is still a kind of timidity, a psychological barrier which doesn't allow women to choose the machine operator's profession'.[24] Whilst it is certainly true that rural attitudes and educational policies combine to create in women such a barrier, this is by no means a sufficient explanation of the phenomenon. A closer look at the conditions faced by women seeking a career as machine operators makes it clear that there are other significant factors which deter women from pursuing this work.

Problems in employment: conditions of work

The major problem faced by women machine operators is the work regime adhered to on most farms. As so few farms operate a shift system, the working day is frequently over ten hours long at the busiest times in the agricultural calendar, most of this being spent in distant fields. For women who have prime responsibility for child care and running the home it is a pattern of work which creates enormous difficulties. Pasha Angelina prizewinners in 1979 noted that, even when conditions were favourable, few farm managements considered a change to shift work which would attract women workers. A prizewinner from Tambov Region revealed that on the state farm where she was employed there was a surplus of labour yet still the women were expected to work a prolonged single shift. These women were given no days off in the summer but allowed extra days in winter to compensate, whilst even during their holidays the management was in the habit of calling them in to work the odd day or two. As a result, many women trained by the state farm itself never took up the work and numbers were dwindling in the women's brigade. Even women with eight or nine years' service as machine operators were leaving because of the hours.[25]

Understandably, many women are reluctant to endure a work schedule such as this, especially on farms which lack crèches and where the care of pre-school children presents a constant worry. It is not surprising to learn that many women face a great deal of opposition from their husbands if they attempt to take up the work. Family conflicts often bring to a premature close a woman's career as a machine operator, as one successful driver observed with some exasperation:

Galina Saranchina completed a training course but her husband forbade her to take up tractor driving. Galya works in the stores now. Surely her husband, an experienced machine operator himself, can understand that the tractor driver's profession is under any conditions and in every sense better than the qualification (if you can talk of such a thing) of a labourer? But then Galina Saranchina is not on her own in running up against obstacles of that sort which many women fail to overcome.[26]

A further discouraging aspect of the work regime is the tendency of management not to observe the lower women's work quota established in law. Many farms, it seems, expect the same quota of work from both men and women but pay the women 10% extra in cash. Experienced women drivers explain that this misses the point of the law which aims to encourage women to enter the profession. For a woman just beginning this work it can be very difficult to meet the same quota as the more experienced men and she may well be inclined to give up her job if she is constantly struggling to achieve this target.[27]

The question of repairs and maintenance is one regularly raised in the press by leading women machine operators. In discussing the conditions which drive trained women away from the profession the 1981 Pasha Angelina prizewinners considered the most common to be poor technical services. They stressed that 'conscientious mechanics' were essential to provide full support for women tractor and combine drivers.[28] Many women, especially those unattached to women's teams, carry out their own repairs and maintenance and regularly complain of a lack of garages in which to do this work. Problems arise in the winter months as these two comments show:

Our collective farm built a garage for the cars but never thought about the tractors. And there's no workshop. It's alright in summer, but in winter? Is it good for you to get under a tractor in a hard frost?

In winter you get up at the crack of dawn and go down to the machinery yard. You get a blow lamp and start to warm up the tractor. While you're thawing it out you're turning into an icicle yourself.[29]

There are complaints that tractors and combines are badly designed from a woman's point of view and efforts have been made, notably by the Minsk Tractor Factory in Belorussia, to produce a tractor which would meet the women's specifications. Poor construction, however, leads to more complaints about endless repairs than about difficulties in operation.[30]

Where women's teams are organised their members often express the view that the work would be made far easier and attractive to women if child care facilities were better developed or if mobile shops and field stations were available to assist them in combining the demands of home and work. Yet for the very many women who work alone alongside men such problems are exacerbated by a sense of isolation. In the Non-Black Earth Zone in particular women are usually scattered in men's brigades and it is therefore far harder to establish special benefits for them. A woman training supervisor recently expressed her concern about the position of these women in a letter to the press. In order to attract more women to the work, she wrote, 'We must clearly set up special conditions for women working alone. We shouldn't be content with just mouthing the slogans, "Women to the tractors!"' Women who work in men's brigades are particularly conspicuous and it can be a daunting prospect even now to drive a machine in full view of one's whole village.[31] Unfortunately there are still many in the countryside who feel that women have no business working with machines and view with some pleasure the prospect of their dismal failure.

Problems in employment: male attitudes

For women who have succeeded in receiving training and are keen to begin work, despite the many problems outlined above, the attitude towards them of managers and colleagues is crucial in determining their success or failure. One well-known woman tractor driver has observed, 'It's extremely important how women are received by men who see the machine operator's profession as practically their monopoly. It has to be said that the reception can be none too friendly.'[32]

Although the 1969 law clearly stipulates that women should have priority in the assignment of new machines, a stream of complaints to the press makes it clear that on many farms this is far from standard practice. It often happens that, when new machines are entrusted to women, male colleagues are quick to express their disgust and their contempt for women's abilities. Many managers themselves simply do not trust women to handle a large machine and are patronising in their treatment of those who know their rights under the law. One woman who asked to be assigned a new machine which had just been given to a male colleague was told, 'It's a heavy tractor, you won't be able to work on it. You'll just spoil it', a reaction which appears to be characteristic.[33]

Women regularly complain that they have received no support whatsoever from management on their farms. Their stories suggest that managers often regard trained women machine operators as a nuisance to be removed as rapidly as possible. A common ploy which, not surprisingly, has a high rate of success, is to assign a woman an ageing and disintegrating machine which will demand endless repairs. With the tractor out of service she is then faced with obstruction by mechanics. Few women are able or willing to withstand prolonged campaigns of this type against them.

In a letter to *Krest'yanka*, Lyubov' Bolgarina of Krasnodar Territory described her two-year struggle with an ancient tractor and deliberate obstruction by the men with whom she worked:

You go to the mechanic and he curses you. He hasn't got time to mess about with your tractor. In working hours he either reads a book or mends his own motor-bike. You go to the fitter and he just says 'You should be more gentle, more gentle ... then you could drive even that tractor.' ... But it's difficult to be more gentle: the steering is faulty, the brakes fail. One summer the unloading conveyor of a sugar beet combine ripped off the cabin roof so for more than a year I have felt everything; snow, wind and stars. The tractor needs repairs but they tell me that there's no room in the workshops.

Even when she was obliged to turn to moonlighters to obtain essential parts she received no assistance from any institution or individual on the farm. The chairperson of the workers' committee met her complaints with, 'If it's hard for you to work in these conditions we can replace you', whilst the mechanic would regularly advise, 'Go and bake pies, Lyubov' Ivanova! Give up this old heap! It'll just fall to pieces somewhere on the road. Can you call this a tractor?!' And she concludes:

I do so wish that managers would treat us women machine operators with some interest and sincerity, that they would use our knowledge and experience properly! I do so wish that a brigade could be completely staffed by women, that we could go to work in high spirits and get some satisfaction from it! We could move mountains! Every year now girls complete courses for tractor

'It's a miserable business, having a woman in the brigade. You can't even make up a threesome!'

(*Krest'yanka*, 2, 1975, p. 27)

drivers, but where are they? Some become milkmaids, others become pig rearers, young people to to the towns to study. At one time on our state farm there were eleven women machine operators, then there were seven, now there are only four. But if the attitude of the management towards us doesn't change soon then there will probably not be a single one left.[34]

The editors of *Krest'yanka* described this story as typical of the treatment meted out to skilled women on farms across the country.

Numerous cases have been reported in the press of more overt discrimination against women which takes the form of a management refusal to assign them machines after training. Five women from one state farm in Stavropol' Territory, for example, described in a letter to the press the gulf between rhetoric and action which they had experienced. They had trained together and planned to start a women's team after qualifying. Yet on returning to their native farms:

Our enthusiasm received no support from anyone. They just talked about the team. They wouldn't give us tractors. We, machine operators, are now working as unskilled labourers wherever they send us. Sometimes we get together and ask ourselves, 'What did they train us for? So much money was spent on us ... We put so much effort into it, and all for nothing.'[35]

The unwillingness of farm managers to employ women in the work for which they have trained or the hostility of male colleagues is sometimes corrected by the intervention of local District Party officials following appeals to the national press. Most women who face these barriers,

'Let's stop messing about with this tractor. We'll give it to the women's brigade, it'll do for them.'

(*Krest'yanka*, 2, 1977, p. 31)

however, are simply forced to accept the inevitability of defeat and seek work elsewhere.

Party support for women: the case of Millerovo

Where efforts have been made to implement the 1969 legislation, women have managed to gain a foothold in the profession of machine operator. One rural district of the USSR has consistently received attention in the media for its success in recruiting women to this work. This is the district of Millerovo in the Rostov Region.

From the campaign's inception in 1969 women machine operators in this area have received the full backing of Region and District Party organisations. As a result, it is claimed, the district has long since ceased to recruit city workers for temporary help with sowing and harvesting. Instead, rural women machine operators now work a third of the total sown area of the Millerovo District. From just fifteen women trained in 1969 the movement has grown steadily until, in 1982, there were 370 women permanently employed in the women's brigades and teams, representing every farm in the district. Every year these women's brigades have recorded higher productivity than the men's brigades in the same region. To gain such a success Party officials have made the establishment of two-shift systems their priority for women's teams and pressure has been brought to bear on any farm where its introduction has been delayed. Experienced and conscientious mechanics are assigned to support all women's brigades and, in addition, the Party ensures that both working and living conditions for the women are of a high standard. Young children are cared for in crèches and extended day groups have been established for all school-age children whilst their mothers are at work. All the women receive specially designed overalls and have access to well-equipped field stations during working hours. Periodic health checks are carried out at the field stations and mobile shops arrive regularly with essential items and goods in short supply. All the women are encouraged to further their skills and education, many have been made members of local Soviets, whilst the thirty-four leading workers have become Communist Party members.[36]

The women machine operators of Millerovo have received a great deal of publicity in both the local and national media. Lyubov′ Tikhomirova, leader of the first women's brigade in 1969, is now a Hero of Socialist Labour and member of the Presidium of the RSFSR Supreme Soviet. Others over the years have been awarded Pasha Angelina prizes. Zinaida Nikolenko, 1980 prizewinner from Millerovo District, was interviewed in the national press about the effect of this publicity in her region:

Nowadays women tractor drivers are in the public eye. They receive honour and respect everywhere. Photographs and stories about them appear in the papers. Not so long ago I wrote a short piece in a magazine about our brigade and I received heaps of letters afterwards saying, 'we want to work in your brigade'. There were even requests from city girls. One of them wrote, 'I dreamed of becoming a model but when I read your article I decided to come to you.'[37]

For the women of Millerovo, working solely with other women has been an important factor in their success. A survey in the late seventies asked a cross-section of machine operators in the district if they would prefer brigades to be mixed now that the women had become established in the profession. Whilst 20% of the men were in favour of mixed brigades, the women were unanimous in their insistence on the value of women-only teams. These, they felt, gave them far greater freedom and self-confidence than they would feel working alongside men.[38]

Individual state farms, notably in Volgograd and Ul′yanovsk Regions, have studied the experience of Millerovo and have had some success in implementing these methods in their own regions.[39] Examples such as these, however, remain a drop in the ocean and have no significant impact on practice in agriculture across the country.

The experience of Central Asia

In Central Asia, where skilled labour is often scarce but an ample workforce of both sexes is available, the employment of women as operators of cotton picking combines frequently takes the form of a social experiment. In these Islamic communities the introduction of women to skilled work remains an essential element in promoting the concept of female equality. For Central Asian women to drive machines is still, on most farms, an achievement of the first order. Attitudes towards training women were extremely hostile during the 1960s and it was common for women to be forced to give up work due to the 'unbearable conditions' created by male colleagues.[40]

Two decades later, attitudes towards Central Asian women contemplating work with agricultural machines appear to have eased considerably. Whilst it is clear than women in this region continue to face discrimination in both training and employment, reports suggest that their treatment is no worse than that of women in other areas of the USSR. Most women graduates of rural vocational-technical colleges in Central Asia fail to make their career as full-time machine operators, an experience which they share with women in European areas. In contrast to other regions, however, Central Asian girls rarely seek employment in the towns if they are refused skilled work on the farms. Strong cultural traditions and family ties lead to low rates of migration to the cities for both sexes. As a result, many trained women work on cotton picking combines during the harvest only and return to manual labour for the rest of the year. In consequence the average length of service of women machine operators in Central Asia is two and a half times less than that of men. According to one source, however, representation of women in the machine operator's profession, in Uzbekistan at least, is now higher than the national average.[41]

In recent years there has been a marked increase in official encouragement of Central Asian women to become machine operators. Komsomol prizes have been instituted at republic level for skilled women and the prizewinners have received a good deal of publicity, both locally and nationally. These women are often recruited into the Communist Party and elected to Soviet organs to promote women's emancipation in their region. Malika Kurbanova, Komsomol prizewinner for Tadzhikistan in 1978, for example, had, at the age of twenty-two, already been chairperson of her local women's Soviet for three years. In a comment characteristic of this new generation of machine operators, she expressed the view of Central Asian women that 'they are not decorations for the home but first and foremost useful members of society. That's why they need to master the new professions more boldly.'[42]

The close link between machine operation and women's emancipation in Central Asia has been in evidence in the 1970s in an experimental programme in Kirgizia. A brigade of girl school leavers on the Frunze collective farm, Osh Region, was formed in 1972 to tend an area of the cotton fields from sowing to harvest. They were to be trained to drive combines and were to live together during the growing season at a purpose-built field station away from their families. The inevitable opposition of the girls' parents to such a scheme was overcome by the persuasion of the farm's chairperson, Ol'maskhan Atabekova. This woman had been in charge of the Frunze kolkhoz since 1953 and had become a well-known and respected figure in Kirgizia. The '16 girls' brigade, as the group became known, was highly successful both as a production unit and as a social experiment. Requests to join the brigade from other girls were so numerous that other brigades were rapidly organised. No doubt the unheard-of independence which the scheme offered was highly attractive to young women whose lives were considerably more restricted than their European counterparts. Komsomol supervision ensured that behaviour at the field station was beyond reproach so that the future of the scheme should not be put in jeopardy. As a visiting journalist described the scene: 'In the evenings after supper the record player is switched on. Girls and boys arrive from other brigades and the place shakes on the open veranda. But at exactly 22.50 the music ends – it's time to stop. Tomorrow they have to get up early.'[43] Since 1972 the example has spread to other farms in the district and many girls have used the scheme as a stepping stone to higher education and vocational training. From the '16 girls' brigade alone, thirty women have, over the years, received higher education and returned to the kolkhoz as agronomists, accountants and teachers.[44]

Temporary machine operators

During the 1970s the process described in Kirgizia whereby machine operators have become specialists has often been seen in reverse in other areas of the USSR. It has become increasingly common for women specialists in areas with chronic labour shortages to take training courses and assist with sowing and harvesting on local farms. Many of these women are Party members for whom the work is initially a Party assignment. In a magazine interview a school headmistress from Krasnodar Territory expressed the sentiment that her involvement in the work was a patriotic duty: 'We are all first and foremost grain-growers because we live on a collective farm. "If you live in the village – master machinery".* Surely that means everybody. The harvest is short but demands enormous effort, from everyone wherever they work.'[45]

The backgrounds of women in these temporary teams are extremely varied. One team, for example, which appears in the fields of the Altai Region year after year comprises an agronomist, a zootechnician, a welder and an accountant. Although their efforts receive much publicity, such teams have little influence in promoting the movement as a whole. As they are employed on a strictly temporary basis no special conditions are arranged for them and, as some of these women have themselves observed, this undoubtedly retards the development of permanent women's teams.[46]

Some concluding remarks

Despite the experience of women in the war years and the publicity which has accompanied the latest campaign, it continues to be a commonly held view in the countryside that the machine operator's profession is not for women. Throughout the 1970s women have regularly demonstrated that they are no less competent than men to do this work. In many cases women have recorded higher productivity than their male colleagues and the view is often expressed that they are more conscientious in their approach to the work. No doubt many who have had to struggle to be accepted in the profession are concerned to prove their worth once employed. Yet despite their record, hostility remains and it is only the fortunate minority who receive the support of their superiors and colleagues. Traditional rural attitudes towards women and work which have been so little challenged in the past have evidently not been modified by the 1969 law. Rural men who, to judge by their rate of turnover in this work, are not enamoured of their

* A popular slogan for agriculture in the 1970s.

working conditions, clearly feel resentment at the privileges offered women under this legislation. This may, in part, explain the obstruction and hostility faced by trained women seeking this form of employment.

The economic problems faced by farms with labour shortages may be a further factor in the reluctance of managers to employ women. The rates of pay and benefits guaranteed under the law make women more expensive to employ than men. At the same time, the range of amenities such as child care, mobile shops and field stations consistently advocated by supporters of women's employment in this sphere represent further costs which managers may fear they will be pressured to meet. Whilst the fulfilment of the current plan remains the essential short-term goal of farm managers and local officials, the outlay which is potentially involved in the employment of women may appear prohibitive, even if future financial benefits could be assured. In such circumstances, managers may indeed feel that it is in their interests to discourage individual women from entering or remaining in this work, for fear of setting a precedent which may have huge financial implications. For most women, observing both the conditions which cause men to give up the work and the endurance required of women seeking to enter it, there is little incentive to pursue training. There is no evidence that the glaring lack of success of this most recent campaign to recruit women will be reversed in the future.

LIVESTOCK WORKERS

The effect of factory farming on female employment

The sharp increase in livestock numbers recorded in the 1950s has been followed by a somewhat slower expansion of animal husbandry. At the same time, however, the levels of mechanisation in this branch of agriculture have increased considerably, as Table 3 shows. Whilst the number of women employed in dairying rose between 1959 and 1970, numbers in fatstock production fell during this period. As the mechanisation of cattle and pig units in particular developed, the representation of women in this sphere of animal husbandry has fallen considerably. The proportion of women employed had declined from 70% to 51% by 1970, as Table 4 illustrates. On the basis of press reports throughout the 1970s it can be assumed that the tendency to employ fewer women when fatstock units are mechanised has

Table 3 *The mechanisation of livestock units, 1963–80*
(as % total livestock holdings)

	Cattle			Pigs			Poultry		
	1963	1970	1980	1963	1970	1980	1963	1970	1980
Water supply	50	68	91	72	81	94	. . .	77	95
Feeding	2	12	45	13	28	66	. . .	38	85
Mucking out	7	30	75	14	42	86	. . .	38	86
Milking	20	56	90						
Complex mechanisation of units	. . .	9	42	. . .	23	63	. . .	23	72

Note: . . . = not available.
Sources: Narodnoe khozyaistvo SSSR v 1980 g., Moscow, 1981, p. 112; *Narodnoe khozyaistvo SSSR v 1963 g.*, Moscow, 1964, p. 337.

continued to the present day. In many cases the employment of men, especially in leadership positions, in mechanised livestock units has been seen as a temporary measure until sufficient women have been trained to operate the new machinery. It has been found, however, that such a policy often leads to the permanent employment of men in these jobs. A journalist visiting a state farm pig unit observed, 'I noticed that . . . all the team leaders were, as a rule, men. As it was explained to me, the machine operator team leaders helped the women in the first place to master the job of operator. They are still helping now because they have more experience.'[47] It is not uncommon for women to be overlooked completely when modern automated livestock complexes are opened on the farms. A report from Kherson Region of the Ukraine, for example, in 1978 showed that men alone were being trained as operators for units such as these and that no effort was being made to retrain experienced women livestock workers for employment in the new conditions. It must be assumed that, in cases of this type, women are simply transferred to other manual jobs when the old units disappear.[48]

Where women are trained for employment in factory farming the change in their work routine can be enormous. Whilst letters still reach the press from women complaining of long hours and few days off in old-style livestock units, employees in modern complexes are working

Table 4 *Women in animal husbandry, 1970*

	Number employed	Women as % all workers	As % all women agricultural workers
Dairy men/women	1,744,607	98	13.8
Cow and pig men/women and calf rearers	846,130	51	6.7
Poultry rearers	133,431	94	1.1
Total	2,724,168	79	21.6

Source: Itogi vsesoyuznoi perepisi naseleniya 1970 goda, Moscow, 1972–4, Vol. VI, Tables 2, 18.

a standard eight-hour day. In addition, higher productivity in factory farming usually leads to better pay. The best of the new complexes also offer a range of amenities which are especially attractive to women: extensive child care provision and free transport, recreational and medical facilities, shops and canteens.[49]

A detailed survey of two factory farming units in Nerekhta, Kostroma Region, in 1973 allows a useful comparison between old and new systems of employment for women. In both the pig and poultry units surveyed occupational segregation was particularly pronounced: almost all those working directly with livestock were women whilst the technicians and drivers were exclusively men. Nevertheless the average pay of a woman livestock worker was comparable, and in some cases higher, than that of a skilled man. Poultry rearers earned between 148 and 169 roubles per month, whilst women tending pigs took home an average of 111 to 219 roubles depending on age, experience and productivity. On a neighbouring collective farm women livestock workers earned on average 101 roubles per month and did not enjoy the shorter working day and less taxing conditions of the factory farms. It should be mentioned that the majority of women in the Nerekhta units were in their forties, most having received no more than a primary education. The automated units therefore offered considerably higher pay in more congenial surroundings than they might otherwise have obtained. The material incentive to women to seek work in factory farming was even more pronounced in the case of unskilled manual workers. Women packers and labourers in the Nerekhta units earned between 109 and 146 roubles per month whilst,

Table 5 *Work schedule on dairy unit of Tsaryuk collective farm,*
Belorussia, 1970

	Begins	Ends
First milking session	4.00	5.30
Cows sent out to pasture	5.30	
Cows driven in from pasture	12.00	12.30
Supplementary feed	12.30	13.00
Second milking session	13.00	14.30
Cows sent out to pasture	14.30	
Cows driven in from pasture	20.00	20.30
Third milking session	20.30	22.00

Source: *Nauchno-tekhnicheskii progress i sotsial'nye izmeneniya na sele*, Minsk, 1972,
p. 92.

as unskilled fieldworkers on a local collective farm, they would have
received an average of only 56 roubles per month.[50]

Sparse information on wage rates in factory farming suggests that
their women livestock workers earn considerably more than the
national average agricultural wage of state farmers. As a result,
workers in modern complexes appear to have become something of an
elite amongst women in animal husbandry. As one journalist described
the change, 'yesterday's peasants are today's rural working class'.[51]

WOMEN IN DAIRYING

Work on traditional farms

Although the job of milking dairy cattle has long been considered
women's work, it is an occupation which, on the majority of Soviet
farms, is far from easy. The traditional system of work employed in
dairying on state and collective farms alike involves milking cows three
times a day. As a result, women are required to work an exceptionally
prolonged shift with breaks of varying length between milking sessions.
Table 5 provides a characteristic example of the work schedule
employed in dairying.

On this particular farm the first milking session began one hour
earlier in hot weather and the final session was completed later at
night. A survey of farms in the Non-Black Earth Zone in 1974–5 found

that, in units where this system was employed, 70% of milking staff were on call between 4 or 5 a.m. and 6 or 7 p.m. A further 14% regularly worked from 3 a.m. to 10 or 11 p.m.[52] In winter when the cows cannot be driven out to pasture the work becomes considerably more demanding. In many cases women are expected not only to milk the cows but also to feed and water them and to clean out the stalls, much of this work being done by hand. As a result, milking itself has been estimated to occupy less than a quarter of total working time on traditional farms. In Siberia, where the winter stalled period is much longer than in European areas, surveys have shown that women in dairy units consider their work to be very heavy and more arduous than that of any other group of agricultural workers. To the demands of the work itself must be added no less than six journeys to and from the workplace every day. The result of working such unsocial hours is that 'women do not in fact feel free from their work at any time of the day or night'.[53]

Not only do women in dairying work extremely long and awkward hours but, for many, holidays are few. In 1974 dairy women worked an average of 308 to 314 days per year. In regions where staff shortages allow few extra workers to cover in case of absence it is not unusual to find women working between 330 and 350 days in the year. As such, milking staff receive less free time than any other group of workers in industry or agriculture.[54]

Information about rates of pay in dairying is very inadequate. Such scant data as are available suggest that women involved in milking may have a higher annual income than tractor drivers. In view of the work schedule on dairy farms, however, hourly rates received by dairy women are rather lower than those of skilled machine operators.[55] It is clear from a variety of surveys that the relatively high pay is a major factor in women's choice of this profession. A survey of women employed on traditional farms in Novosibirsk Region during the late sixties found that 35.6% of them were married women with three or more children and a further 30.4% were either widowed or divorced with three or more children. Similar results were recorded on collective farms in Orel Region in the same period. Here 30% of women livestock workers were widows: almost all the widows on the farms being employed in this branch of agriculture. In all cases these women were attracted by the material rewards of a job which provides a constant income throughout the year. The women surveyed in Novosibirsk Region observed that no other work was available which could offer

such a level of pay. The pressing need for financial security undoubtedly induces women with heavy family commitments to endure
the rigours of work in dairying. The resulting workload which these
women face leaves them virtually without any free time to
themselves.[56]

Innovations in dairying

The mechanisation of dairy farms has increased dramatically since
1960. At that time the overwhelming majority of dairy women milked
by hand. Today, only 10% of dairy cows in the USSR are hand-
milked. In consequence, the risk of premature arthritis in the hands,
formerly the major occupational health hazard of milking staff, has
been greatly reduced.[57] On the most modern farms fully automated
milking parlours have been introduced. In many of these the cows
stand on a rotating drum as the milking machine is attached. The
operator stands at a lower level than the cows to avoid bending and
uses a hose to wash the udders which eliminates the need to fetch
buckets of water for this job. In the majority of cases, however, milking
machines are introduced into existing buildings and fitted into existing
work schedules. As a result mechanisation alone has proved insufficient to attract young women into dairying. In response to the
problem of staff shortages and in an attempt to boost productivity
through reorganisation, the 1970s saw the introduction of a variety of
new working systems on dairy farms.

As units have been mechanised, managements have frequently used
the opportunity to introduce a system based on two, rather than three,
milking sessions per day. As the total staff required on dairy units is
often reduced when the work is automated, it has been possible to
employ permanent deputy dairy women to cover in case of absence.
This has allowed the introduction of a five-day week on many farms
during the last decade. Table 6 shows an example of a dairy woman's
daily work schedule under this system. As this example illustrates,
milking twice rather than three times concentrates the working day
into two distinct units, in this case between 6 and 10 a.m. and between
3 and 7 p.m. On most farms employing such a system a seven- or eight-
hour day appears to be standard. In many units the reduction of staff
through mechanisation has also brought about increased specialisation, whereby a proportion of dairy women are concerned exclusively
with cleaning the cows and operating the milking machinery whilst the

Table 6 *Work schedule on dairy unit of Kotel'skii state farm, Leningrad Region, 1971*

	Begins	Ends
Preparation for milking	6.00	6.30
Milking	6.30	8.00
Cleaning feeding troughs and gangways	8.00	8.30
Feeding	8.30	9.30
Supplementary milking of newly calved and high-yielding cows	9.30	10.00
Tethering and cleaning cows after pasture	15.00	16.00
Preparation for milking	16.00	16.15
Milking	16.15	17.45
Feeding	17.45	18.45
Supplementary milking	18.45	19.10

Source: P. S. Shelest, *Odna sel'skaya sem'ya – shtrikhi k sotsial'nomu portretu sel'skogo rabochego 70-kh gg.*, Moscow, 1972, p. 132.

remainder are transferred to permanent work feeding the cows and cleaning the unit.

A refinement of the new split shift system has been the introduction of the two-shift system on the most progressive farms. The new feature of the working day under this arrangement is the introduction of team work. A single and often very large group of animals is milked and tended by one woman on the morning shift and by her partner on the afternoon shift. The actual hours worked in each shift vary quite widely from one unit to another but are usually a maximum of eight hours. Under this system women generally change shifts each week and, where there are sufficient staff, a five-day week is usual. The standardised working hours which these innovations permit have proved very popular to women whose lives are thus no longer dominated by the demands of the farm. As one young woman explained her approval of the system: 'If I'm working on the first shift I'm home by 7 o'clock in the morning. In the next hour I clean up and take the children to the nursery school. The nursery and the primary school are not far from the house. At eleven I'm back at the unit to get the group ready for my partner.'[58] These new work schedules have received the approval of both the agricultural workers' trade union and the USSR Ministry of Agriculture. Both these bodies favour the introduction of a standardised working day and five-day week throughout the dairy industry as a means of attracting and retaining a stable, skilled workforce.[59] Yet the systems have been adopted only on a minority of farms to date. Many managers are evidently of the opinion that new working schedules can only be operated in modern, purpose-built dairy units. Experience has shown, however, that the system can be successfully employed in old units which have a reasonable degree of automation. The transition to the standardised working day in dairying is frequently seen as a long-term objective to be achieved as old buildings are brought up to modern standards and new units are put into operation.[60]

The new systems are not without their critics amongst dairy women themselves. For older women with many years of experience tending a single group of cows the innovations bring problems of adjustment. The introduction of team working means a loss of pride in their skill and prestige for those who obtained high levels of productivity under the old system.[61] A further criticism stems from a fear of being burdened with far more work than before. With the introduction of the new system women usually become responsible for far larger groups of cows and the work, however highly mechanised, is thus a good deal more intensive, as this account of a modern milking parlour indicates:

As three cows are being milked on the left-hand side of the milking parlour, the operator, Valya Nikitina, drives out from the right-hand side those which have already been milked, and the next three come in to replace them. The work goes on without a break; there's no time for a breather or a chat. It was not for nothing that Valya said before the shift, 'In our unit it's like the textile factory where I used to work, you don't get time to turn round.'[62]

To older women such a scheme of work may appear unacceptable, particularly if there is some doubt as to whether adequate cover will be provided in cases of absence. As a dairy woman on a new unit in Kemerovo Region expressed her fears:

The two-shift system is not for me ... I won't be able to manage it. I've been working here for fifteen years; my strength isn't what it was. If I have thirty cows now I shall have to milk sixty then – my partner and I will join our groups together. But just imagine if my partner doesn't turn up one day? Then I would have to milk sixty cows twice in one day.[63]

Anxieties such as this are not entirely unfounded. A 1982 estimate indicated that there should be at least 200,000 deputising dairy women across the country as a whole to allow for days off and cover in cases of illness. At the time, the total employed was around 50,000 short of this target.[64] Where the new systems are employed they are often accompanied by a tightening of labour discipline to avoid the problems created by absenteeism. Model dairy units may well become a focus of attention for local Party activists as the pressure for higher productivity increases. On a highly automated unit in Tomsk Region, for example, the brigade leader described how local Communists were in the habit of conducting lightning 'raids' once or twice a week to 'expose the bad workers'. For a worker's name to appear in the activists' satirical paper was, she maintained, 'more dreadful than being deprived of a bonus'.[65]

The increased pressure of work on modern units is, for many women, outweighed by the benefits which it brings. Not only is the working of unsocial hours kept to a minimum but, as the system becomes established, most farms report increased productivity and can afford to pay higher wages. As on the modern fatstock units, employees on the new dairy complexes often enjoy the additional benefits of canteens, shopping and recreational facilities. The Deputy Minister of Agriculture, L. Kuznetsov, in 1981 wrote in support of improvements such as these: 'We must think about providing hot meals, about bringing a supply of food and consumer products for working women straight into the units, about providing transport for those who live far from work, about in-service training for the young and about housing. Then the problem of staff shortages will disappear by itself.'[66] Where the two-shift system has been successfully introduced and concern has been displayed for women's conditions of work, surveys have indeed shown that the number of young women employed in dairying has increased dramatically.[67] It is clear, however, that on many farms today the ideas of the Ministry are no more than desirable targets for the future. The reality of dairying for most women employees remains very different.

Problems and complaints

The problem of excessive working hours remains unresolved on many dairy units in the USSR. On small units in particular, difficulties in replacing staff on leave are often acute, with the result that not only holidays but also days off are not granted. A steady trickle of complaints published in the national press emanates from dairy women who have been working seven days a week for a considerable period. With the intervention of the press, local Party and Soviet officials are pushed into taking action in cases such as these. In a typical example from Ivanovo Region in 1982 a meeting was held for both the dairy women concerned and responsible local officials with the result that deputising staff were appointed to provide days off for all employees. The dairy women involved were to receive double pay or time off in lieu for overtime worked. It seems to be a common practice, however, when units are short staffed to pay women for compulsory overtime rather than to organise leave.[68]

A survey of state farms in Moscow Region in the early seventies found the level of mechanisation to be the major cause of dissatisfaction amongst animal husbandry workers.[69] Where machinery has been installed in dairy units this is by no means the end of manual labour for many women. It has been admitted by the Ministry of Agriculture that the milking machinery currently in use is in need of improvement and that the supply of spare parts is inadequate and subject to delay, 'Insufficient mechanisation of processes in animal husbandry, machines standing idle in the units through a shortage of spare parts undoubtedly slow down the growth of productivity and aggravate the already acute problem of the shortage of livestock workers.'[70] Inspections of dairy units carried out on behalf of the national magazine *Krest'yanka*, and pieces of investigative journalism prompted by women's letters of complaint have revealed the effect of this state of affairs on the working day. In units where technology has been installed women are to be found milking by hand, carrying milk in buckets or carting feed manually to the cattle. In one unit in Belgorod Region a new feed conveyor was in operation for only two or three weeks of a five-month period due to constant breakdowns: 'We complained to the brigade leader and the specialists and the manager', the dairy women recalled, 'but we got the same reply from all of them: there are no spare parts!'[71]

The problem of repairs is not infrequently aggravated in such cases by the apathy of management. Where new complexes are planned or under construction, poor conditions for women on existing units may simply be ignored. This inertia is felt not only over the question of spare parts but extends to the organisation of work schedules, of a sufficient supply of winter feed and to the repair and cleanliness of farm buildings. An inspection of units in Khar'kov Region found the following example:

We don't milk by hand but we carry the milk to the depot in buckets – there is no milk conveyor. And we distribute the feed manually although there are

feeding operators on the staff. Last winter we were quite short of feed so we
decided to feed the cows ourselves. Who knows better than a dairy woman how
much to give to a cow so the yields don't fall? That, of course, was an emergency measure. But now everyone's got used to the idea that a dairy woman
is a herder and feeder as well. The conveyors haven't worked for a long time.
We have nothing but pitchforks left in reserve.[72]

Krest'yanka informed its readership in 1982 that 'disturbing letters'
had been received from Buryatiya, Kursk, Belgorod and a list of other
regions describing similar problems, compounded in places by erratic
supplies of disinfectant and soap and a lack of hot water. Complaints
have also been published about units which become surrounded by
mountains of manure around which constant detours have to be made
with heavy buckets of feed. The disinterest of management in
conditions on outdated dairy units is constantly raised in the press in
response to women's letters. Protests at a lack of concern for livestock
and dismissive attitudes towards the workforce are aimed at staff at all
levels from brigade leaders and specialists to top management on the
farms.[73]

It might be concluded from the content of women's complaints that
the new dairy units, whilst improving working conditions for some
employees, actually encourage a deterioration in conditions for the
remainder. What is certain is that the example of the modernised units
and the reorganisation of the working week has shown women on old-
style dairy farms what can be achieved. It seems probable that the
frequency of complaints reflects not so much a worsening of conditions
as a new intolerance amongst women towards management neglect. A
recent letter from a collective farm in Ivanovo Region provides a good
example of the growing assertiveness of dairy women in the face of
inaction by their superiors. To their credit, the women describe a
deplorable situation with humour and irony:

Our unit is divided into two yards – the old and the new. The new one is clean,
warm and has mechanised feeding. It's not work – it's sheer pleasure. So if you
meet a smiling dairy woman you know she's from the new yard.

But ours is the old one. The building is decrepit and raging winds howl around
it like on the open steppe. We have more cows than the new yard but there's
not a trace of mechanisation. We drag hay and silage from one end to the
other, clambering over enormous steep-sided mountains of manure. That's
why we come to work at four in the morning.

We went to see the boss of our kolkhoz. However you look at it, we said, our
yard doesn't correspond to the spirit of the times. But the boss looked at us

reproachfully and said. 'Every unit is needed, every unit is important, and yours – even more so. It's a working museum on our own kolkhoz. We certainly appreciate everything else in comparison with it.'

We fell silent listening to these words of wisdom. And then, put to shame, we made our way back to our yard. We didn't look at each other as we went. We felt awkward. So, it seemed, an honour like that had been conferred upon us – our yard was to remain as a living embodiment of the unit of the past so that against it today's achievements in animal husbandry could be observed more clearly. And we hadn't seen things in perspective. We had had no idea.

Now of course we understand our historic mission and are prepared for the good of the cause to be museum exhibits. But if only they'd raise our wages a bit. We work manually but we get the same as the dairy women in the new yard. We talked about this to the boss but he replied 'It's too late!' And said not another word.

What 'it's too late' means the boss didn't explain. And we are afraid to ask. What if we show up our limited mental outlook again? After all, who knows what our boss might be hinting at?[74]

Letters such as this often lead to radical changes for their authors. As the striking results of press intervention are published they doubtless encourage others to adopt a similar line of attack.

In recent years concern has been expressed over the effects of poor working conditions on women's health. Surveys have found that dairy women fall ill more often than agricultural labourers. Many days are lost through accidents and through chest and intestinal infections caused by unhygienic conditions and prolonged hours spent in a humid atmosphere. Women working the traditional single shift regularly complain of a lack of sleep. Where work has intensified with the introduction of the new system, there has been an increase in back problems and disorders of the arms and hands in dairy women employed in units with inadequate mechanisation.[75]

A work study report on a dairy unit in Chelyabinsk Region indicated the principal causes of strain in such cases. The unit employed a two-shift system under which each dairy woman was responsible for seventy cows during her nine-hour shift. Feeding was done by hand and involved each woman in carrying between sixty and seventy buckets of mash a total distance of over 1,000 metres at each feed. In addition she would also distribute between 240 and 280 kilos of hay and the same amount of straw or other bedding material by hand each shift. As a hose was not provided for washing the udders, each woman fetched five or six buckets of hot water during milking. Milking itself took up between two and two and a half hours and, although mechanised, 'the operator ... works for more than half this time in an uncomfortable position'.[76] During the late seventies studies of this type have been followed by official inspections of health and safety provision for women livestock workers. Although some efforts have been made to provide special medical services for dairy women, for example through regular courses of physiotherapy and massage, there has been criticism that farms ignore safety regulations and do little to prevent occupational disease.[77]

Staff shortages in dairying

The combination of poor management attitudes and a punishing work schedule evokes protests and attempts at change in some dairy women. In others the response is simply to look elsewhere for employment. Surveys have shown that those who remain in dairying despite the conditions do so primarily for economic reasons. As they grow older, however, and unable to cope with the physical strain of the work, women often transfer to agricultural labouring jobs. Younger women with several children also often find the workload beyond them and are similarly obliged to accept less well-paid work. Amongst the youngest group of workers, researchers have found an extremely high degree of dissatisfaction with the job. The majority of young dairy women on old-style farms see their occupation as a purely temporary means of employment before entering college or finding work in industry or the service sector.[78]

For women who have grown up in the countryside and have worked with livestock for many years the decision to leave is often made with regret. Experienced workers in animal husbandry commonly express a love of animals amongst their reasons for remaining in the work, the following comment being characteristic, 'Some people think our work is uninteresting but our hearts ache if we know that the cows haven't been fed.'[79] A long letter from a woman with a background such as this was published in the national newspaper *Sel'skaya zhizn'* (Rural Life) in 1980:

Not long ago I changed my job. From the dairy unit on the 'Native Land' kolkhoz I moved to a bakery. I didn't leave because I was looking for an easy life, not by any means. It was a difficult step for me; after all I'd worked with livestock for eighteen years. I loved my job and was proud of it. I swapped the unit for the factory because they don't care about dairy women on the kolkhoz, they get no attention and no concern.

The writer goes on to describe the conditions on the farm: little mechanisation, poor accounting leading to huge fluctuations in pay, managers and specialists who continually passed the buck, staff shortages leading to few and irregular days off. In eighteen years she had never once had a holiday. She compares all this with the excellent conditions on the neighbouring 'Dawn' kolkhoz and expresses mixed feelings at being virtually driven out of the job:

Now I'm a baker, everything's going fine for me at the bakery. But I often think, perhaps I wasn't right to leave the kolkhoz. I gave up a job I loved and which I'd given so many years to instead of helping to put things right with my friends, with the whole collective. And what's more, I miss my former charges, the cows. Here's something for the managers of the 'Native Land' kolkhoz to think about too. I am certain that if they looked after the livestock workers there like they do on the 'Dawn' kolkhoz, dairy women wouldn't leave the unit.[80]

Observing the plight of women of their mother's generation young girls today are refusing to work on units with archaic conditions and indifferent management. Reports from many areas demonstrate the willingness of school leavers to take up work in dairying where processes are mechanised and shift systems are introduced. When these are lacking young women are conspicuous by their absence from the units; few are prepared to sacrifice their social and family life to the demands of the evening milking session. As a woman journalist recently observed, 'Amongst the girls whom I managed to talk to I noticed a barely-hidden alarm at the very words "dairy woman".'[81]

The results for the farms can be catastrophic. In the Non-Black Earth Zone in particular the situation has become critical. In 1982 Novgorod Region was short of 600 dairy women, whilst Pskov Region needed 5,000 extra workers in livestock farming. In 1980 a state farm director in Vologda Region confessed, 'We are taking men away from their work, turning fieldworkers and drivers into dairy women. It's bad for the cows without women's hands but there are getting to be less and less of them in the countryside.' In Ivanovo Region managers of industrial enterprises were at one stage taking it in turns to milk the cows on certain of the region's farms. Dairying suffers from a high turnover of women recruited to help solve the problem, leaving many units with an ageing and low-skilled workforce. In Pskov Region in 1982, for example, 2,916 dairy women were over the national retirement age, whilst only 685 were under thirty.[82] Where staff shortages are acute, farm managers find themselves caught in a vicious circle: with so few employees it is virtually impossible to introduce a two-shift system, and without a two-shift system new workers cannot be recruited.

Since the late seventies the Party has taken some action to alleviate acute problems such as these. In the three years to 1981, 381,000 young people were directed into animal husbandry under the auspices of the Komsomol. This has been promoted as a patriotic duty and was described by Leonid Brezhnev as 'a sign of civic maturity, convincing evidence that the younger generation has the interests of the country at heart'.[83] Since the 26th Party Congress in 1981 whole classes of school leavers have been urged to remain on their native farms, usually for a one-year period, the girls setting up Komsomol youth teams in dairying. The sudden arrival of large numbers of young women in previously understaffed dairy units has resulted in some cases in the introduction of new work schedules and better conditions. It seems doubtful, however, that the Komsomol's campaign will prove to be more than a cosmetic measure aimed at papering over the cracks. The fundamental problems for women in dairying seem unlikely to be addressed as long as production can be guaranteed by a succession of purely temporary workers.

Recent employment trends

The highly mechanised dairy complexes which provide improved conditions for women remain the most attractive workplaces for young women beginning their working lives in farming. Automation in dairying, however, in its most advanced forms, reduces the workforce substantially.[84] As a result, attractive job opportunities in this area of agriculture remain restricted. It is significant, therefore, that women increasingly find themselves competing with young men for positions in automated units.

Between 1959 and 1970 the proportion of women amongst milking personnel decreased slightly in all major regions of dairy farming.[85] It can be assumed on the basis of press comment that this trend has continued. The title 'machine milking operator' has been introduced on mechanised farms in preference to the designation 'dairy woman' or 'dairy man'. The emphasis on the technical aspects of the work which this new title implies, together with full-scale mechanisation, has enabled some young men to overcome the traditional prejudices which dairying inspires. In recent years men have appeared regularly in the lists of prizewinners in dairy competitions; in 1983 a man from a

Kaluga Region state farm became USSR machine milking champion. One of the most highly automated dairy complexes in the Soviet Union, situated near Riga in Latvia, is staffed exclusively by men. To those who express surprise at the employment of men in this time-honoured female occupation the reason can be easily explained. In the words of two male prizewinners, 'It's a machine operator's profession now.'[86]

In Central Asia, the introduction of fully automated units has not been necessary to draw men into dairying. Where only simple technology has been installed men have often been involved from the first in the operation of the new machinery. By 1970 in Kirgizia, for example, 49% of milking was done by machine. Although women monopolised work with dairy cows, one survey found that only 0.1% of dairy women actually operated milking machinery.[87]

In European areas men are far from endangering women's predominance in dairy farming. Yet the recent trend is of importance for women precisely because men are entering the profession as an elite workforce in the most attractive and prestigious units. At a time when so many young women are rejecting traditional employment opportunities on old-style dairy farms it is significant that automation is opening up this sphere of agriculture to men. As in fatstock production, recent examples in dairying show that it is by no means automatic that women will benefit from technological progress.

AGRICULTURAL LABOURERS

Despite increasing investment in mechanisation, Soviet agriculture remains highly dependent on manual labour. One estimate from the late seventies suggests that 65% of agricultural work is done manually, compared with less than 40% of work in industry. As a result, a large group of workers is employed by the farms as agricultural labourers in arable farming and horticulture. Between 1959 and 1970 the number of general labourers working in agriculture was almost halved, falling to under 13 million. Nevertheless, employees in this category still amounted to 56% of the agricultural workforce. In addition, a further 4% of workers in farming were employed in non-mechanised work in horticulture.*[88]

Table 7 shows the representation of women amongst agricultural

* These include the occupational categories listed in the Soviet census as workers in plant propagation and feed production, orchard and vineyard workers, vegetable and melon growers.

Table 7 *Women agricultural labourers, 1959 and 1970*

	1959	1970
Workers in plant propagation and feed production	432,464	438,337
as % all so employed	70.7	74.4
as % all female agricultural workers	2.2	3.5
Orchard and vineyard workers, vegetable and melon growers	123,001	229,478
as % all so employed	64.3	72.0
as % all female agricultural workers	0.6	1.8
General agricultural labourers	15,932,948	9,117,308[a]
as % all so employed	65.8	72.2[a]
as % all female agricultural workers	80.7	71.3[a]

[a] Owing to the incomplete data on female occupational categories in the 1970 census, these figures represent estimates which are undoubtedly higher than the true figures. On the basis of female representation recorded in the 1959 census, I estimate that the total number of general agricultural labourers may be exaggerated by as much as 290,000, which would reduce the percentage quoted by approximately 3%.

Sources: *Itogi . . . 1970*, Vol. VI, Tables 2, 18; *Itogi vsesoyuznoi perepisi naseleniya 1959 goda, SSSR (svodnyi tom)*, Moscow 1962, Table 46.

labourers from 1959 to 1970. As the Table illustrates, women are over-represented in this section of the agricultural workforce. Increased mechanisation has been accompanied by a contraction of the labour force and a greater degree of specialisation amongst agricultural workers. Although the number of women employed as general labourers fell by more than two-fifths in the eleven years between censuses, the representation of women amongst these unskilled and non-specialised workers actually increased. In consequence, the largest single category of women in the agricultural workforce today is still that of the general labourer.

Employment in the private sector

A further category of agricultural labourers are those employed by private agriculture. This group comprises those who, in Soviet censuses, are said to derive their principal means of subsistence from private subsidiary agriculture. A great many rural women, of course, whilst employed on state or collective farms also work part-time on their private plots. The labour input of these women to private agriculture and the importance of the plots both for the rural family and for the state is considered in Chapter 2 below.

Throughout the period from 1960, over 90% of those employed exclusively in private agriculture have been women. By 1979, however, only 0.8% of rural women were employed solely in the private sector.[89]

The proportion of rural women employed in private agriculture varies considerably from one region to another. The majority of women employed only in the private sector are either elderly or mothers of large families. Republics with ageing rural populations or with high birthrates, therefore, number amongst those in which a higher than average proportion of rural women are employed in private farming, notably Lithuania and Tadzhikistan. This does not, however, provide of itself a sufficient explanation for the pattern of regional variation observable for female employment in the private sector, and it would appear that other local, historical factors may have a role to play. The nature of the work performed by women in private subsidiary agriculture is discussed at greater length in Chapter 2. The following observations on the nature of women's employment as agricultural labourers are, therefore, confined to the socialised sector.

Seasonal employment patterns

The short growing season characteristic of much of the USSR produces sharply seasonal patterns of employment in arable farming. A survey of 1,036 collective farms in the RSFSR in 1967 found that more than half the total labour input in arable farming was recorded between July and October. By contrast, only 14.7% of the hours worked were recorded between December and March. [90] The content of the work of agricultural labourers as well as the hours involved fluctuates considerably by region and according to the demands of the farming year. The results of a survey of six state farms in Belorussia in 1971 provide an example of the jobs undertaken by agricultural labourers during the course of a typical year in this region:

January to March   carting manure
April   sorting potatoes

May	loading, transporting, planting and weeding potatoes
June to July	cutting and ricking hay, carting and stacking hay in barns
August	drying grain after rain during harvest, stacking straw, drying and sorting grain in the stores
September to October	lifting potatoes and other root crops
November to December	sorting seed in grain stores, carting manure[91]

As arable farming and horticulture demand a far larger workforce in summer and autumn than in winter, many workers are, in effect, seasonally unemployed. As the majority of general labourers are women, so the majority of those facing seasonal unemployment are likewise women. Although women predominate in livestock farming with its constant demand for labour throughout the year, only one in five female agricultural workers is employed in this way. The permanent labour force on the farms is therefore predominantly male as agricultural machine operators can be transferred to work transporting fertilisers and feedstuffs or repairing machinery in winter. Similarly, male manual workers are preferred for employment in various types of repair and construction work during the winter months. In consequence, a pattern emerges of relatively stable employment for men throughout the year whilst many women, with the major exception of animal husbandry workers, remain underemployed.[92]

The 1967 survey of the RSFSR cited above found that 86% of the able-bodied men compared with only 62% of the able-bodied women working on collective farms in the peak months of July to October were also employed between December and March.[93] As these figures cover all occupations on the collective farms it may be assumed that the fall in demand for women labourers in the winter was considerably greater. A survey of seven kolkhozes in Stavropol' Territory in the mid-seventies, for example, found that two-thirds of women agricultural labourers worked only occasionally in the winter. Seasonal patterns of employment appear also to be subject to a good deal of regional variation in line with agricultural specialisation and the available labour supply. In Tadzhikistan and the Caucasian republics, for example, it has been said that half the women who work in July are not at work in December. Similarly, on the cotton growing kolkhozes of Southern Kirgizia, where the overwhelming majority of women work as field labourers, more than a third of total hours worked by women were recorded during cotton picking from September to November, whilst only a tenth of total hours were worked between December and March.[94]

For agricultural labourers who are employed in winter, the length of the working day appears to differ widely according to the needs of production. A survey of women engaged in fieldwork on state and collective farms in Rostov Region in 1973–4 indicated a contraction of no more than forty minutes of the working day from summer to winter, the working day on state farms, however, being around an hour shorter than on the collectives. A similar survey of Stavropol' Territory showed the working day of women fieldworkers to be, at six hours, more than two hours shorter in winter than in summer. In the Ukraine, however, women labourers on collective farms in one district were found to work three times longer each day in June than in January.[95]

The unskilled and seasonal nature of agricultural labouring makes this the least well-paid occupation on the farms. Surveys indicate that low pay is a major cause of dissatisfaction amongst this group of workers.[96] Yet the hours of work and seasonal unemployment which depress gross earnings appear to be acceptable and even attractive to certain groups of workers. Women with young children, for example, may transfer to a labouring job to escape the work regime in dairying. Although a labourer's wages appear to be between a half and a third of earnings in animal husbandry, these women find the work convenient where child care provision is limited and see it as a form of temporary part-time work.[97] Similarly women under twenty wishing to enter higher education may take on a labouring job as a temporary, intellectually undemanding means of earning a living which allows maximum time for study. Available data suggest that women who decide on such a course of action may well have already received a higher level of education than their male counterparts and thus express a great deal of dissatisfaction both with their pay and with the monotonous and exhausting character of the work.[98]

Gang labour in the fields is employed from spring to autumn: from sowing, through weeding to harvesting and, later, in preparing crops for storage or processing. Women's labour is employed in all weathers in the cultivation of fruit, vegetables, sugar beet and rice. As late as 1973, 80% of the work involved in the production of sugar beet was done by hand. In recent years, however, the mechanisation of beet cultivation has increased dramatically: in Kiev Region of the Ukraine, for example, it was reported that by 1981 the manual labour required to produce 100 kilos of beet had fallen to half 1979 levels.[99] It would appear, however, that the drilling of sugar beet seed is less carefully controlled than, for example, in Britain, and that spraying to keep down weeds is less commonly undertaken. As a result, many fundamental operations in beet cultivation are carried out manually by women. A woman sugar beet grower from Vinnitsa Region of the Ukraine described what is involved in thinning out sugar beet seedlings:

The main thing is not to make a mistake when, straining your eyes and summoning all your patience, you try to leave the strongest seedlings in the rows, not to litter them with sickly shoots. Up to thirty sprout in every meter but you only keep six or seven. You have to leave enough room for the root to grow between each seedling that you keep. Altogether up to 400,000 seedlings are pulled up from each hectare. And you have to bend over every one of them, have a long look at some of them; you don't choose immediately as if one were as good as another. And from the very first the weeds have to be pulled up. Your back aches and your feet get heavy. That's what it's like, forming the crop.[100]

It is scarcely surprising that women regularly involved in this work have a saying, 'You wash your family in sweat whilst the harvest is growing.'[101]

Technological change and the status of women's work

The changing nature of sugar beet production with the growth of automation provides a graphic example of the rigid occupational segregation which characterises Soviet agriculture. As men monopolise the job of agricultural machine operator in every sphere of arable farming so, as machines have been introduced into beet production, the leading teams of workers have become male or are led by men. There have been very few attempts to train experienced women sugar beet growers to operate the new machinery. Those who have sought training and employment in machine operation have faced the problems common to all rural women who try to enter this male domain. Consequently, it is all too evident that women are becoming a second-class workforce on the sugar beet fields. As one journalist, attempting to put the matter in a kindly light, described this

'This is for you, men, as the stronger sex!'

'But you won't be able to manage a machine like that, girls, so you get the easier tools.'

(*Krest'yanka*, 2, 1975, p. 27)

development, 'the men have the machines, the women have years of experience, natural patience and the knack of dealing with this capricious crop'.[102]

There is evidence that women do feel upset at the way in which their work has been devalued with the advent of mechanisation. Some have complained that the men receive both honours and high financial rewards for their work whilst the women still labour from dawn till dusk as their grandmothers did. Others have complained that the needs of women manual workers are not taken seriously and that their heavy work is made more difficult by the poor organisation of rural services and nursery schools at peak periods.[103] What is certain is that manual labour holds very little attraction for school leavers and, as a result, the work remains firmly the province of middle-aged and elderly women for whom fieldwork has become a way of life.

As manual labour remains an essential element of horticulture the ageing of the female workforce has become a matter of concern in certain areas. In the words of a sugar beet team leader in the Ukraine:

Those of us who are used to manual work are getting older. When we finish work, who will grow the the beet? Young girls today have secondary education so of course it's hard on them to become labourers. Unskilled work scares them off. There's no way out of this. We need 100% mechanisation in beet production. There's no question about it. But until the technology is developed it's essential to raise the status of manual work in operations which decide the fate of the harvest.[104]

The question of 'raising the status of manual work' has given rise to a variety of experiments with bonus systems and revised work schedules. Shift working has been introduced on some farms during the busiest months, shortening the women's working day from eleven or twelve hours to a standard seven hours. Other farms have employed a system whereby each woman labourer is responsible for a given area of land from sowing to harvesting. She receives a monthly wage during the growing season and a cash bonus at harvest time for every 1% over the plan target which she can produce. In addition, certain districts have introduced a range of honours for manual workers, bestowing on the most successful the titles 'Master vegetable grower' and 'Master of agriculture'. Judging by press reports the new systems have proved highly popular with the women concerned.[105]

In recent years these initiatives have been supported by occasional articles in the press which paint glowing portraits of leading women manual workers. Such articles appear to be in part a response to criticism of the heavy emphasis in the press on the activities of machine operators. Rural women activists in a reported meeting with journalists, for example, commented, 'We can't manage yet without manual work in the countryside yet editors pay little attention to the people who are employed in it.'[106] In an attempt to redress the balance, lengthy articles on the lives and achievements of brigade leaders in horticulture have been published, each of them stressing the exceptional qualities and personal authority of these women. Articles referring to manual labour almost invariably describe it as being performed by 'highly skilful ... genuinely golden women's hands'.[107] Yet the descriptions of the working day contained in these attempts to add dignity to manual work provide in themselves an explanation for the absence of young women from the fields. A trade union official from the Ukraine described the effect on women labourers of weeding vegetables:

Who doesn't know how hard it can be to weed tomatoes, cucumbers or cabbage by hand! The women would work until dinner time when they could hardly stand from tiredness. A hot meal would be brought to them in the fields but they wouldn't even look at it; they just wanted to rest in a bit of shade. Heavy work caused illness. One wouldn't turn up for work, then another ... the farm looked for a way out for a long time. But are you likely to find one when the basic tool of production in weeding is the hoe?![108]

Whilst the most backbreaking labour may be relieved by more widespread application of herbicides, it is clear that there remains no shortage of tasks in which monotony and fatigue are the order of the day. Recent Soviet research into occupational health has established a connection between the heavy physical work performed by the majority of rural women and the increased incidence of heart disease, and especially of hypertension, amongst this sector of the population. One survey for example, found that rural women in Moscow Region were one and a half times more likely than rural men and three and a half times more likely than urban women to suffer from heart disease.[109] As mechanisation increases and improves there is little to prevent young women seeing manual labour as a job without a future. No amount of talk about 'golden women's hands' can disguise the fact that the work demands enormous physical effort for very little material reward. In the eyes of many, and often of the women themselves, the job performed by the majority of women in Soviet agriculture remains a singularly unattractive profession.

WOMEN IN INDUSTRY AND THE SERVICE SECTOR

In recent years the expansion of rural services and industrial enterprises has begun to provide an alternative for women to employment in agriculture. The development of industry and the service sector has, however, been subject to a great deal of regional variation. The employment of rural women in these branches of the economy fluctuates enormously from one region to another according to the availability of this type of employment and the influence of cultural factors. Although the census provides a breakdown of the workforce to republic level only, the available data are indicative of general trends in current rural development.

In 1970, 13% of employed rural women in the USSR worked in industry. In the RSFSR, however, and the Baltic republics of Estonia and Latvia the figures recorded were between 18% and 20%. At the other end of the scale, less than 5% of rural women worked in industry in Azerbaidzhan and the Central Asian republics, with the exception of Kirgizia. Similarly the service sector, including health and education, employed considerably more women than the national average in the RSFSR, Estonia and Kirgizia, reaching its peak in Kazakhstan where it employed 25% of working rural women. Once again the three Central Asian republics of Uzbekistan, Turkmenia and Tadzhikistan were at the bottom of the league with the service sector employing between 8% and 11% of the female rural workforce.[110]

Despite the growing numbers involved there is little information available on the rural women employed in these sectors of the economy at anything other than specialist level. One of the few sociological surveys of rural industrial workers was carried out in 1971 in Belorussia. This found that the majority of rural industrial workers were men; a finding in line with national trends. Men were employed in heavy physical work in brickworks and in factories producing peat and alcohol, whilst women were to be found in large numbers only in enterprises connected with the processing of dairy products and the production of linen.[111]

Belorussian rural factories were found to attract a far younger workforce than was characteristic on the farms. In industry, 18% of male employees and 23% of female employees were under thirty, whereas only 7% of the collective farm workforce was in this age group. Women industrial workers, the survey discovered, were generally rather less well-educated than the men, although the reverse was true amongst the youngest groups of workers. The discrepancy between grading and skill levels of men and women at work was, however, far larger than their educational differences. Whilst 30% of men and 40% of women rural industrial workers had received only a primary education, only 28% of men compared with 65% of women were classified in the bottom three grades of the workforce. In consequence, more than a quarter of the men but a mere 2% of the women were in the top two grades. In addition, many rural factories recruited unskilled workers on a seasonal basis in accordance with the needs of production. These workers were found to be almost exclusively female: women, it was discovered, sought seasonal industrial employment as a form of part-time work to fit in with domestic commitments.[112]

The development of factories on state and collective farms to combat seasonal agricultural unemployment is leading increasing numbers of women to divide their working year between industry and farming. The very limited data which exist as to the effect of this trend on female employment suggest that this pattern of work is most characteristic of young rural women: in one survey 81% of women employed in this way were under thirty-five. Though available data show the majority of those who work in both agriculture and subsidiary industries to be women, one survey found that the women employed in this way spent far less of their working year in industrial employment than did the men: 41% of the days worked by women compared with 65% of the days worked by men were spent in industry. Nevertheless, the financial benefits of industrial employment for collective farm women were considerable, with 61% of their annual income deriving from their industrial employment.[113] The introduction of industry to the farms has proved attractive to women not only for its material rewards but also because it can offer a standardised working day.

In recent years greater attention has been paid to the question of introducing industry to the rural areas of Central Asia. The policy has been seen both as a means of providing employment for the growing and underutilised labour force in these areas and as a spur to migration to the towns for the largely static rural population. The hope has been expressed that by mastering urban professions in their native villages young people in Central Asia will be encouraged to consider a move to nearby towns which are at present highly dependent on a skilled workforce recruited from other republics.[114] The growth of mechanisation in agricultural production has decreased employment opportunities in this area, especially for women, whilst large families and inadequate child care facilities make it difficult for women to seek full-time non-seasonal work. It would appear that many young women would be happy to work in rural industry yet suffer from a lack of skills. A survey of five districts of Tadzhikistan, for example, published in 1975, revealed that more than half the women who expressed a wish to work outside the home had no marketable skills whatsoever and were therefore overlooked when rural industry recruited new staff or trainees.[115] Branches of major industrial enterprises, mostly in textile manufacturing, are being developed in heavily populated rural areas of Uzbekistan. It has been admitted that the unskilled nature of their predominantly female workforce has created problems in the initial stages, with productivity in the rural factories at only 30% of that of the parent enterprise. One report, for example, commented, 'it should be said frankly that amongst the 200 employees per shift at the weaving mill the five women work supervisors from Fergana simply get lost and are not able to help everyone'. As the policy has the blessing of the Communist Party at the highest levels, however, such factories may well appear throughout Central Asia.[116]

Education, welfare and consumer services are, at all levels, dominated by women. Few data are available on the unskilled and semi-skilled workers in these fields, yet it would appear that women who take unskilled work in clubs, canteens, shops or libraries may be considerably better educated than their counterparts in industry or agriculture. The report of a survey carried out in the late 1960s under the auspices of the Belorussian Academy of Sciences concluded: 'The influx of workers with relatively high levels of general education into this sector is completely understandable in view of the limited choice for women of skilled professions in rural areas.'[117] It would seem that women are attracted to these jobs which make few demands of their abilities by better working conditions than may be found in farming.

Work in the service sector is invariably portrayed in the press as an extension of a woman's nurturant role. Articles regularly emphasise the importance of the job of cook or canteen worker, especially during harvesting. At this time of year the volume of work in catering increases dramatically as the workforce swells and a mobile meals service is often provided for workers out in the fields. Journalists stress that catering numbers amongst the 'caring professions' and that its employees have an important role in boosting the morale of agricultural workers, as the following characteristic extract makes clear: 'The ability to create home comfort at the field station, to crack a well-timed joke and in this way to raise the spirits of the grain growers, and above all to give them a satisfying meal – all of this marks her out as the head cook of the collective farm canteen.'[118] As the provision of services in rural areas, notably in catering and child care, follows the demands of agricultural production, employees in these areas may be hired on a seasonal basis only. Like horticultural labourers, unskilled workers in the service sector may find themselves unemployed in the winter months.[119]

WOMEN IN THE RURAL INTELLIGENTSIA

The majority of specialists, 56% of the total employed in rural areas in 1970, were women. As in unskilled and semi-skilled rural professions a considerable degree of occupational segregation was in evidence amongst the rural intelligentsia. Women formed 75% of what Soviet sociologists term the non-productive intelligentsia: that is, specialists in education, health and culture. Amongst the productive intelligentsia, specialists directly concerned with agricultural production, women formed only 31% of the workforce.[120] There is little reason to suppose that a radical change in this pattern of employment has taken place since this date.

Specialists in health, education and culture

The predominance of women specialists in rural health and education mirrors the representation of women in these professions in the economy as a whole. Throughout the 1970s women have formed 71% of all Soviet teachers in general educational schools. In 1970, 74% of doctors were women; a figure which had fallen to 69% by 1979. The representation of women amongst paramedical staff is still higher. In 1970 women made up 83% of all Soviet medical assistants (feldshers) and midwives and over 99% of nurses. In addition, 65% of cultural workers in this same year were women.[121]

As the rural intelligentsia is considerably less diverse and less highly skilled than its urban counterpart, teachers form a major element in it. In 1970 teachers formed 30% of the rural population with higher or specialised secondary education compared with only 6% of the urban population with this degree of educational attainment.[122] Surveys suggest that teaching is slightly less feminised in rural than in urban areas but that women teachers in rural schools, as in the towns, are concentrated in class teaching and are under-represented amongst head teachers. Across the country as a whole around a third of secondary school head teachers are women. As a result, men predominate at the top of the pay structure in teaching although surveys have shown that their length of service and level of qualification differ little from that of women. To illustrate the disparity between men and women in posts of responsibility, a survey of rural teachers in Novosibirsk Region in 1967 found that, of the 70 men and 564 women questioned, only 51% of the men compared with 82% of the women were employed at the basic level of class teacher.[123]

Rural schools have a less highly trained and younger workforce than urban schools. Graduates of pedagogical institutes are, where possible, directed into their first appointment in a rural school where they are expected to remain for the initial three years of their career. Although this system provides staff for remote areas which would otherwise experience extreme difficulty in attracting qualified teachers, it means that rural schools suffer from a high turnover of young and inexperienced staff. Many return to the towns at the earliest opportunity whilst the overwhelming majority of teachers remaining in rural schools are themselves of rural origin. It is a regular practice for schools suffering severe staff shortages to recruit local young people for the work who then become qualified as part-time external students of teacher training colleges.[124]

In order to encourage graduates to remain in the villages and to form a stable workforce in the schools a range of benefits is available for rural teachers. Young teachers with higher or specialised secondary education are eligible for state loans of up to 1,000 roubles over a period of five years. All teachers are entitled to free flats with heating and lighting, or assistance with these if living in their own home. In an attempt to attract well-qualified men into rural schools, teachers with higher education are exempt from military service throughout their period of employment in a rural area. Articles appearing in *Krest'yanka* magazine in 1980 on these provisions for rural teachers evoked many letters from women who were clearly unaware of their entitlements.[125]

Ignorance of the law or a failure by local authorities to act upon it leads to problems for many rural teachers. Poor planning and liaison between construction agencies results in a lack of housing for teachers when new schools are built. In consequence, teachers are often housed in dormitories or taken as lodgers by local people. Women teachers with young children find the lack of pre-school facilities in rural areas a problem which may oblige them to look for work elsewhere.[126]

For women teachers, however, a major reason for leaving the village is the need to keep a private allotment and the consequent lack of free time which they enjoy. Surveys in Novosibirsk Region in the late 1960s indicated that women teachers had one and a half times less free time than their male colleagues as a result of their involvement in private agriculture. As a result, 48% of the men and 76% of the women teachers surveyed said that they found their work very tiring. It was found that the total amount of time spent by women working for their school, in the home and on the plot often averaged between eighty and eighty-five hours per week.[127] Although efforts have been made by some state and collective farms to provide local teachers with farm produce, thereby removing the necessity for a plot, it has been noted that insufficient attention has been paid to the problem. It is not surprising, therefore, that women graduates of urban institutes are often unwilling to take up work in the village. 'Where there's a cow, there's no teacher', is the terse observation on the subject said to be current in the countryside.[128]

Small rural institutions with few staff present similar problems for both teachers and doctors, demanding of them a broad general knowledge and reducing the opportunities for specialisation. The demands of rural conditions on medical staff are particularly high. In the countryside doctor–patient ratios are considerably higher than in the towns: 17.9 doctors per 10,000 rural population as against 34.5 per 10,000 urban population in 1974. As in teaching, medicine suffers from a high staff turnover and acute localised staff shortages have been reported.[129] The resulting workload on individual doctors may be extremely heavy, prolonging the working day and allowing little or no free time. The shortage of qualified doctors in the countryside has made the paramedical worker (the feldsher, nurse or feldsher-midwife) a key figure in rural health care. Paramedical staff have far higher responsibilities in primary care and diagnosis than do their equivalents in the towns and the pressure of work upon them appears to differ little from that of rural doctors.[130]

Rural doctors now receive higher pay than their urban counterparts; in 1972 doctors with higher educational qualifications received a starting salary of 100 to 110 roubles per month in the towns, 110 to 138 roubles in the villages. It is clear, however, that this provides insufficient compensation for the rigours of the job in the countryside. Problems with housing affect medical as well as teaching staff; a survey of medical staff leaving their posts in Moldavia found unsatisfactory living conditions cited twice as often as the reason for resignation in the villages as in the towns.[131] An additional problem for rural doctors is the provision of transport necessary to attend emergencies and the lack of hard-surface roads. As one survey has revealed the doctor is more often than not obliged to reach the patient on foot. Taking into account conditions such as these the authors of this survey conclude: 'It is not surprising that by no means all young specialists find in themselves the strength and desire to overcome these difficulties. The village frightens them and, after working for three or four years, they are keen to settle in the towns.'[132]

An extremely rapid turnover of staff is also characteristic of rural cultural workers, though for rather different reasons. Unlike doctors and teachers, women employed in rural clubs rarely have a higher education. Indeed, more than half of the rural cultural workers have received no special training for the job whatsoever. Most club workers are employed in their native villages, very many of them being recent school leavers who have taken the job as a temporary measure.[133] The role of cultural workers in the countryside is potentially highly complex. A survey carried out in Belorussia in 1969, for example, found that they were expected to cater for the tastes of the broad mass of the population which was both elderly and poorly educated, as well as for a small group of well-educated and skilled young people. The lack of training or experience and the youth of many club workers inevitably created difficulties when faced with such a task. 'Having experienced the bitter taste of several failures', this survey stated, 'many of them ... hand in their resignations and change not only their place of work but also their occupation.'[134] It would appear that it is this lack of professionalism which contributes to the dismissive attitudes towards them said to be displayed by many farm managements. Disinterest on the part of farm officials in the intended role of club workers diminishes the prestige of the job. As a result, a large-scale RSFSR survey in 1979 found club workers spending a significant amount of their time on activities which were wholly unconnected with culture, such as taking inventories of livestock or helping with work in the fields.[135]

During the 1970s an attempt was made to combat the inadequate preparation for their jobs characteristic of most rural cultural workers. Fifteen Institutes of Culture have been opened, twelve of them in the RSFSR, to produce a graduate labour force for rural clubs. However, the RSFSR survey cited above discovered that the innovation had not been a great success. It was found that both students and teachers at the institutes felt that the profession of cultural worker enjoyed little prestige. A mere 1.7% of first year and 0.8% of final year students wanted to work in rural clubs, whilst more than 27% admitted that they wanted to be professional musicians or actors but had been unable to get into the relevant college. When asked which qualities they felt were lacking in graduates, both staff and students responded, in order of importance, the ability to organise, a love of the profession, professionalism, initiative, general culture and erudition. This indictment of the training offered by the new institutes and of the quality of their rural intake mirrors the cynicism which I found amongst certain teachers at the Institute of Culture in Minsk. As one remarked of the students, 'they know nothing when they arrive and less when they leave'. It is a state of affairs which has led commentators to assume ironically that the institutes are preparing their students from the villages for work in the city.[136]

Common to all branches of the rural non-productive intelligentsia, then, are the problems stemming from a complex and demanding job, poor living conditions and the unhelpful attitudes of local farm managers. By comparison with the urban intelligentsia, rural specialists also frequently suffer from a sense of isolation and may experience greater difficulties in establishing personal relationships. Sociologists have paid some attention to the question of marriage and family life amongst rural specialists, seeing in the demographic structure of the villages a reason for the return of so many qualified women to the towns. More teachers, for example, remain unmarried in the countryside than in urban areas. In an overwhelmingly female profession, a survey of Novosibirsk Region in the late 1960s found that 24% of urban teachers but 40% of rural teachers were unmarried. Similar results were recorded by a survey of Sverdlovsk Region some five years later.[137] The lower rate of marriage amongst rural teachers reflects the problems of adaptation to rural life, including those experienced by rural girls who have studied in the city, and the difficulty of finding a partner to conform to expectations. In Sverdlovsk Region it was found that only 19% of teachers' husbands had a higher education, compared with a figure of 49% in the towns. Just under half the urban teachers in the sample but only 28% of rural teachers were married to men who worked as specialists.[138]

The tendency of young women to move to the towns in search of a husband has led at least one sociologist to suggest a form of 'marriage bureau' for undergraduates to help stabilise the workforce of rural specialists:

It would be advisable for the Komsomol committe of higher education institutions to arrange inter-college meetings of students studying for agricultural specialisms (agronomists, vets, agricultural engineers etc.) with students from teacher training, medical and cultural institutes. The organisation of such contacts may facilitate the establishment of young families orientated towards permanent settlement in the countryside.[139]

It is a suggestion which underlines the pronounced division by sex of professions engaged in by specialists in the Soviet countryside.

Table 8 *Women specialists on state and collective farms, RSFSR, 1975*
(as % of all employed)

	State farms	Collective farms	In the whole economy[a]
Chief agronomists, zootechnicians and veterinary surgeons	20.5	23.3	
Agronomists	34.2	34.0	
Zootechnicians	53.3	58.1	
Veterinary surgeons, feldshers and technicians	44.9	33.1	
Chief engineers	0.4	0.4	
Engineers, technicians, mechanics, heads of repair workshops	5.0	1.1	48.0[b]
Economists	64.9	59.7	86.0[c]
Accountants	80.5	64.9	89.0[d]
Controllers	60.4	48.1	69.0

[a] Figures from 1970.
[b] Chief engineers, engineers and technicians.
[c] Economists and planners.
[d] Accountants and book-keepers.
Sources: V. I. Staroverov, *Sotsial'naya struktura sel'skogo naseleniya SSSR na etape razvitogo sotsializma*, Moscow, 1978, pp. 265–6; *Itogi ... 1970*, Vol. II, Table 19.

Specialists in agricultural production

The representation of women amongst specialists in animal husbandry is steadily increasing. By 1980 over 45,000 women were employed on farms as zootechnicians, 54% of the total, and a further 43,000 were employed as veterinary surgeons or their assistants, 37% of the total. The representation of women amongst agronomists appears to have fluctuated considerably since 1960. In 1980 over 28,000 women held such posts, 30% of the total.[140] Men, therefore, continue to predominate amongst agricultural specialists. Soviet farms, however, employ a range of specialists involved either directly or indirectly in agricultural production, and the representation of women varies enormously from one occupation to another. Table 8 illustrates the pattern of female employment at specialist level in the RSFSR in 1975.

The representation of women amongst agricultural specialists is considerably diminished at chief specialist level. In occupations other than the principal agricultural specialisms a clear split emerges between technical professions and those concerned with planning and accounting. Whilst women predominate amongst the latter group of specialists, their proportion is insignificant in technical occupations. This fact becomes the more striking when the employment of women on the farms is compared with that in the economy as a whole. Whilst the professions of economist and accountant are considerably less feminised on the farms than in the rest of the economy, the discrepancy between farm and non-farm employment of women as technical specialists is truly enormous. Although almost half the engineers and technicians in the RSFSR are women they hold only 3% of these jobs on state and collective farms. This pattern is characteristic of the whole of the USSR. Although the number of women engineers and technicians on the farms is slowly growing, by 1980 their representation had reached only 5.2%.[141]

Female representation amongst agricultural specialists varies significantly from one region to another. In 1970, women made up 36% of Soviet agronomists, zootechnicians and vets. The proportion of women in these occupations, however, ranged from over 47% in Estonia and Latvia to 12% or less in Uzbekistan, Turkmenia and Azerbaidzhan.[142] In Islamic areas the employment of women as agricultural specialists has been hindered by traditional attitudes which have made it difficult for women to seek training in institutes far from their native villages or to find employment after training. As a result, although numbers are increasing, native Central Asian women form a minority of women specialists in many areas of their region.[143]

Rural sociologists have observed that there appears to be no good reason for the maintenance of such pronounced occupational segregation at specialist level. Describing the under-representation of women amongst specialists in rural Azerbaidzhan in the mid-1960s one writer made the following comment, equally applicable in today's conditions:

All this cannot be explained by the position of women in the family or their inability to carry out these jobs. In the opinion of the author, occupations and work in agriculture which could easily be undertaken by women should be offered to them wherever possible ... This would eliminate the artificial split between the use made of men's and women's working time.[144]

V. I. Staroverov, a prominent rural sociologist, commenting a decade later on the development of overtly 'male' and 'female' specialisms, noted that women's share of the 'male' professions could be significantly increased.[145] It seems clear that the rural bias against women and technology which is so apparent at machine operator level is not easily removed by women attaining higher qualifications. Conversely, there is little evidence that young men are developing an interest in traditionally 'female' specialisms. Many writers have stressed the undesirability of an overwhelmingly female teaching profession, for example, yet it would appear that occupations deemed to be 'women's work' have low status in the eyes of young men in the villages, as this comment suggests: 'We need to raise the prestige of the professions of teacher, cultural worker and doctor in the eyes of young men ... The predominance of female labour in the non-productive sphere serves as a peculiar psychological barrier to men working here.'[146] Although the growth in numbers of women specialists in most areas of the USSR has, since 1960, outstripped that of men, the pattern of growth has been far from even in all occupations. Women monopolise the service sector, planning and accounting on the farms whilst work in technical fields remains virtually closed to them.

WOMEN IN MANAGEMENT

In a country in which almost half the agricultural workforce is female, women remain grossly under-represented in management. Table 9 shows the prevailing status hierarchy in state and collectivised agriculture. The employment of women at the highest level of state farm director or collective farm chairperson has remained almost static since 1960. Of nearly 47,000 top management posts in agriculture, women occupy a mere 817. At the level of deputy chairperson or sector manager women do slightly better, making up 6% of all those employed. The general rule applies to all these occupations that, the lower the level, the greater the representation of women. Although women's share of management positions in animal husbandry is growing, it remains disproportionately low when considered against the predominance of women in this area of farming. Approximately three out of every four workers in the major branches of animal husbandry are women, yet they hold only 37% of supervisory posts in this sphere.

Table 9 *Women in collective and state farm management, USSR, 1980*

	Total number employed	Women employed	% women employed
Collective farms			
Chairperson	25,923	499	1.9
Deputy chairperson	20,824	1,528	7.3
Field brigade leader	116,361	11,344	9.7
Livestock brigade leader or head of livestock unit	71,662	24,978	34.9
State farms			
Director	20,825	318	1.5
Unit or sector manager	41,217	2,459	6.0
Field brigade leader	112,135	18,167	16.2
Livestock brigade leader or head of livestock unit	78,815	31,424	39.9

Source: Narodnoe khozyaistvo (1980), pp. 285, 287.

There is little available data from which to assess the degree of regional variation in management posts held by women. The 1970 census does, however, provide a breakdown by republic of women's representation amongst brigade leaders. In 1970, 17% of leaders of brigades of all types were women. In the Baltic republics women's share ranged from twice to three and a half times the national average. At the other end of the scale the proportion of female brigade leaders was less than half the national average in Moldavia, Georgia and the Central Asian republics, with the exception of Kirgizia.[147]

Sociologists and Party officials alike in the USSR have advanced two major reasons for the predominance of men in agricultural management. The first is the burden of domestic responsibilities which women bear; the second is the underestimation of their abilities by those responsible for deciding promotion. These two elements in women's failure to gain responsible jobs were summarised by Eduard Karbovskii, deputy chairperson of the Kazakhstan Council of Ministers, as follows:

As far as women are concerned, there are two circumstances which still hinder us. In the first place, we know of course that neither the shining successes of the scientific and technical revolution, nor the growth of male consciousness, has yet freed a single rural woman from housework. And secondly, we have learned to manage with male managers whilst women's psychology and the social psychology of female collectives also differs from ours.[148]

Management jobs on Soviet farms are characterised not only by heavy responsibilities but also by particularly long working days. The lack of free time experienced by many managers makes the work extremely difficult for women with family commitments. As a result it is not uncommon for women to refuse promotion in order to avoid increased stress and overwork. As Viktor Orishchuk, Ochakov District Party secretary in the Southern Ukraine, explained:

After an exhausting day one has to find in oneself the energy, for example, to sit down with a book or an abstract and prepare for the next day ... It is evident that a woman on whose shoulders lies the main burden of concern for the running of the home and the children's upbringing at times finds herself faced with an unhappy dilemma: work or home? And so we lose high class specialists and good, competent managers.[149]

The underestimation of women's capacity for management is characteristic not only of the farms but also of non-productive rural specialisms. A survey carried out in Belorussia in 1970 found that women formed a majority of the rural intelligentsia and had higher educational attainment than their male counterparts yet held only a third of management posts. The authors of the survey concluded that men were clearly given preference in promotion 'without sufficient reason' for such a bias.[150] Orishchuk, interviewed on the subject of women in management, observed how common it was amongst male officials not to expect women to succeed in management. He provided the example of finding a field brigade in disarray with production halted at the busiest time of the year. On discovering that the brigade leader is a woman, he remarked:

That explains it, you say to yourself, they need a strong man in the job to get things in order. Afterwards, when everything has turned out alright, you remember what you thought and feel annoyed: surely there are a few weak brigade leaders amongst the men too? Why did you think that? Or you might hear a state farm director say with pride, 'In this sector of ours such and such a woman is working. It's a serious situation there, but she's coping.' And he even sounds a little surprised![151]

The question is often raised as to whether the qualities required in a manager, such as firmness, toughness and efficiency, are not in conflict with what is termed a woman's 'essential femininity'. Orishchuk was of the view that 'femininity ... in no way hinders a person from successfully managing a collective, and it may frequently help'. He observed that from personal experience he had found women managers to be both more persistent and consistent than men in correcting shortcomings at work and less tolerant of failures to deliver on time.[152] Other commentators have referred to women's maternal qualities as an asset in management, as in the following characteristic example: 'Her collective is one big happy family and the state farm director treats people with a mother's warmth and care.'[153]

Whatever the qualities women may have to fit them for management posts it remains a fact that few women rise to the top in farm management. In this, the role of the Communist Party is crucial. The position of kolkhoz chairperson, for example, has been on the Party appointment list, the *nomenklatura*, since the 1950s. This means that no such appointments can be made without Party approval. In practice, the kolkhoz chairperson is almost invariably a Party member. Staff to fill other managerial and specialist posts on the farms are usually selected by the chairperson together with the District Party first secretary. The under-representation of women in the Party is, therefore, a significant factor in their lack of occupational mobility. The Party not merely reflects the low status of women in the rural workforce but effectively reinforces it by failing actively to recruit them as Party members and assign them to leadership positions.[154] It may be significant that where women do succeed in becoming directors and chairpersons they are often said in the press to have taken over farms described as the 'most backward in the district' or in 'a critical condition'. It is a phenomenon which gives ground for speculation that women are more likely to be entrusted with farm management when there is little damage left to be done.[155]

In 1961 Nikita Khrushchev made the following observation at a farm conference in Kiev:

You are well aware of the enormous role which women play in all aspects of the building of communism. But for some reason there are few women in this hall. You can take a pair of binoculars if you like to make them out. How do you explain this? It may be said that it is mainly managers who are present here. It turns out it is the men who do the managing and the women who do the work.[156]

The situation which prompted Khrushchev's crude but pointed comment has altered very little since the early sixties. The odds are still stacked against women succeeding in management as overwork,

UNUSUAL SITUATIONS
'You just check stock today, girls, and I'll carry the sacks, don't you worry.'
(*Krest'yanka*, 3, 1975, p. 29)

prejudice and, not least, Party control bar their way to promotion. As one journalist, echoing Khrushchev's sentiments, noted, 'The strong and healthy man is to be found sitting behind an office desk, whilst out in the fields where there is mud, dust and heavy physical work, there is the woman.'[157]

WOMEN'S RESPONSES TO RURAL EMPLOYMENT

As has been outlined above, women predominate in low-skilled work in the rural labour force. They find it difficult to obtain promotion and to enter work with a high technical content; a factor which is ever more significant as production becomes more highly automated. How do women themselves react to this state of affairs? The findings of social scientists and complaints published in the press suggest that many women feel their powerlessness acutely and are unhappy at the restricted occupational choices available to them in the countryside.

Surveys indicate that men are far more likely than women to be engaged in the work of their choice. In consequence, men are usually more satisfied with their jobs than are women. A survey of over 3,000 men and women in the RSFSR in the early seventies provides a characteristic example of attitudes to work. It was recorded that 68% of men and 32% of women questioned were working in the profession of their choice. By contrast, 39% of men and 61% of women felt that they had had little or no choice in finding employment. Dissatisfaction with their work was expressed by 15% of the men and 23% of the women questioned.[158] Smaller surveys undertaken in Western Siberia during the 1970s have elicited a similar response. More than twice as many women as men said that they did their present job as no other work was available. It was noted, however, that the number of women expressing open dissatisfaction with their work was not a great deal higher than the number of men. Women frequently declared themselves satisfied with their work as there was no alternative to it; a view which indicates a degree of resignation amongst women in this situation. It is significant that women were less satisfied with their work in areas which permitted an element of occupational choice. Work satisfaction also varied according to the level of development of rural settlements. In outlying villages with few or no public services women expressed the highest degree of dissatisfaction with their work, due primarily to the extremely heavy burden of domestic labour and private agriculture. It was, however, discovered that rural development did not necessarily lead to higher levels of job satisfaction amongst women. One report commented, 'urbanisation improves employment conditions for men more than it does for women'.[159] As we have seen, agricultural improvement may actually lead to a deterioration in women's employment prospects in the socialised sector, consigning them to unskilled manual labour and seasonal unemployment.

Women's attitudes to their work modify considerably after marriage and especially, the birth of children. Surveys have found that single young women are more interested in furthering their education than are men of the same age and marital status, yet, when their children are born, they are far more concerned than men with their children's welfare and the need for financial security. As their ambitions to train for a new profession diminish and family commitments grow, women express more frequently their dissatisfaction with work and their desire to change their job.[160] Diminished work satisfaction amongst women with young children is explained as the result of restricted occupational choice becoming still more curtailed by the demands of child care, as in this comment by a Soviet economist: 'The heavy involvement of collective farm women in private subsidiary agriculture and domestic labour is a significant influence on their choice of occupation. Collective farm women are often obliged to choose not the qualified work for which they have trained but that which gives greater possibilities for looking after the private plot and the family.'[161] As might be expected, it is the better educated rural women who are most unhappy with the work which is available to them and the very limited opportunities for promotion or change.[162]

In such a situation it is scarcely surprising that women often react sharply to those who take advantage of their positions of authority. An analysis of complaints to Party committees from rural women undertaken by one rural sociologist revealed that the majority were concerned with indifference or rudeness towards them by male superiors. Women complained about management attitudes more often than about poor work organisation or heavy work. In this survey, 6% of women workers said that they were experiencing difficulties at work because of poor management whilst 9% of women who had changed their place of work had done so because of problems with their superiors.[163]

Rudeness and unpleasantness appear to be not uncommon features of worker–management relations on Soviet farms and letters to the press make it clear that women find it upsetting to become the target of verbal abuse and condescension. As one woman tractor driver expressed this, 'Our boss . . . does not see that in front of him is a woman who is older than he is, a mother whose child might be ill, simply a human being who gets flustered when someone shouts at her.'[164] In addition to complaints of this type the magazine *Krest'yanka* has published a number of more serious cases in recent years. These usually involve fraud, theft or drunkenness by men in managerial positions in addition to rudeness towards women workers. Between 1980 and 1982, 20% of complaints by women published in this magazine concerned poor management. From mid-1979 to mid-1980 details were printed of eight cases in which women's complaints to the magazine had resulted in the reprimand or, more usually, the sacking of a manager. Local Party committees, reporting back to the magazine, invariably state in such cases that the women's complaints were found to be fully justified and cite 'rudeness to subordinates' amongst the reasons for dismissal. In all but one case managers were sacked only when rudeness was accompanied by habitual drunkenness or criminal activity; the exception appears to have been a case of sexual harassment of women workers by a male brigade leader.[165]

It is clear from magazine articles that women who complain about their working conditions or management atttitudes often face further unpleasantness when their protest comes to light. As a result, it is not uncommon for letters to the press to be anonymous or for those who speak out to find themselves without the support of their colleagues. A situation of the latter kind was described by a dairy woman from a state farm in the Komi Autonomous Republic in North European USSR. She had protested about the constant drunkenness at work of a male cowherd, but the women with whom she worked were unwilling to support her in her complaint. In consequence, she became the target of rebukes and unpleasantness from her superiors, from the state farm director down. The seriousness of the situation is attested to by the fact that she, together with her husband and two sons, as a result left the farm where she had lived all her life and moved south to Georgia.[166]

Sadly, high-handedness and barely-disguised contempt for women employees on the part of certain managers pervade women's letters of complaint and the pieces of investigative journalism which they prompt. The following extract from an investigative article is illustrative of such attitudes. Written by a journalist visiting a Belgorod Region collective farm in late 1979, it describes a meeting with dairy women who had sent an anonymous letter to the press describing their deplorable working conditions. In the course of the meeting the secretary of the farm's Party committee put in an appearance:

At this point Abakumov came into the room and at once everyone fell silent. Why? Surely these complaints should be addressed to him, the secretary of the collective farm Party committee, in the first place!

'Comrade Tisheninova, why didn't you come to the office for your diploma?' in a severe tone he asked the leading dairy woman who had the highest yields for the first nine months of 1979. 'People waited for you for nothing.'

'I didn't know, no one told me', the award-winner defended herself in embarrassment.

'Well, we'll look into it. They sent someone specially for you!'

That was the first that Raisa Stepanovna Tisheninova, winner in socialist competition, heard about her award. Surely they could have presented her with her diploma there in the unit, they could have said a few warm, heartfelt words and shaken her hand in the presence of her colleagues. But she was not congratulated; rather she was given a dressing-down. And all because she had dared to take part in a discussion of a serious situation in the dairy unit.

'They don't spare their criticism here', one of the women smartly summed things up, 'that's why no one wanted to sign the letter.'

But as everyone knows, you can't fight facts. They speak for themselves. And no amount of pleading inexperience by the young Party committee secretary, V. Abakumov, can justify his arrogant, almost dictatorial tone in the discussion with the collective farm women.[167]

Whilst it remains impossible to assess the prevalence of such attitudes on the part of farm management or the scale of women's reaction to it, it is evident that many women are resentful of those who abuse their position. Some are clearly not prepared to put up with a combination of appalling conditions and patronising management. The action which they take varies enormously according to local circumstances. In some cases a complaint to local Party or trade union officials may suffice, in others the support of the national press has to be enlisted. Very occasionally women may take the drastic and, under Soviet law, punishable step of strike action to convince management of the legitimacy of their grievances.[168]

It may be significant that none of the cases cited in the press concerns a woman manager. As there are few women in posts of responsibility, particularly at the higher levels, this may not seem surprising. Alternatively, it may indicate a more sympathetic attitude towards women workers by their female superiors. If greater sympathy is in fact displayed by women managers then it undoubtedly stems from an appreciation of attitudes and problems common to most women in the countryside. Klavdiya Abramova, sector manager of a state farm in Rostov Region, thus explained her attitude to the women employed under her:

Sometimes the dairy women or calf rearers are late for work and the herders have to wait for them. There's a conflict and the women should be punished. But of course they have their children, husbands, a cow, their plot – there's hardly time to turn round. I too have a cow, a piglet, chickens and a plot. I too get up early and am still on my feet late at night. So I understand our women.[169]

It seems reasonable to assume, if this comment is characteristic of women in authority, that the benefits of promoting more women into management posts would accrue not merely to the individuals involved. Women workers at all levels would no doubt see their conditions improve if managers were to display rather more sensitivity towards them.

In the present situation, management remains a fundamentally male prerogative. For every woman specialist or high level manager, in agriculture at least, there are a further fifty women engaged in arduous physical labour in the fields or livestock units. The heavy physical burden which women bear, their limited job opportunities and restricted promotion prospects are said to be due not only to the structure of the labour market, but also to the restraints imposed on women by their role within the family. In the next chapter the present nature of the rural family is examined along with the role of the state in both removing and imposing constraints on women as wives and mothers.

2

Women in the rural family

THE DEVELOPMENT OF THE SMALL FAMILY

The 1960s saw a significant decline in the Soviet birthrate. This
stemmed in part from a change in the structure of the population: as a
result of the drop in births during the war there were fewer young
women than usual entering the most fertile age groups in the early
sixties. The main reason for the decline in births during the decade
was, however, a general move towards a smaller family size. In rural
areas the fall in the birthrate was made more acute by the migration of
young people to the cities in the more developed regions of the country.
Table 10 shows the change in birthrate in both urban and rural areas
between 1960 and 1980.

The gap between urban and rural birthrates narrowed significantly
during the 1960s. In the following decade the national birthrate
increased slightly, yet by 1980 the rate remained well below that of
1960. National figures, however, concealed a very considerable degree
of regional and ethnic variation across the USSR. In 1980, birthrates
in the Union republics ranged from fourteen births per thousand
people in Latvia to thirty-seven per thousand in Tadzhikistan.[1] The
recent increase in the Soviet birthrate has therefore been chiefly due to
the growth in population in Central Asia and rural parts of the
Caucasus. Figure 5 illustrates regional variation in urban and rural
family size. In European areas of the country and across the RSFSR no
more than 8% of urban families with children under sixteen had three
or more children. In fact, in these areas, the one-child family had
become the norm by 1975. Rural families in these areas were more
likely to have two children than were urban families, yet over 73% of
families in each European republic had no more than two children. In

Table 10 *Births per 1,000 population, USSR, 1960–80 (selected years)*

	Urban	Rural	Average
1960	21.9	27.8	24.9
1965	16.1	21.1	18.4
1970	16.4	18.7	17.4
1975	17.2	19.6	18.1
1980	17.0	20.4	18.3

Source: Narodnoe khozyaistvo (1980), p. 31.

the republics of Central Asia and the Caucasus a minority of families, even in the cities, had only one child. More than half the rural families with minor children in Armenia, Azerbaidzhan, Uzbekistan and Tadzhikistan had three or more children. In Azerbaidzhan and Tadzhikistan, approximately one in three rural families with children under sixteen had at least five children. There are, thus, enormous variations in demographic trends between the more developed regions of the European USSR and Siberia and the underdeveloped republics of the South with their predominantly Islamic cultural heritage. For the overwhelming majority of the Soviet population living in European areas and Siberia, small families have become the rule over the last two decades. It is to these areas which most of the comments in this chapter will apply.

Although small families are now typical of the countryside in these regions, the rural birthrate remains higher for women of all fertile age groups than in towns. Rural women are far more likely than urban women to continue childbearing into their thirties: the rate of births to women over thirty in the countryside is more than double that in the towns.[2] This fact does not simply reflect the continuation of traditional attitudes and behaviour but mirrors the particular living and working conditions of the countryside. Rural housing is far less cramped than city flats and relatives or neighbours are often more readily available to help with child care. Seasonal agricultural work continues to serve as a form of part-time employment for women with young children, whilst the countryside itself forms a less hazardous environment than the town in which to raise them. The pace and nature of rural life provide fewer disincentives than city living to women who would like to have more than one child.

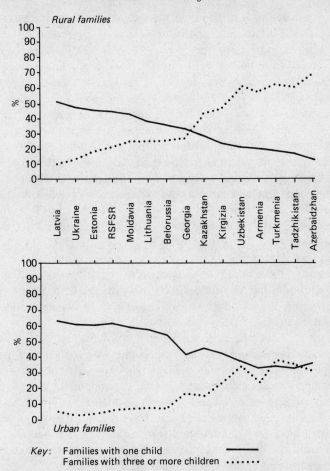

Figure 5   Size of families with children under sixteen, by republic, 1975
(republics in descending order of those with highest proportions of one-child
rural families)

Source: Zhenshchiny v SSSR, Moscow, 1975, pp. 92–5.

ROMANCE AND THE CHOICE OF A HUSBAND

The development of the small family in rural areas provides an
important indicator of changing attitudes towards marriage and
family life. Over the past two decades the extension of secondary
education from eight to ten years and increasing geographical

mobility, together with the impact of the mass media, have hastened the spread of urban ideas and values into the countryside. Although the choice of marriage partner in the villages inevitably remains more restricted than in the towns, the urban influence has had a profound effect on women's attitudes to personal relationships and expectations of marriage. Surveys of rural attitudes conducted since 1960 have shown an increasing concern for emotional fulfilment in marriage by both men and women, with the majority seeing love, friendship, mutual respect and trust as essential to a successful marriage.[3]

In recent years, the women's press has taken up the theme of love and family relationships and has been deluged with letters from women, and from men also, anxious to comment on published articles and to share their own experiences and opinions. Extracts from these letters which are published, notably in the magazine *Krest'yanka*, represent no more than a fraction of the total response to articles on the family, nor is it possible to assess the extent to which published letters reflect an editorial bias. In the absence of more reliable information on attitudes and behaviour in this sphere of human relations, these letters do, however, provide a fascinating glimpse into the lives and emotions of their authors.

From the tone of recent articles it might be assumed that rural women are becoming ever more preoccupied with romance, or 'Love with a capital L', as one journalist described the phenomenon. Certainly, teenage girls whose letters are considered in *Krest'yanka*'s equivalent of an agony column appear to consider the act of falling in love as an unrepeatable event: 'What if it's my destiny [to marry him] and because of my parents I have let it pass me by?' 'I know that love comes once in a lifetime and I have fallen in love for good. But the one I love has married someone else. What am I to do now?'[4]

Young unmarried girls are not, however, alone in their view of romantic love. Older married women, and a good many male correspondents to *Krest'yanka*, characteristically describe their experience of love as enriching and uplifting, as these women's comments show:

Not everyone experiences a great love; it's a gift.

I have been in love too. When I went to work I couldn't wait for the evenings when we would see each other. I would wait for him after work with my heart bursting.

If I go to the town where he lives I am always talking to him in my thoughts, as if he were with me. I feel young again and glad to feel him near me. I am happy that he exists and that I experienced such a feeling.[5]

As these extracts suggest, the experiences described by older women were often shortlived and involved difficult personal decisions. The notion of self-sacrifice to preserve an existing marriage and the juxtaposition of love and suffering is a common theme of many of these letters. The idea of the 'happy pain', as one woman put it, of an existence transformed by love, however fleeting, recurs again and again. It would appear that the publication of such letters has produced a powerful impression on many readers. One correspondent expressed the view that at forty-one with 'a wonderful husband' and 'two marvellous children', she had thought herself fortunate, until she read these letters about love and realised that she had never experienced it:

I envy those letter writers: they have all loved someone. It doesn't matter if it was unrequited or if they were married, it doesn't matter what their relationship was with the one they loved. The main thing is that they know what it is to love. But I feel hurt: am I any worse than other people, or am I just unfeeling?[6]

The desire to experience romantic love and to seek emotional fulfilment in marriage marks a decisive break with the pragmatic attitudes towards personal relationships which women were obliged to adopt in the past. Yet there is evidence to suggest that the utilitarian view of marriage characteristic of traditional village life has far from disappeared. Many women correspondents who write eloquently of the joys of love make it clear that such emotions did not guide their choice of a husband. Typically, women explain that they got married because everyone else was getting married or because it was time to settle down. Though many such marriages were contracted in the 1960s, the pressure to conform has evidently not diminished. A letter from a young woman published as recently as 1981, for example, announced that she intended to get married to someone she had just met as, at the age of nineteen, she was afraid of being left on the shelf.[7] The nature of rural life, however, continues to make the hasty choice of a marriage partner somewhat less hazardous than in the towns. In a small community the habits and character of a prospective partner are likely to be a matter of common knowledge, thereby reducing the risk of unpleasant revelations after the wedding. Commenting on romantic attachments formed by older school students in towns and villages one researcher observed, 'In rural areas where all the pupils are well known to each other and receive public appraisal of their behaviour from the entire adult population of the village, cases of infatuation with physically attractive but shallow boys or girls are significantly rarer.'[8]

Letters have been published in the women's press taking issue with the current preoccupation with romance and stressing the need to consider the practical aspects of family life. A particularly forthright view was expressed by two sisters from Smolensk Region. Aged eighteen and twenty-one, they claimed to be 'normal, average, modern young women' expressing the view of the majority in writing:

You won't get fat on love alone. And emotions, if they exist at all, often only last until the wedding. The main aspect of love in our rationalist twentieth century is the material one. After all, what sort of a husband is it, even if you love him passionately, who only earns 100 roubles a month? How is he going to support a family?[9]

Surveys of rural opinion, however, suggest that this is probably a minority view. A study of a rural district of the Chuvash Autonomous Republic in Central European USSR in 1973, for example, revealed that only 8% of women and 12% of men of Russian ethnic origin approved of a couple marrying without love. Amongst the Turkic Chuvash of the same district with their Islamic heritage less than one in four men and women approved of such a marriage.[10] It would appear that rural young women seek qualities in their future husbands which extend far beyond a large wage packet. Honesty, fairness and an ability to stick to one's principles are sought-after characteristics in a marriage partner.[11] Whether the high estimation of love and personal qualities such as these have actually changed the nature of marriage for rural women in recent years is, however, a very different matter. As one girl from the Crimea wrote, 'I dream about my ideal, but just try and find him – it's a problem!'[12]

AGE AT MARRIAGE: REGIONAL VARIATIONS

Since 1960 a clear tendency towards younger marriage has emerged in European areas of the USSR. The age at which a first marriage is contracted has fallen in both urban and rural areas of the European USSR and Caucasian republics with the exception of Moldavia and Azerbaidzhan. As the trend towards earlier sexual activity and, hence, earlier marriage, has developed in these regions, the trend in Central Asia has been in the opposite direction. In those Central Asian republics where the marriage age has traditionally been very low the sixties and seventies have seen a growing acceptance of secondary education for girls and, in consequence, a delay in the arrangement of their marriages. Figure 6 illustrates the changing rate of marriage

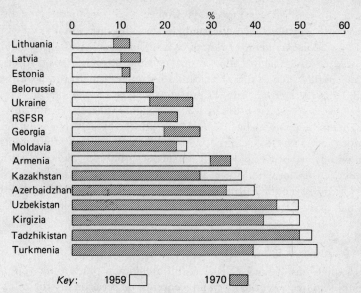

Figure 6   Percentage of rural women married in eighteen to nineteen age group, by republic, 1959 and 1970 (republics in descending order of those with lowest proportions of women married at this age in 1959)

Source: Itogi ... 1970, Vol. II, Table 6.

amongst young rural women between 1959 and 1970. Although the gap between the rates recorded for the Union republics narrowed somewhat, there remained huge variations between regions. At the two extremes in 1970, a rural women in Tadzhikistan was four times more likely to be married under the age of twenty than her counterpart in Estonia.

The Family Law of 1968 established the minimum age for marriage as eighteen for both sexes with a provision for the lowering of this age by no more than two years by the Union republics. Marriage of a minor continues to be punishable by imprisonment under the Central Asian republics' Criminal Codes. In addition, individuals remain liable to prosecution for involvement in forced marriages, the abduction of women, payment of bride price or the practice of *kaitarma*.* It is clear that such offences have by no means died out in Soviet Central

---

* *Kaitarma* involves the withholding of a bride or the abduction, usually by her parents, of a newly married women from her husband's home until the bride price is paid in full.

Asia. In the villages especially, women not infrequently remain excluded from social activities and female seclusion is still practised in places.[13] The payment of bride price is still extremely widespread and is said to have reached startling proportions in prosperous districts. The continuation of this practice has been found to exert a negative influence on the education of Central Asian women: as submissiveness and obedience in a wife are by tradition highly valued, a significantly higher bride price can be obtained for a girl who has not completed her education. There is, therefore, a strong financial incentive for parents to withdraw their daughters from school.[14] The prevalence of such practices and of what Soviet social scientists term 'feudal attitudes' towards women in Central Asia provide evidence of the cultural gulf which exists between these areas and the European regions.

PARENTAL INFLUENCE IN MARRIAGE

In rural areas of the USSR it is still a common practice for young couples to live with the husband's parents, or occasionally the wife's parents, when they are first married. In 1970 approximately one in four rural married couples under the age of thirty-five were said to live with their parents.[15] A Belorussian survey of housing needs in the mid-seventies revealed that almost a third of villagers questioned thought that young people should live with their parents after marriage. In fact, in this same republic, it appears to be customary for young couples to do this, at least until they have children, and their own house has been built.[16] The extended rural family is, however, very much a thing of the past. The average rural family in 1970 had 4.0 members whilst the average urban family size was 3.5. By 1979 these figures had fallen to 3.8 and 3.3 respectively.

The nuclear family is, therefore, characteristic of both urban and rural areas, totalling approximately three-quarters of the families in both cases.[17] By no means all elderly people in the countryside now live with younger relatives. A higher proportion of elderly women live alone in the villages than in the towns. Approximately a quarter of rural women over the age of sixty live alone; in Estonia the figure rises to 42% whilst in Central Asia it is nearer 10%. Over 90% of rural pensioners living alone are women.[18]

Surveys of opinion make it clear that the influence of parents over the personal relationships and the marriages of their children has waned considerably in recent years. In the more developed regions only a minority of rural inhabitants, even in the most elderly age groups, still think it necessary for young people to seek parental consent to marriage. By contrast, the overwhelming majority of rural Uzbeks of all ages believe parental consent a necessity before a marriage can be contracted. In the Chuvash Autonomous Republic in the early seventies more than two-thirds of both Russian and Chuvash villagers said that they would not disapprove of a young couple who married for love against the wishes of their parents.[19]

For young couples living with their parents relations between the generations appear to have relaxed considerably. In the early sixties it was not uncommon for a family such as this to keep a common budget in which all items of expenditure had to be approved by the oldest member of the family. Cases were noted in which the daughter-in-law continued to be regarded as the family's servant. The organisation of the family's budget and allocation of its resources were said to be a major source of conflict between the generations. Young couples in the villages today appear increasingly unwilling to accept the dictates of older relatives in their personal affairs.[20] Nevertheless, the traditional figure of the despotic mother-in-law has not entirely vanished from the rural scene. *Krest'yanka* magazine has occasionally published letters from young married women describing the misery of living in the home of an in-law who is habitually critical and patronising. As one of them explained,

I am afraid of hearing one more time that I am not mistress here, that I am not in charge of anything. Of course I know only too well that I am not mistress here, that I have come to this house like a lodger, that the allotment belongs to her and her son. Why does she have to remind me about it all the time? Is it just to belittle me yet again?

An interesting and perhaps significant aspect of these letters is the fact that each was written by a young woman from a large and poor family who has married into a prosperous household.[21]

A rather different story but one which is most revealing of the persistence of old peasant attitudes was published in the press in 1979. The case concerned an elderly woman in a village in Primorskii Territory in the Far East of the USSR whose son had been left a widower with a six-year-old daughter. The woman was at pains to find her son a new wife to look after him as soon as possible after his bereavement. After intensive enquiries she eventually heard of a young divorcee with a child living in a neighbouring village and despatched her son to visit them. On the day after the son's visit his mother stepped in to arrange the match, with the businesslike comment, 'we won't spend a long time thinking about it. I can see that you like each other, so why don't you live together? We'll take you to live with us, Shura.' So the arrangements were speedily concluded though the marriage remained unregistered. Some time later the mother decided that the relationship which she had engineered was not a success and advised her son to take Shura back where she had come from. Only at this point did the young woman finally express her feelings at being treated as 'a kind of object . . . like a pair of trousers that you take back to the shop'.[22]

As these examples indicate, the downtrodden daughter-in-law is still occasionally to be found in rural families. Yet even in cases such as these, authoritarian attitudes do not go entirely unchallenged. Whether the women involved seek a way out through education or in leaving the family, as in two of these cases, or simply relieve their feelings by writing to the press, the traditional responses of resignation and submissiveness have become increasingly rare in young rural women.

THE 'HEAD OF HOUSEHOLD' IN THE RURAL FAMILY

It is still common for villagers to live in houses built by their grandfathers and even great-grandfathers, and to use household articles which have served more than one generation. This tendency is also apparent in the spiritual side of daily life. In public opinion traditional views and ideas about the domestic regime, about rituals and about the role and position of women in family life change very slowly.[23]

This observation made by a Belorussian sociologist in the early seventies has often been echoed by social scientists describing the tenor of modern rural life. In particular, the conservatism of rural public opinion is frequently stressed. As women's views of marriage change and both their confidence and concern for the quality of relationships develops, new attitudes and old habits not infrequently collide within the rural family. A letter from a young man seeking legal advice from a national magazine provides a brief example of this phenomenon. He and his wife were in disagreement about where they should live and he concluded, 'Everybody thinks that a wife should live where her husband lives, but she says "there's no such rule!", which of us is right?' In response the paper pointed out that there had indeed been 'no such rule' since 1917, whatever local opinion might believe to the contrary.[24]

The recognition by family members of a 'Head of Household' is often used by Soviet researchers as an indicator of the tenacity of tradition within the rural family. Whilst emphasising that the title usually has no more than formal significance today, sociologists have noted its continued acknowledgement in the countryside compared with its decline in usage in the towns.[25] A major reason for this is undoubtedly the preservation of the title 'Head of Kolkhoz Household' on collective farms. The person who bears this title in each kolkhoz family is held officially responsible for the fulfilment of the family's financial obligations towards the government. In addition, the family's house, private plot and outbuildings are registered in this person's name. Thus, government policy itself contributes in this case to the persistence of traditional rural attitudes.

Where a 'Head of Household' is named in rural areas it remains usual for that person to be a man. Throughout the 1960s it was reported that rural women, as tradition demanded, were deemed to be the heads of their households only when they had no husband. The chief exception to this rule were women who had re-married and whose second husband had come to live in their home. Amongst young couples living separately from their parents the man would almost invariably be regarded as head of the family, even where both partners had equal social and economic status in the community. Researchers reported that it apparently did not occur to many women to consider themselves as candidates for the title. When asked the question, 'Who is the head of your family?' women of all ages were said frequently to respond with surprise, 'Who could it be but my husband?'[26] This acceptance of the man's automatic right to be seen as head of the family no doubt explains the response to census questions on 'Head of Household' in 1959 and 1970. In 1959 women were recorded as heads of 37% of urban families and 43% of rural families in the USSR. By 1970 these figures had fallen to 30% in both cases, doubtless reflecting changing demographic patterns as the effect of the Second World War on the male population diminished.[27]

Although men usually retain their customary title in the home it is clear that women today exercise a great deal of authority within the rural family. In interviews in Moscow and Minsk in 1980, two prominent writers on the rural family, Maya Pankratova and Lidya Filyukova, both expressed the view to me that it is women who define the lifestyle of the family, who take the lead in deciding how both money and time should be spent. This opinion is supported by sociological surveys which show that rural women play the decisive role in family decision making.[28] In Pankratova's opinion the growing authority of women within the family is based on the improvement in their education. The dearth of skilled work of an intermediate level for women in the countryside has meant that women, far more than men, have become polarised either into work which demands little or no education or that which demands a good deal of specialised training. In consequence, amongst rural couples, women are not infrequently better educated than their husbands: a study of Central Russian villages showed this to be the case in from a third to a half of families. Surveys have shown that, when a wife is better educated than her husband, the gap between their educational attainment is often greater than between spouses where the husband has received more education than the wife.[29]

Despite the growth in female education and the influence of women in domestic decision making, an examination of the roles played by husbands and wives in the contemporary family reveals a situation which is far from egalitarian. The paradoxical nature of the woman's role in the Soviet family today was summarised by a writer in the magazine, *Nedelya* in 1977:

If the head of the family is defined – as sociologists now define it – as the one who performs the essential managerial and regulatory functions, then it is the woman who better fits the description ... The woman has so much authority within the family that husbands are heard more and more often to say of their wives 'I'll ask the boss', or 'The boss will be angry'. At the same time the woman doesn't seem quite the family's head either, since she is also its busiest servant. Women acutely sense the ambiguity of their role.[30]

In the next section an analysis of domestic roles played by men and women provides the basis for an examination of the persistence of sexual inequality within the rural family.

THE DIVISION OF LABOUR WITHIN THE RURAL FAMILY

'Marital relationships in our country are constructed on an essentially new foundation and in the overwhelming majority of cases are characterised by mutual love and respect, equality of husband and wife, mutual assistance in daily life and joint responsibility for the raising of children.'[31] This statement provides a typical example of the claims commonly made by Soviet writers as to the present nature of the family. Closer acquaintance with the division of labour currently practised in the Soviet family, however, demonstrates that such claims are, at the very least, exaggerated. As Viktor Perevedentsev, a prominent Soviet economist, has noted, although women throughout the USSR now have higher educational attainment than men and form a majority of the country's specialists, they continue to perform almost all the housework. As a general rule, the burden of domestic labour borne by women increases dramatically both on marriage and on the birth of their first child. Similarly, when either the working day or working week is reduced, much of the time gained is spent on housework by women but on leisure by men.[32]

In rural conditions, domestic labour is particularly arduous and time consuming. In consequence, rural women spend considerably longer working in the home than do urban women. A large-scale statistical survey of the RSFSR in the late seventies found rural women bearing an average total workload of eighty-eight hours per week, the greater part of their working time being spent in the domestic economy rather than on the state or collective farms. As a result, rural women had, on average, only eleven hours per week free time, less than half that available to urban women.[33]

The nature of domestic labour in the village

Essential services

The last twenty years have seen a significant increase in the supply of public utilities to rural homes. By the mid-seventies, it was claimed that 99% of rural homes received gas. Other services, notably the provision of a mains water supply, have been far slower to develop. The expense involved in providing such facilities to small communities scattered over vast areas has proved prohibitive. As a result, by 1976 almost all privately built rural housing and two-thirds of the housing stock of state and collective farms were still without running water, mains sanitation or central heating.[34] What this means for women with the responsibility for running a home can be readily imagined. Only a minority of women as yet escape the heavy work of fetching water from the nearest well for all daily needs. As many families continue to rely on the traditional stove to provide heat throughout the winter months, firewood preparation, in which men play a leading role, is a major occupation for the family in the autumn. Many rural families continue to use the traditional Russian steam bath, with the family bath house usually built alongside their living quarters. Preparing firewood and fetching water for the bath is extremely time consuming but, as yet, no portable steam boilers have been produced to simplify the process and communal facilities have not proved an acceptable substitute.[35]

Experiments in high-rise living were introduced into the countryside in the early seventies. It was felt that the construction of flats on the urban model would prove a more economical means of providing housing with full amenities for rural inhabitants. Although the new blocks appear to be attractive to young people, they have proved most unpopular with the mass of rural dwellers: 'Why pull a peasant away from the land and settle him on the fifth floor?', being a typical comment.[36] Reactions such as these coupled with disaster stories from the victims of shoddy workmanship in the new flats have led to the abandonment of this housing policy. Since 1978 the construction of new detached houses in the villages, with allotments and sheds attached, has been officially encouraged as a means of bringing better facilities to rural inhabitants. More radical proposals for modernising rural homes have included the suggestion by Perevedentsev that plans to build new housing and install gas and water supplies should be reconsidered. Instead, resources should, in his view, be diverted to the total electrification of existing rural homes. In this way, he argues, rural women would reap the benefits of electic cooking, heating and the pumping of water from local wells. As a result, young people might be encouraged to stay in the village and the entire operation would save the state money. At the moment, however, there appears to be no plans to put such a proposal into effect.[37]

Washing and cleaning

The shortage of public services, and especially the lack of a water supply to so many rural homes, makes housework in the villages considerably heavier and more complicated than in the towns. The absence of running water makes washing and cleaning, even with the advent of domestic appliances, a time consuming business. It is still not unknown for women in the more isolated settlements to do their washing in the river. A city woman exiled to a Siberian village in the 1960s described the process:

I have learned how to launder under the conditions here. It is interesting that as a child my idea of a village was associated with peasant women rinsing their laundry in an ice hole, and now this association has been confirmed. Here only things like washing and rinsing, especially in freezing weather, are considered difficult.[38]

Since the mid-sixties, however, the production of washing machines has increased dramatically: by 1981 official figures stated that 58% of rural families possessed one, compared with only 12% of rural families in 1965.[39] It might be expected, however, that the ownership of domestic appliances would be less widespread in the less developed regions of the country. As the British writer on Soviet women, Alix Holt, has pointed out, time budget analysis is not easily applied to an activity such as housework.[40] Nevertheless, the data collected in such studies do provide a rough indication of the way in which women spend their time within the home. Surveys from various areas suggest that women spend two to three hours per week washing if they have a washing machine, rising to between four and five hours if washing is done by hand. The average appears to be nearer four hours if ironing is added to the time spent on laundry.[41]

Public laundries are few and far between in the countryside although they often form part of service complexes (*Dom byta* or House of Everyday Life) which are now appearing in rural settlements. As in the towns, rural women are often suspicious of the quality of public laundry services and hence reluctant to make use of them. The head of one *Dom byta*, anxious to release local women from the scourge of the weekly wash, described how she had had to extol the virtues of the new laundry in the village club and before the start of film shows in order to get the women to make use of this facility. In a few places, launderettes have begun to appear on collective farms at the request of local women.[42]

The amount of time which women are said to spend cleaning their homes varies enormously from one survey to another. It seems to depend less on the availability of labour saving devices than on the age of the women questioned. Women working as agricultural labourers generally spend more time cleaning than, for example, dairy women who have a longer working day. Yet it is the oldest women, irrespective of employment, who spend the longest cleaning the house; a pattern which can be observed in other areas of housework.[43] As rural housing is far less cramped than urban flats, women usually have a larger area to keep clean. Vacuum cleaners are said to be owned by 15% of rural families though, as with washing machines, demand is said to have grown considerably in recent years as more soft furnishings have appeared in rural homes.[44] Carpets remain a luxury item and, as such, are usually used as a decorative wall hanging. Floors still have to be washed down or swept with a rush broom.

Cooking and shopping

Preparing food is the major element of housework for rural women, taking up around half the total time spent on domestic labour. Surveys from the 1960s reported that women were still in the habit of rising early to prepare the family's food for the whole day and then leaving it in the traditional stove until it was required. In warm weather women would prepare food outdoors on primus stoves, a practice still common in the south of the country. Electric and gas cookers have now replaced the Russian stove in many rural homes, whilst 65% of families are now said to own a refrigerator.[45] Few of the electrical kitchen gadgets on sale in the cities are in use in rural homes. Although items such as electric kettles or water heaters have proved popular it has been reported that rural dwellers find many appliances inconvenient, unproductive or complicated to repair, whilst many apparently feel that electric or gas cookers cannot compete with the traditional stove for reliability or versatility.[46] In areas where bread is unavailable in the shops the time which women spend cooking is dramatically increased; one survey of Stavropol' Territory in the mid-seventies found that baking bread added at least seven hours a week to the total time spent on food preparation. The supply of bread to rural shops has, however, substantially improved in recent years and the majority of rural women are now able to purchase it. Convenience foods are far less readily available in rural areas than in the towns, yet they are clearly in demand by women.[47] Although a good deal of attention has been given in recent years in the press to the standard of rural cafés and restaurants they remain too few to provide a realistic alternative to cooking meals at home. Rural shops frequently fail not only to provide convenience foods but also the most basic food items. As a result, the keeping of a private plot and livestock is an absolute necessity in most villages.

As there are few shops to visit and much less to buy, shopping takes up far less time in the countryside than it does in the town. It is a situation which finds little favour with rural women. A survey of collective farms in the Rostov Region in 1973 and 1974, for example, found that a third of the men and women questioned thought shopping facilities were poor.[48] The women's press publishes a constant stream of complaints about rural shops and services. The most common complaints are of erratic opening hours and deliveries, persistent rudeness from the assistants together with their habit of reserving items in demand for friends and relatives. Reviews of shopping facilities in the countryside by journalists have revealed problems through short-ages similar to those which beset the towns. A review of rural shops in Khar'kov Region in 1981, for example, found them to be stocked with expensive, cellophane wrapped 'gift' packages, yet totally lacking in such items as soap powder, children's toys or wellington boots, let alone articles which were in general demand nationally. The in-adequacy of rural shops obliges women to make regular trips to the towns for essential items on their days off. A 1975 survey in the RSFSR suggested that two-thirds of rural families made these shopping trips to the towns, especially for the purchase of non-food items and domestic appliances.[49]

Many villagers find it necessary to travel to the towns to have their possessions repaired, or alternatively they attempt repairs themselves. Service outlets in rural areas are still very few and both their availability and quality vary enormously. In 1978 the value of services used per head of the population over the year was calculated as 17.9 roubles in rural areas and 30.4 roubles in urban areas: services supplied to urban dwellers therefore being rather less than double those supplied to rural dwellers.[50] The repair of consumer goods is a particularly thorny problem in rural areas and the subject of regular complaints to the press owing to shoddy workmanship and inter-minable delays. Consumer complaints also frequently focus on the poor quality of purchased goods of all descriptions from non-flammable matches to collapsing tables or headscarves which dye the wearer's face in wet weather. It must be said, however, that such creations are by no means peculiar to the Soviet Union. Where the situation for the consumer does, however, differ considerably from that of Britain, for example, is in the question of seeking redress in such cases. Matters are often put right, or money refunded, only after a prolonged consideration of the question by the press and the management of the institution at fault.[51]

Housework in the countryside, then, demands significantly more time and energy than in the towns. Rural women generally have more space to clean, larger families to cater for and fewer labour saving devices and public services than are available to urban women. Though consumer goods are now more widely available and are often given as prizes for achievements in production they do not necessarily improve the lot of women in the home. The home of a dairy woman in Belorussia which I visited in 1980 provided a graphic example of this. In twenty-five years' service she had won a great many prizes, a large number being on display in her living room. The array of carpets, cut glass and china which met the eye was of an abundance and quality which clearly astonished the urban academics who accompanied me. Yet all this was in stark contrast to the spartan kitchen with its tiny sink, scrubbed wooden table and no running water and to the earth closet at the end of the yard. In these less than ideal conditions the luxury items which she had been given no doubt created a good deal of extra work for the aesthetic pleasure which they afforded.

Private subsidiary agriculture

Private agriculture remains of enormous importance to family income in the countryside. It provides essential food items which would otherwise be unavailable to rural families and extra cash through the sale of surplus produce. It has been estimated that approximately 80% of privately grown produce is consumed by the producers themselves, providing around half the rural family's food.[52]

The contribution of the private plot to both incomes and agriculture is still very high. In 1970 the private sector accounted for almost a third of gross agricultural production and for approximately one sixth of the total real income of the Soviet population. These figures appear the more impressive when set against the area of land involved; since the early 1960s private holdings have occupied around 3% of the total sown area of the USSR.[53] Table 11 provides a more detailed breakdown of the contribution made by the private sector to Soviet agriculture. Although both the proportion of essential food products grown on plots and the private holdings of livestock have declined by comparison with 1966, private production has remained at a significant level.

A campaign was waged against private agriculture between 1958 and 1965 on the assumption that the socialised and private sectors were inevitably in competition with each other for labour resources. Restrictions were eased in 1965 but fell far short of an encouragement of private farming. The economist, M. Makeenko, writing in 1966, observed that 'Some economists regard private subsidiary agriculture not as being socially necessary for the normal reproduction of labour power but as an aspiration towards money grubbing engendered by the "dark forces" of the peasant psychology.'[54] As Makeenko pointed out, even if rural wages were to be raised considerably, the socialised economy would not be able to provide all the produce required by

Table 11 *The contribution of private subsidiary agriculture to USSR agricultural production and family income (in %, selected years)*

	1966	1970	1978	1983
% produced on private plots				
of meat	40	35	29[a]	29
of milk	39	36	29[a]	25
of eggs	68	53	34	30
of potatoes	60		61	
of vegetables	40			
of wool		20		24
% livestock held on plots				
cows	42	39[b]	30	31[c]
goats			76	77[c]
sheep	21	21[b]	18	19[c]
pigs	31	25[b]		20[c]
% collective farm family income				
provided by plots	37[d]	32	25	26

[a] 1965 figures.
[b] 1971 figures.
[c] 1977 figures.
[d] 1984 figures.

Sources: M. Makeenko, 'Ekonomicheskaya rol' lichnogo podsobnogo khozyaistva', *Voprosy ekonomiki*, 10, 1966, p. 61; *The USSR in figures 1977*, Moscow, 1978, pp. 122–3; *Narodnoe khozyaistvo SSSR v 1978g.*, Moscow, 1979, pp. 196, 211, 245, 392; *Narodnoe khozyaistvo SSSR v 1983g.*, Moscow, 1984, pp. 258, 262, 413.

rural families. His view that the private sector should therefore be seen as an 'organic part of the socialist economy' was not, however, widely supported.[55] Throughout the late sixties and early seventies sociologists were in the habit of viewing the reduction in size of the private plot as an indicator of cultural development in the collective farm peasantry.

Since 1976 private subsidiary agriculture has received greater attention and encouragement from the Soviet government as a means of solving the problem of shortages in urban shops, especially of meat and dairy products. In the wake of more relaxed official attitudes the press has given considerable attention to the question of improving productivity on private plots and to the ways in which co-operation between the state and private sectors can be developed to the benefit of both.[56]

The years of discouragement of private agriculture have not been without their effect, however. It has been reported that rural young people in particular regard the keeping of a plot as unprestigious and uninteresting, an occupation only suitable for old women. They are said to be far more interested in spending their days off in cultural pursuits than in gardening.[57] Certain writers have pointed out that villagers are unlikely to be encouraged to increase their involvement in private farming unless the collective farms provide more help and better organisation, perhaps with the aid of some small-scale mechanisation. At present, the small sizes of the plots make the use of farm machinery impossible. A 1973–4 survey of Rostov Region found that only 17% of collective farmers and 28% of state farmers had piped water on their allotments, fewer than 7% had garden sprinklers, whilst only 1% owned wheelbarrows.[58] In the time-honoured tradition, therefore, the majority of the work involved in producing more than a quarter of Soviet agricultural output is done by hand, by women, as an extension of their domestic labour.

Male and female roles in domestic labour

The contribution made by men to the domestic economy is considerably greater in the countryside than in the towns; a fact which results very largely from the necessity for private farming. The range of tasks which must be carried out in the successful running of a home in the countryside is far broader than it is in the towns. The distribution of these essential tasks between the men and women of the rural family is still largely determined according to custom. Traditional concepts of what constitutes 'men's work' and 'women's work' in the domestic sphere have by no means disappeared from the countryside. As a result, men are to be found preparing the soil of the allotment in preparation for planting, and building or repairing shelters for livestock. Where necessary, men procure and prepare firewood and clean out the yard. They also feed and water livestock, fetch water and tend the allotment on their day off. Younger men may entertain fewer prejudices about work in the home which would once have been seen as beneath their dignity. Nevertheless, women continue to bear the brunt of the work involved in the day to day running of the home. Tending the plot, preparing animal feed and caring for livestock are

Table 12 *Total workload of industrial workers, state farmers and collective farmers, RSFSR, selected surveys, 1963–70 (in %)*

	Comparative workload by social group[a]		Comparative workload by sex[b]	
	Men	Women	Men	Women
Industrial workers	100	100	100	132
State farmers	115	107	100	122
Collective farmers	139	117	100	111

[a] Where the workload of industrial workers = 100%.
[b] Where the male workload = 100%.
Source: V. D. Patrushev, 'Socioeconomic Problems of the Free Time of the Rural Population', *Soviet Sociology*, Fall 1978, p. 23.

primarily seen as women's responsibilities. In addition, cooking, cleaning, washing and shopping, the major elements of domestic labour in the cities, are overwhelmingly the responsibility of women in the villages.

The additional components of domestic labour in the countryside, however, produce a tendency towards the equalisation of the total workload of men and women when compared with the workload of urban inhabitants. Time budgets carried out in four European regions of the RSFSR in 1963 and 1970 form the basis of Table 12 which illustrates this point. In this survey, hours worked in socialised agriculture were longer for the men and shorter for the women than they were in industry. Living in the countryside and working in agriculture extended the total workload for men far more than it did for women. For men on collective farms it was their contribution to private farming which raised their workload so decisively. All the women in the survey had a greater total workload than the men. Yet amongst industrial workers, where the men's contribution to domestic labour was far more limited, the gap between the total hours worked by women and men was much greater than on state or collective farms.

The relationship between work in the socialised sector and in private farming is an extremely complex one, not least because both involve seasonal patterns of labour. As might be expected, low wage-earners in general have larger plots, are more likely to keep a cow and hence spend more time in the private sector than do high wage-earners. Families in remote and underdeveloped villages rely more heavily on the food which they can produce themselves than families in more developed areas and therefore often spend more time in private farming. Conversely, families within easy reach of urban centres may devote a good deal of attention to private farming and especially to the production of foodstuffs which command a high price in city markets. The income generated by work in the socialised as against the private sector may largely determine which sector takes preference at any given season of the year. In a survey of collective farms in one district of the Ukraine in the mid-seventies, for example, it was found that management had great difficulty persuading people to work on the collective lands once soft fruit had ripened on the private plots. Collective farmers preferred to spend their time picking their home-grown strawberries as the crop was such a profitable one.[59]

Such variations in the attention paid to private farming make the assessment of labour input by sex highly problematical. In 1966, able-bodied men in the RSFSR were said to spend an average of 9% of their total working time in the private sector. The comparable figure for women was 35%. Figures from 1967 put the proportion of working time spent in private farming rather higher: in Western Siberia where the highest proportion was recorded for private farming, the figure for women was 60% of total working time compared to 11% for men. M. Fedorova, writing in 1975, claimed that women in the RSFSR worked 30% less than men in the socialised sector. Patrushev's study of Rostov Region state and collective farms in 1973–4 found women's contribution to private farming to be similar or slightly less than men's. At the other end of the scale a study of Novosibirsk Region found women to contribute 70% of the total working time spent in private farming in the least developed villages.[60] These studies indicate that women tend to spend longer working on their allotments on working days than men do. On days off, however, men work the larger share of time on the plots whilst women turn their attention to other aspects of housework, as will be examined below.

A small-scale time budget survey of agricultural workers in the Caucasus District of Krasnodar Territory in 1975–6 is not atypical of male and female patterns of activity described in larger studies. The data provided in this study are particularly useful in that they allow a comparison of the demands of domestic labour on two groups of male and female workers with similar work commitments in the socialised

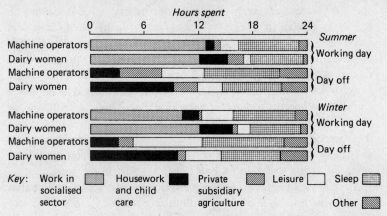

Figure 7   Time budgets of machine operators and dairy women, 23rd Party
Congress collective farm, Caucasus District, Krasnodar Territory, 1975–6

Source: A. M. Krylov, A. I. Slutskii and A. A. Khagurov, 'Analiz byudzheta vremeni
kolkhoznikov i rabochikh sovkhoza kak sposob izucheniya sotsial'nykh problem
upravleniya kolkhoznym kollektivom', *Nauchnye trudy Kubanskogo universiteta*, 205, 1976,
pp. 141–66.

sector. Figure 7 illustrates time allocation by male machine operators
and by dairy women over an average twenty-four-hour period in
winter and summer, on working days and days off. As the Figure
shows, there were striking differences between the ways in which these
men and women spent their time. In summer the women worked
shorter hours for the collective than the men but worked far longer on
the plots; women's total working time thus amounted to sixteen and a
half hours per day, two and a half hours more than the men. They also
did more work in the home, making their total working day four hours
longer than that of the men. In consequence, the men enjoyed both
more leisure time and more sleep than did the women. On days off the
disproportionate burden carried by women in domestic labour
became still more apparent. In summer the men worked longer hours
in private agriculture than the women, yet the women spent longer on
housework and child care, the total time involved being swelled by
trips to town. In winter the gap between male and female domestic
labour on days off widened still further. Whilst the men spent the
overwhelming majority of their time, nearly seventeen hours, sleeping
or relaxing, the women spent more than ten hours a day on domestic
labour and journeys to town.

A very similar pattern of labour was observed by Patrushev in Rostov Region in 1973. The women collective farmers in his study did seven times more housework per week than the men, over one third of it, notably washing, shopping and baking, being performed at weekends. Most rural workers still work a six day week, whilst at the peak periods of sowing and harvest, even their one day off has a tendency to become a shortened working day. This concentration by women, therefore, of major domestic tasks at the weekends means that they rarely have a day for leisure and relaxation. Patrushev found women's average total workload in socialised and domestic labour never fell below eight and a half hours any day of the week.[61]

A further telling factor to emerge from Patrushev's study was that the unequal burden of domestic labour on rural men and women had actually become more unequal in the decade preceding his survey. Between 1963 and 1973 the average time spent by men on housework had fallen by a half to 3.3 hours per week. For women, housework had increased by 14% to twenty-four hours per week. The reason for such a radical drop in the time spent by men would appear to be the introduction of gas and electricity into rural homes which removed the need for men to prepare firewood for the stove. A major element in the increase experienced by women was the rise in time spent shopping, resulting from improved rural services and shopping facilities. Patrushev thus views the increase in the time spent by women on domestic labour as a positive phenomenon, reflecting an improved rural standard of living. However, as domestic work for women expanded in nearly all its aspects over the decade it is difficult to see how figures demonstrating the failure of men to participate at anything other than a perfunctory level can be interpreted in such a way.[62]

Unfortunately, little statistical information is available as to the organisation of domestic labour within the family unit. As might be expected on the basis of the evidence presented above it is the wife who performs most of the housework. Such data as are available suggest that occupation is an important factor in determining the division of domestic labour between the husband and wife. A 1966 survey of Moscow Region villages found that in the families of unskilled or semi-skilled agricultural workers domestic tasks were more likely to be shared equally between spouses than in families of managers or specialists. The proportion of couples sharing housework fell from 29% in unskilled families to 18% in specialists' and managers' families.[63] In

'You're suffering from nervous exhaustion.' 'I think I probably overdid it yesterday, I was cleaning and cooking all day!!'

(*Krest'yanka*, 3, 1978, p. 31)

low income families the wife's wage is extremely important and less likely to be seen as a supplement to the family income. This may be a major factor in the more egalitarian approach to housework in such families. It might be expected, however, that men and women in the higher occupational groups with better education would be more likely to espouse the notion of shared domestic tasks. There is evidence to suggest, however, that in such families the factor of time outweighs the possible influence of raised consciousness. A study of collective farmers in Kostroma Region in 1972 found that where both spouses worked in animal husbandry 20% of husbands did no work at all in the home or plot during the winter months. Where both spouses were specialists, however, no less than 40% of husbands did not participate in domestic labour or private agriculture.[64] As has been observed in Chapter 1, women's promotion prospects are damaged by the burden of work which they experience in the home. The data from Moscow and Kostroma Regions indicate further that the wife's work in the home frees her husband for study and the improvement of his skills and hence furthers his career prospects to the detriment of her own. Women, it would appear, are constrained to sacrifice their own time and labour to facilitate the occupational mobility of their husbands.

Table 13 *The provision of rural pre-school child care facilities, USSR,
1960–80*

	Number of permanent institutions (thousands)	Increase (1960 as 100%)	Children enrolled (thousands)	Increase (1960 as 100%)
1960	27.2	100	863	100
1965	35.0	129	1,479	171
1970	41.2	151	1,901	220
1975	50.7	186	2,542	295
1980	58.7	215	3,450	400

Sources: Sel'skoe khozyaistvo SSSR, Moscow, 1971, p. 676; *Narodnoe khozyaistvo
(1980)*, p. 409.

Child care: state provision

The assistance in child care given by the state to families with pre-school children has increased considerably since 1960. Table 13 shows the rise in provision of permanent child care facilities in rural areas to 1980. The number of permanent day nurseries (children 0–3 years old) and kindergartens (children 4–7 years old) in the countryside doubled during the period whilst the number of children on roll increased fourfold; the most rapid period of expansion being from 1960 to 1965.

Despite the significant increase in facilities, permanent places for pre-school children continued to be available only for a minority of the age group in rural areas. On the basis of census returns for 1970 it may be estimated that approximately 12% of rural children and 51% of urban children of pre-school age were provided with permanent nursery places. By 1980 it was reported that approximately 25% of rural pre-school children had permanent nursery places.[65] Rural child care provision showed varying degrees of development in the fifteen Union republics in 1970. Only the RSFSR, Estonia and Kazakhstan recorded levels of provision above the national average. As might be expected, few rural children received permanent nursery places in much of Central Asia and Azerbaidzhan, whilst provision was surprisingly poor in Lithuania, Belorussia and Moldavia. In the two last named republics the gap between urban and rural provision was particularly wide as the proportion of urban pre-school children enrolled in these areas was above the national average.

Child care facilities are by no means evenly distributed across rural areas within the same republic. In 1977 it was reported that over half the collective farms in the RSFSR had no permanent facilities. At the same time 15,000 nurseries were unevenly distributed amongst 18,000 state farms: whilst some state farms had two or three nurseries, 'thousands' were said to have none at all. Throughout the 1970s the number of additional rural children of pre-school age catered for in seasonal nurseries, i.e. those functioning only during peak agricultural periods, has been reported as 2 million.[66]

As the prime responsibility for child care rests with women it is they, rather than men, who are most affected by a shortage of facilities. The attitude of rural women towards child care facilities has undergone a significant change in recent years. As late as 1970 a Belorussian rural sociologist noted that there was a need for work amongst women to publicise the new facilities and encourage their use.[67] Yet over the last decade in particular, rural women have become vocal in their demands for child care facilities to be extended to all areas as a priority. The letters received by the press on the subject show the provision of nurseries to be a major concern of women in the countryside and that the year by year increase in provision by no means matches demand. Indeed, the publicity received by women's letters of complaint in recent years has undoubtedly encouraged others to bemoan the situation in their own villages.[68] Over the last decade *Krest'yanka* has published women's complaints from all over the RSFSR about the shortage of nursery places and the delays involved in building new facilities. Cases have been publicised in which nurseries have been closed for repairs for up to five years or in which a newly built nursery has been used for some other purpose, for example, as a hostel for groups of workers. It has been stated in the press that public money allocated for expenditure on rural nurseries has not been fully taken up. In 1979, for example, the plan for nursery construction on state farms was fulfilled by only 51% in Belorussia, 61% in Azerbaidzhan and 64% in Tadzhikistan. Converting earmarked expenditure into bricks and mortar has evidently proved problematical in many cases.[69]

An editorial in *Krest'yanka* in December 1980 reported on the results of women's complaints presented by the magazine to the responsible authorities. Whilst some of those approached were said to have responded at once and opened nurseries as quickly as possible, others were said to have responded to their enquiries in a cursory fashion or not at all. It is often said that farm managers see the provision of child care facilities as a low priority. The women writers of letters to the press perceive this as highly counter-productive. They describe local management worrying about production and labour shortages whilst able-bodied and skilled women who would like to work sit at home caring for pre-school children.[70] Although nursery construction may well bring about long-term benefits to the farms, it seems probable that delays are created by the more immediate demands of production facing farm managers.

For women with young children who go to work despite the lack of nursery facilities, there are a variety of approaches to the problem. The traditional solution has been to leave young children in the care of their grandmothers, yet grandmothers today are very often well below retirement age themselves. Amongst couples who live with their parents, however, it is the grandmother in the majority of cases who has the prime responsibility for the care of pre-school children. There is also evidence to suggest that very young children may be sent to live with grandparents on a long term basis to enable their parents to stay in full-time employment. A study of Tambov Region revealed that, on average, 2% of rural children did not live with their parents. Most of these children were orphans. In the age group two to three, however, 7% of children did not live with their parents. This 5% increase on the average rate was largely accounted for by children who could not be accommodated in nurseries and of whom the grandparents therefore had temporary care.[71]

Where there are no nurseries and no one is available to mind young children, working women are obliged either to leave them at home unsupervised or take them to work with them. Both methods are practised and result in women constantly worrying about their children's safety and their own ability to hold down their job. A state farmworker in the Far East described how even the seasonal nurseries on her farm were no longer functioning. With two children aged three and four she faced a constant battle over her employment:

In 1977 I only managed to work on the state farm in spring. And even then all three of us came to the livestock unit – me with my pitchfork and the kids running around the cow shed. Towards winter I began to miss too many working days: in the cold, wet weather you couldn't bring children to the cow sheds. Our director says he will sack me for not going to work. Surely he has no right to do that in such a situation?[72]

As might be expected, it is proving increasingly difficult to persuade young couples to remain on farms such as these.

The problems involved for women in combining work and child care are not, however, always resolved by the opening of a new nursery or kindergarten. Complaints reveal that the opening hours of these facilities may not correspond with rural work schedules or that, where a considerable distance has to be travelled, local transport may not provide a service to take the children to the nurseries. In addition, nurseries are not infrequently reported as closed during the winter months owing to inadequate heating. Women often express concern at the quality of existing facilities. One survey indicated that almost a third of rural women sending their children to nurseries did so with some reluctance and would have preferred to leave them at home if possible.[73] A major reason for the lack of confidence of women in the care provided by kindergartens is the shortage of trained staff. It has been admitted that, on collective farms in particular, regulations on pay and conditions for workers in child care facilities are often broken. The long hours and lack of holidays imposed on them leads to a high turnover of staff, particularly of those who are qualified, with the result that the farms often rely on elderly local women to run their nurseries. Local apathy to pre-school education has been blamed for this state of affairs. Farm managers, it is said, prefer to employ 'semi-literate old grannies' as they create less trouble than young specialists for whom suitable conditions would have to be created. Other complaints by women which appear with some regularity in the press concern poor hygiene, monotonous food, a lack of toys and overcrowding in dismal or damp conditions.[74]

Although rural women express serious reservations as to the condition of existing nurseries there is no doubt that they see an extension of well-run facilities to the countryside as highly desirable. Young women especially who have a relatively high level of educational attainment themselves view nursery schooling as a modern and enlightened way of raising children.[75]

Parental roles in child care

Rural time budget studies are unilluminating on the subject of child care as they provide insufficient analysis of their samples according to family size and age of minor children. As would be expected, studies show a dramatic fall in the free time enjoyed by rural women with the birth of each child. Unfortunately, there appears to be no comparable study of the effect of the birth of children on the free time enjoyed by rural men. What is clear, however, is that in urban and rural areas alike, the prime responsibility for child care falls to women. As it is women who are obliged to give up work if there is no one else to mind their children, so it is women who take time off work to care for children when they fall sick. Under Soviet law leave of absence to care for sick children is permitted to both men and women. In practice, however, 98% of such leave is taken by women. The amount of time which women lose from work through child care is substantial. A survey of women machine operators in Rostov Region between 1974 and 1976 found that one in five cases of absence from work was caused by the care of sick children, representing over 11% of the total days lost by these women.[76]

Parental responsibilities in the contemporary Soviet countryside are not, however, confined to care for a child's physical development. Moral and intellectual qualities are also expected to be fostered by the home environment which, in many cases, means the mother. A survey of parental roles in villages of Orel Region during the seventies found that in 40% of families the wife had sole responsibility for the upbringing (*vospitanie*) of children.[77] A significant proportion of women questioned in this and other surveys on attitudes towards children confessed to experiencing difficulties in raising them. The problems fall into two main categories. On the one hand they involve the lack of time which women had to spend with their children, coupled with a lack of knowledge of child development. In one study, for example, collective farm women were asked whether they often talked to their children. Most of them replied, 'what is there to talk to them about? Our children know more than we do nowadays.' On the other hand, problems stemmed from the attitudes of husbands both towards their children and towards their wives. Women cited indifference and the lack of help or understanding from their husbands as creating difficulties in child care. Other major problems were said to be caused by drunkenness, rudeness and condescension by men towards their wives.[78]

Very occasionally an account appears in the press of an attempt to combat prevailing male attitudes to child care and housework. In 1980 the teacher of a rural nursery school in Arkhangel'sk Region described her approach to the problem:

Not long ago we held a fathers' evening . . . I suggested before beginning the discussion we should listen to the children – what do they think of you, how do they see you? And I switched on the tape recorder . . . Everyone grew quiet and pricked up their ears. 'My daddy never plays with me or takes me for walks', came a voice from the tape. 'When daddy's drunk I'm frightened of him.' 'On his day off daddy takes me for walks; he tells me all sorts about the trees, about the street, about birds.' 'My daddy gets tired after dinner, lies on the couch and watches television, but mummy washes up and does the washing. Mummy says "clear the table", but he replies, "clear it yourself".'

That night quite a few left the kindergarten shame-faced. We are not in town here, everyone knows everyone else and could easily recognise the children by their voices. Some of them were indignant – what a thing to do, playing a tape! it's outrageous! – but I thought, if it's hit home then it's been some use.[79]

Initiatives such as this appear to be few and far between or, if they do occur, receive scant publicity. The low level of participation by rural men in child care mirrors their behaviour in other areas of housework. In concluding this analysis of domestic labour in the countryside the reasons for such manifest inequality between husbands and wives are examined in the light of current Soviet political theory and government policy.

THE PERSISTENCE OF INEQUALITY WITHIN MARRIAGE

Writing in 1976 one Soviet rural sociologist observed, 'A person's psychology changes rather more slowly than the material basis of his or her life. There still remains a considerable gulf between the proclamation of political equality and legal regulation of equal rights and actual equality in practice between men and women in family and personal relationships.'[80] Nowhere is this gulf more apparent than in the question of domestic labour. Though the problem was acknowledged by Lenin himself shortly after the Revolution it remains unresolved in the Soviet Union today. Indeed, an Uzbek writer, commenting on letters to the newspaper *Pravda* in 1975, echoed Lenin's famous comment that 'The old master-right of the man still lives in secret':

The preconception that domestic concerns are strictly and completely the responsibility of women must be considered the most bigoted and obsolete way of thinking. What about husbands, older sons and brothers? At meetings, some of them speak out in favour of equal rights for women, whilst at home they conduct themselves like rich landowners of the old regime.[81]

As the evidence of time budget studies and surveys shows, such attitudes are not confined to Central Asian society. In the USSR, as in the West, publicly voiced opinion on the issues of housework and child care may bear little relation to private behaviour. A Belorussian survey of 1971, for example, found that 85% of rural men thought husbands should play a full part in helping their wives in the home or, in a small minority of cases, that couples should share housework equally. In practice, however, in over 80% of the rural families surveyed, the men helped either irregularly or not at all.[82]

Rural sociologists have criticised men's avoidance of housework, their refusal to do 'women's work' and the lack of respect for their wives which accompanies such behaviour as numbering amongst the 'significant survivals of the past' in the contemporary countryside.[83] Yet how far can the present distribution of domestic labour within the rural family be characterised as a 'survival' of the old peasant mentality? If indeed it is no more than a vestige of the old order, why has so little progress towards its eradication been made almost seventy years after the accession to power of a party committed to women's emancipation?

Rural conservatism

It must be said that rural conservatism undoubtedly has a part to play in dissuading young couples from attempting an egalitarian approach to their roles within the home. In the 1960s women themselves, especially the elderly, were reported to be the major supporters of the status quo. It was said that they were scornful of men who helped their wives with housework and censured women who received such help. 'She rules him with an iron rod', or 'He's at his wife's beck and call' were remarks said to be in common usage in such cases. A survey of Russian villagers in the Chuvash Autonomous Republic in 1973 found the overwhelming majority to be in favour of a man helping his wife around the home. Both men and women were, however, far more cautious as to the type of work which a man should do. Only a third of men and 40% of women approved of men doing 'women's work' such as washing, cleaning floors or milking.[84] Such a traditional view which regards the major components of housework as beneath the dignity of a man was the subject of a comment by a Soviet writer in 1977:

From my own experience in the countryside, I know that in the rare cases (perhaps one or two out of every ten marriages) in which a new husband takes on some 'female' domestic duties, this invariably leads to trouble. The first to learn of this 're-arrangement of the world' are the husband's parents, followed by relatives and neighbours. Through concerted efforts, they usually manage to break up the marriage. More recently, I have found that the same situation obtains in the city, the only difference being that 'public opinion' exerts greater pressure in the countryside.[85]

As this comment suggests, and as surveys quoted above show, the failure of men to take an equal share in domestic labour is as prevalent in the cities as in the countryside. The 'double shift' which women perform in the socialised and domestic economy is a recognised fact of life in both urban and rural areas. The CPSU Programme of 1974 announced that 'remaining inequalities in the position of women in daily life must be completely eliminated', whilst Leonid Brezhnev, speaking to the 16th USSR Trade Union Congress in 1980 admitted, 'We are still far from having done everything possible to ease the double burden which [women] bear at home and at work.'[86] The universality of women's exploitation within the home would suggest that to dismiss it as a 'survival' of the old peasant or bourgeois mentality provides an insufficient explanation for its persistence.

Socialisation

In recent years, certain rural sociologists have looked to the process of socialisation in home and school as a source of the prejudices apparent in the distribution of domestic labour. Rural children today still do a great deal of work in the home and on the plot. It has been found that the jobs undertaken by boys and girls differ considerably from each other and follow very closely the pattern of domestic labour practised by their parents. Thus, boys are to be found working on the plot, helping to prepare fuel and animal feed and cleaning the yard. Girls also work on the plot and tend the family's cow and, in addition, help look after younger children, shop, cook, clean and care for clothes. From an early age, therefore, girls are far more heavily involved than boys in domestic labour.[87]

Such an approach to housework, fostered in young children in the home, is allowed to go unchallenged in the schools. Indeed, not only is the traditional view of appropriate sex roles not tackled through the educational system, but is in fact positively reinforced by the school curriculum. At the most obvious level, differentiation of school activities by sex can be commonly seen in work-training classes in secondary schools. In addition, craft and domestic science lessons are regularly confined to either boys or girls on traditional lines. Such stereotyping can in no way be seen as the unconscious product of traditional attitudes. It is, by contrast, actively promoted by current educational thinking. As recent British research has shown, parents and teachers are being specifically exhorted by Soviet educational theory to differentiate between the upbringing of girls and boys in order to ensure the development of what are deemed appropriate feminine and masculine behaviour and characteristics.[88] The social psychologist I. S. Kon, in a statement characteristic of this trend in educational theory, has insisted that it is necessary to 'Train, and train again, girls to be girls and boys to be boys, so that we will then see in them the women and men we want to see.'[89] In recent years an increasing number of pamphlets and articles have been explicitly devoted to these themes. At the same time, official acceptance of a sexually dichotomised process of upbringing has been reflected in the tenor of reporting in the Soviet press. Thus, a report from a village school in Zaporozh'e Region describes how fifth-form boys do woodwork whilst the girls have a lesson on 'milk and milk products'. The girls cook pancakes for break, the article continues, 'for their classmates, "the joiners". And of course, they don't forget themselves.' Or, in another characteristic example, a photograph showing a group of girls cleaning the windows of a new village store bears the caption, 'Who else but girls should look after the tidiness and cleanliness of house and street? No surprise either that these same girls should have been asked to tidy up the newly built shop.'[90]

In the light of the adoption of such a line by many educationists and its reflection in school and media alike, the reluctance of the press to advocate the equalisation of responsibilities within the home appears more understandable. Over the past two decades media encouragement of male participation in domestic labour has, with rare exceptions usually connected with International Women's Day (8 March), been confined to a cursory 'My husband helps me with everything' in interviews with leading women workers; a statement which, in itself, encourages the notion that the principal responsibility for housework and child care rests with women. The March edition of *Krest'yanka* in 1983 provided a rare example of media promotion of shared roles within the home. The front cover carried a large colour photograph from a Lipetsk Region state farm of a man in an apron chopping onions and inside described the democratic approach to housework adopted by him and his wife. In addition, the centre pages carried an article entitled 'A Man In The House', urging men not to restrict their domestic activities to 8 March. Alongside the encouragement to husbands to venture across the threshold of their own kitchens, the writer felt it necessary to include advice of a more elementary nature. 'Try to adopt a few rules: don't leave your things wherever they happen to fall. When you come home from work put your clothes on a hanger, clean your shoes, and, incidentally, find a permanent place for them. Tidiness will gradually become a habit and will make life a lot easier for you and your wife.'[91] As this extract suggests the sharing of domestic tasks between husband and wife is not likely to be achieved overnight. Yet it cannot be said that the considerable resources of the Soviet press have been harnessed in an attempt to improve the situation. Though 'A Man In The House' for example, became a regular feature in *Krest'yanka*, its adventurous introduction was immediately superseded by advice on do-it-yourself, and even this was dropped entirely from the magazine within a matter of months.

The reticence of the press on this subject is mirrored in the writings of Soviet social scientists and statements by political figures. Despite the massive amount of evidence now available on the problems of inequality within the family the most common official and academic response to the question of women's 'double shift' is to advocate improved consumer services, labour saving devices and child care facilities. Though all these are desirable elements in the alleviation of the burden of housework it is most unlikely, given current economic priorities, that sufficient resources would be diverted into these areas to release women from their domestic functions. Though surveys have shown that women would welcome an improvement in consumer services, it has been found that they would favour a more equal distribution within the family of domestic responsibilities. Despite traditional prejudice against men's involvement in 'women's work' in the villages it is clear that there are now plenty of rural women who would like to see a less rigid division of labour within the home. In 1982, for example, *Krest'yanka* printed what was described as 'a curious letter' from a man in Penza Region who explained that cooking for his family was his hobby, and who offered several recipes for the use of readers. The magazine received 'hundreds of letters from grateful and delighted women readers' in response to this item.[92]

The principal reasons for the marked reluctance in published writings and official pronouncements seriously to consider a redefinition of traditional domestic roles, coupled with the act of fostering sex-appropriate behaviour in children and young people, are in part historical and in part a response to current problems. They stem both from classical Marxist theory on the family and the history of the 'woman question' in Soviet ideology and from demographic developments in the USSR today.

Ideology and family policy

Classical Marxist ideology on the subordination of women, notably as expounded in Engels' *Origin of the Family, Private Property and the State*, holds that women's oppression has an economic foundation and is inextricably linked to the development of class society. Women's emancipation, he states, will be achieved only through the abolition of private property followed by the mass entry of women into social production which is to be facilitated by the socialisation of domestic labour and child care. Classical Marxist theory, therefore, calls for the socialisation rather than the equalisation of domestic responsibilities. There is little attempt to deal with the problems of relations between the sexes as it is assumed that, with the destruction of the class relations from which they derive, the exploitation and oppression of women will eventually wither away.

Throughout the 1920s the 'woman question' was a source of much debate and experiment in the USSR. In 1930, however, with the abolition of the Zhenotdel, separate work with women ground to a halt and women's issues were given low priority in the push for economic expansion which characterised the next decade. As the triumph of socialism was declared, the woman question ceased to be a topic for debate. The ending of the class struggle and, hence, the liberation of the working class, so official theory ran, had brought about the liberation of women. In the Soviet Union in the 1930s, however, only the first of classical Marxism's prerequisites for the emancipation of women, their entry into social production, had been realised. The socialisation of domestic labour had manifestly not been achieved. Nevertheless, under both Stalin and Khrushchev, Soviet ideology proclaimed the solution of the 'woman question' as one of the 'great achievements of Soviet socialist construction'.[93] In such an ideological climate, therefore, discussion of sexual inequality clearly became impossible.

As Mary Buckley, the British researcher on women and ideology in the USSR, has shown, the acknowledgement of the existence of sexual inequality has re-emerged only in recent years.[94] Since 1967, Brezhnev's introduction of the concept of developed socialism into

Soviet ideology has allowed theorists to argue that socialist society passes through different stages of development. Developed socialism is seen as a protracted period of socialist construction following the attainment of socialism in the 1930s. During this stage, it is main-tained, the prerequisites of communism are gradually established. As socialism in the USSR at the present time is, therefore, held to be inadequately developed, it may be admitted that the 'woman question' likewise has not been fully resolved. The position of women at any given time is now said to be tied to the level of socialist development. Though the ultimate emancipation of women, it is maintained, is guaranteed by socialism, the attainment of equality may now be characterised as a long and protracted process. The introduction of the concept of developed socialism, therefore, meant that the recognition of sexual inequality and a discussion of the means by which it might be eliminated once more became acceptable elements of Soviet social science after a silence of some thirty-five years. This official acknowledgement of the complexities of women's emanci-pation from the late sixties gave some grounds for optimism that the re-definition of male and female roles within the family might at last be attempted.

During the 1970s rural sociologists numbered amongst those who voiced criticisms of the unequal roles played by men and women in the home. Those who examined the domestic burden shouldered by rural women saw the need for a profound change in attitudes towards housework and child care. The root of the problem was identified by these writers as lying in the differential treatment of boys and girls by parents and teachers. Thus, one rural sociologist criticised the prevailing division of labour between sons and daughters in the rural family as one which 'cannot help but form, and indeed does form, a view of housework as a "woman's affair"'.[95] Very occasionally concern was expressed at the role played by the educational system in sex-role socialisation. The author of an unpublished dissertation in 1977 stressed the need for schools to counteract the negative influence of parental behaviour. This he defined specifically as the effect on boys of their fathers' behaviour and attitudes, particularly in such matters as their lack of help in the home, lack of understanding and condescen-sion towards women and heavy drinking. Instead, he contended, the education of boys in schools was primarily orientated towards 'teaching them to be men', whilst the need remained for them to be taught that all family members should share domestic tasks.[96]

Although the issue of sexual equality has been allowed to re-emerge since the late 1960s, few Soviet academics have presented an analysis such as this. It is surely significant that the most trenchant comments on the subjects of sexual stereotyping in education and inequality within marriage are to be found in works which are unavailable to the general public.[97] Published academic writing regularly evades the issue of the husband's role within the home or acknowledges the existence of a problem obliquely by reference to other socialist countries. In a recent example of this technique, one sociologist, writing on the development of the small family in the USSR, quoted data from Poland on male attitudes to domestic labour and commented, 'many men are psychologically unprepared for an equal distribution of domestic responsibilities'; an observation which could be extended only by implication to the Soviet context.[98] In their references to the experience of other socialist countries, however, Soviet academics do not appear to have considered the position taken by the Cuban government on this question. The Cuban Family Code of 1974 states that both partners must share domestic tasks and child care equally when both husband and wife are in full-time employment. This provision of the law is read out at marriage services and has received a great deal of publicity in the country.[99] Whatever the results of this policy, such a radical response to sexual inequality is evidently not viewed as a proper subject for debate in the USSR. On the basis of published academic writing it may be concluded that the refinement in political theory which has permitted sexual inequality to be acknowledged has allowed only for a limited discussion of its origins and possible eradication. For the most part, analyses of women's oppression within the home continue to follow the orthodox Marxist line in calling only for increased socialisation of housework and child care.

A significant factor in the restriction of debate on sexual inequality has been increasing government concern about the falling birthrate. In its attempt to encourage women to have more children the government has adopted a pronatalist line which espouses traditional notions of femininity and masculinity. In the mass media, persistent references to women's 'natural' qualities, the essentials of femininity and women's innate fitness for child rearing and home making have gone hand in hand with changes in population policy. Recent changes in educational theory are in line with these developments and, indeed, give journalistic writing its authority. It hardly needs to be said that this revival of sex-stereotyping is completely at odds with

Marxist–Leninist orthodoxy. Far from permitting a genuine re-appraisal of sex roles in the home, it seems probable that current family policy will perpetuate sexual inequality in the family, the school and society at large. The nature and implications of these developments for rural women are examined in greater detail below.

CURRENT POPULATION POLICIES

The scale of the problem

The decline in the birthrate experienced over much of the USSR since the early sixties has been a cause of concern for Soviet planners throughout the 1970s. A low birthrate coupled with an ageing population have produced a sharp decline in population growth in European areas. In Central Asia the decline has been far less significant as the birthrate has remained high in a region with a far more favourable population structure. The result of such trends has been an increasing polarisation in the rates of growth experienced in these regions of the USSR.

Over the country as a whole the natural growth rate has fallen by more than a half since 1960 to 0.8%. As Table 14 shows, however, the fall has been most dramatic in European areas and Siberia. In the largest republic, the RSFSR, the growth rate in 1979 stood at less than a third of its 1960 level. In consequence, population growth in Central Asia has become a major element in the growth of the Soviet population as a whole. In 1979, for example, only 9% of Soviet citizens lived in Central Asia yet this region was responsible for 30% of the entire USSR population growth.[100] The rapid growth in population in this labour-surplus region which is characterised by its strong cultural traditions and static population has proved particularly worrying when contrasted with the decline in natural growth in regions of labour shortage. The problems involved in producing population policies to meet this complex situation have been regularly debated by academics in recent years.

Recent legislative change

Following the 25th Party Congress in 1981 new measures were enacted to increase maternity and child benefits. As the birth of a third child to a family was seen as decisive for the reproduction of the population,

Table 14 *Natural growth rates by republic,
1960 and 1979 (in % per year)*

	1979	1960
Latvia	0.1	0.7
Estonia	0.3	0.6
Ukraine	0.4	1.4
Lithuania	0.5	1.5
RSFSR	0.5	1.6
Belorussia	0.6	1.8
Georgia	1.0	1.8
Moldavia	1.0	2.3
Kazakhstan	1.6	3.1
Armenia	1.7	3.3
Azerbaidzhan	1.8	3.6
Kirgizia	2.2	3.1
Turkmenia	2.7	2.6
Uzbekistan	2.7	3.4
Tadzhikistan	3.0	2.8

Source: V. Perevedentsev, *270 millionov,*
Moscow, 1982, p. 9.

maternity benefits were re-organised with this in mind. Instead of a gradually increasing benefit from the birth of the third child onwards, the state now pays a grant of 50 roubles on the birth of a first child and of 100 roubles to both the second and third child, the grant remaining as before to subsequent children. The promotion of the three-child family, implying, as it does, an increase in births in European areas and a decrease in Central Asia, neatly avoids the necessity of producing different benefit laws for different regions, an option undoubtedly rejected as politically unacceptable.[101] New maternity leave provisions were, however, to be phased in between 1981 and 1983 on a broad geographical basis from north to south. Partially paid maternity leave was to be extended to the child's first birthday in the first instance to women in the Far East, Siberia and the Far North. Maternity pay was likewise set at 50 roubles per month in these regions, 35 roubles per month elsewhere. Additional unpaid maternity leave could now be taken until the child reached the age of eighteen months, whilst paid leave to care for sick children was to be extended to fourteen days per year during the 11th Five-Year Plan. The 1981 legislation also provided for an extra three days paid holiday per year for women with two or more children, with an option to take a further two weeks unpaid leave by arrangement with management. In addition, measures have been taken to extend part-time work and home working for women with children, and to increase and improve available popular literature on marriage, child care and demography. The aim of this provision is stated as 'the strengthening of the family as one of the highest moral values of socialist society'.[102]

In the rural press these measures were accompanied by editorials urging collective farm managements to take a fresh look at provision for working mothers and by examples of farms which had their own 'population policies'. The most striking case concerned a kolkhoz in Gorky Region which had suffered from labour shortages and an ageing population. Alongside an improvement in housing and services on the farm, management had instituted its own range of maternity benefits. By 1980, women on the farm received six months' paid leave on the birth of a second child, one year for a third child and eighteen months for a fourth child. As a result, it was claimed, within ten years the number of children under twelve on the kolkhoz had grown from 100 to 400; as the chairperson concluded, 'There it is, the collective farm socio-demographic policy in action.'[103]

The 1981 legislation, however, whilst extending some benefits and redefining others, is by no means the first attempt in recent years to enable women to combine the dual roles of worker and mother. Throughout the period since 1960, working women have been eligible for maternity leave for eight weeks before and eight weeks after the birth of a child. Additional unpaid leave could be taken by women until the child reached the age of one. Maternity pay was available to state employees according to their union status and the length of their uninterrupted employment until 1973 when all women employed by the state became eligible for benefits equal to previous average earnings. Maternity grants and pay were only extended to collective farm women in 1965.[104] On medical advice a woman may be transferred to lighter work during pregnancy without a loss in average pay. This provision extends also to nursing mothers and to women with children under the age of one. Dismissal of a woman from work on the grounds of pregnancy has been a criminal offence since 1960, yet cases of this type continue to be reported. A Supreme Soviet Commission in 1973 found there to be 'serious shortcomings' in the application of these laws in the workplace, particularly in regard to the transfer of pregnant women to lighter work. Cases of unfair dismissal in connection with pregnancy were said to be not uncommon in the service sector, health, education and on state farms. The courts are said to be reluctant to order adequate compensation to be paid in such cases. It would appear that the press may be a more fruitful avenue of complaint than the courts for women who have not received their entitlement under the law.[105]

The limitation of family size

Existing legislation clearly did little to encourage women in the sixties and seventies to have larger families. Surveys of opinion amongst both urban and rural women indicate that their view of the ideal family size is invariably larger than the number of children which they intend to have themselves. As might be expected from birthrate statistics rural women both intend to have more children than urban women and regard a larger family as preferable. Opinion as to how many children constitute an ideal family varies in a predictable manner according to region and ethnic group, rising from two to three children in rural Estonia to six or seven in rural Uzbekistan.[106]

Progress in disseminating contraceptive information and appliances has remained very slow, especially in rural areas. Neither the pill nor inter-uterine devices are widely available in the villages. As a result, women are obliged to rely on less reliable barrier methods and on abortion as a major means of birth control. Information on the use of contraception and the prevalence of abortion remains scant, yet data suggests that the more developed the region, the more likely women are to practice contraception and hence avoid abortion.[107] The unreliability of contraceptives and the reluctance to use inefficient and uncomfortable methods do, however, pose problems for women in all areas. A survey of Kalinin Region in 1971 found that 47% of rural women and 57% of urban women seeking abortions had used contraceptives. Reliable contraception was also cited by women in Chuvash villages in the mid-sixties as necessary to obtain their desired number of children.[108] A family planning service is still in its infancy in the villages, as a recent comment by the USSR Minister of Health indicated:

If for some reason a women either cannot or does not want to have any more children, then it is the duty of the doctor to let her know what the modern methods of contraception are, how to avoid abortion and to keep one's health and fitness for work. We are taking steps so that the women's consultations will work in this directions.[109]

This move towards the development of contraceptive services at a time when women are being encouraged to have more children has undoubtedly been prompted by concern at the effect of repeated abortions on women's health and on infant mortality. Abortion is said to be no less prevalent in rural areas than in the towns. The most significant difference in requests for terminations in town and country is that rural women are less likely to abort a first pregnancy and are generally older than urban women seeking abortions. In the Kalinin Region survey for example, two-thirds of rural women seeking abortions were aged twenty to thirty-four whilst three-quarters of the urban women were in this age group.[110]

In the countryside, however, the picture is complicated by the practice of illegal abortion. In 1966 it was reported that some 16% of all abortions carried out in the USSR were incomplete i.e. performed outside medical institutions and necessitating subsequent professional treatment. The number of illegal abortions was said to have fallen by more than a half in rural areas between 1955 and 1965, the most significant decline being recorded in the Baltic republics and the Ukraine.[111] It is clear, however, that illegal abortion has by no means disappeared from the countryside today. In 1978, for example, an article on abortion in *Krest'yanka* laid great stress on the need to avoid illegal operations because of the risk of infection. Women undergoing such abortions were urged to seek medical assistance immediately afterwards before the onset of septicaemia. A major factor in the persistence of illegal abortion must surely be the problems involved in seeking medical attention in many villages. Letters to the press indicate that inadequate health provision is a major problem in some areas.[112]

Although illegal operations are seen as an additional health hazard for women, popular medical articles have in recent years also urged women to avoid legal abortions. Abortion is cited as a cause of pelvic inflammatory disease, secondary infertility, miscarriage and prematurity. Women are warned that these health problems create marital difficulties: 'After an abortion, family dramas often arise as a woman suffering from a gynaecological illness cannot lead a regular sex life. This sometimes results in the breakdown of a marriage.'[113] Such scant data as are available suggest that abortion may indeed cause considerable problems for women's health. Amongst women agricultural machine operators surveyed in Rostov Region between 1974 and

1976, for example, gynaecological ailments accounted for over a quarter of requests for sick leave. Of such cases, 11% were directly due to abortion, whilst a further 41% concerned pelvic inflammatory disease. Of medical consultations sought by this group of women, 37% resulted from gynaecological complaints. No rural surveys appear to exist on the prevalence of secondary infertility or other symptoms resulting from abortion. A Moscow survey in 1972, however, found that more than two-thirds of infertile women in the sample had become infertile after repeated abortions; in more than half of these cases infertility had developed during the first five years of marriage. Two Western researchers, C. D. Davies and M. S. Feshbach, writing in 1980, made the connection between abortion, the increase in premature births and the rise in infant mortality which has occurred in recent years. Clearly, Soviet writers themselves see a link between the regular practice of abortion and complications in subsequent pregnancies.[114] As a result of the prejudicial effect of abortion on women's health and hence on the birthrate, contraception is now seen as preferable. Nevertheless, in the current pronatalist climate, writers in the popular press have tackled the subject with little enthusiasm. The article in *Krest'yanka* cited above, for example, contained a great many warnings as to the risks involved in abortion yet failed to give full support to the use of contraception. Women were simply informed that contraceptives could be harmful if used without medical supervision and that they should see a doctor if for some reason they could not have a child.[115]

Rural women questioned as to their reasons for seeking an abortion often cite financial difficulties in their answer. Whilst women in the towns regularly give overcrowded housing as their reason, women in the countryside are more likely to blame the lack of nursery facilities. However, the major reason for abortion stated by women in Amur Region in 1969 and Kalinin Region in 1971 was simply a desire not to have any more children. Rural women, therefore, request abortion when they consider their families to be complete and this may bear no relation to their financial situation or to material problems such as housing or nursery places. In the Amur survey it was noted that the more highly educated the woman the fewer births she had and the fewer abortions she had. Family planning was found to be related to a woman's view of how many children she felt were desirable and thus, in two cases out of five, her reason for seeking abortion was said to be 'unclear', i.e. nothing hindered the birth of another child except the woman's own desire to avoid it.[116] In order to boost the birthrate, then, it would appear that the state needs not only to produce better material conditions for mothers but also to change the desire of most women to limit their families to one or two children.

Pronatalist propaganda

In recent years the resources of the mass media have been increasingly employed in an effort to change women's attitudes to motherhood. The examples given below are typical of press comment aimed at rural women in European areas and Siberia where the birthrate is low. In line with the promotion of the three-child family, articles aimed at women in Central Asia concentrate on women's role in production and in the wider society with the aim of restricting births in these areas by drawing women out of the home.[117]

During the late seventies, growing concern over the fall in the birthrate led to an upsurge in overt pronatalist propaganda in the Soviet press. Articles with titles such as 'The Village of Heroines' or 'The Greatest Happiness' appeared with clockwork regularity in rural newspapers and magazines, extolling the virtues of large families. The 'Heroine-Mothers' of ten or more children who were featured in these accounts offered the opinion that couples should have at least three children and encouraged other women to follow in their footsteps; 'I wish you, dear women, as many children as I have', said a Moldavian mother of twelve, 'and that they would be as good as mine are. Children are a great happiness. I should know that. Believe me.'[118] In one extraordinary example the village of Borki in Khar'kov Region of the Ukraine was featured. With a population of just over 2,000 the village boasted 152 large families and twenty-eight 'Heroine-Mothers'. Examples were given of families where a mother, daughter and daughter-in-law all bore the title 'Heroine-Mother'. In the particular 'moral climate' thus created in this village there was said to be only one divorce in every hundred families. The journalist authors of articles such as these were full of praise for the effect of this abundance of children on the women concerned and often portrayed happy motherhood as a source of physical beauty. Similarly, it was claimed that large families had a profoundly beneficial effect on individual children, both physically and psychologically: 'Children from large families are more hard working, more independent, more modest and have more respect for their elders.'[119]

During this same period the emphasis on women as mothers was underlined again and again in official statements and slogans. The approved slogan for women in 1979, for example, on the 62nd Anniversary of the October Revolution, ran: 'Long live Soviet women – active builders of communism! Glory to mothers who give out the warmth of their hearts in raising their children as worthy citizens of their socialist Motherland!'[120] Eulogies to women indulged in by the Soviet press every 8 March (International Women's Day) commonly portray women as the mysterious source of the life force. The male authors of such pieces, whilst placing women firmly on their pedestals, have a curious habit of equating the glories of womanhood with passivity. The implication of much of this writing is that women are the givers of life and love, the guardians of life-enhancing qualities and moral values, whilst men are made for action and for the protection of these unfathomable creatures of destiny. A particularly striking example of the genre appeared in the newspaper *Sel'skaya zhizn'* on the eve of International Women's Day, 1980. Its Ukrainian author began his piece in praise of rural women with the following words:

The longer we live on this earth, the more deeply and acutely we feel that all that is best in this world comes from Woman, from her kindness and generosity with which only nature itself can be compared. I think that it is for just this reason that down the centuries we men have tilled our land, built houses and palaces, avidly sought to fly in the sky, ploughed the oceans, created music, invented the wheel and the atomic reactor, loaded upon ourselves the most difficult and exhausting work, because we wanted to understand the source of the greatest wonder of all, given to us for all these labours, the name of whom is Woman.[121]

It would be misleading to suggest that all men invited to contribute to the celebration of International Women's Day in the popular press produce quite such startling results. Nevertheless, the frequent adulation of women for little other than their mothering qualities strikes an oddly discordant note in a country in which women have made such an enormous contribution to economic growth.

The development of a model of femininity to be emulated by Soviet women has become an increasing preoccupation of journalism in recent years. The 8th of March eulogies, whilst representing a particularly unsubtle aspect of this new concern, nevertheless form an integral part of it. This presentation of an ideal of femininity for women to follow is inextricably linked to current population policies. It represents a move away from overt pronatalist propaganda to an attempt to redefine women's self-image and to re-kindle their interest in home and family. By the early 1980s the link between images of femininity and the promotion of motherhood had become more explicit. Through interviews in *Krest'yanka* with leading stage and film actresses, motherhood was extolled as the highest expression of femininity. The delivery of this message to rural women by glamorous stars of the screen is in stark contrast to the interviews of the late seventies with the village 'heroines' and their enormous families. Larisa Malevannaya took the leading role of Vera in the much publicised and widely shown film 'Late Encounters' (*Pozdnie svidaniya*, Lenfil'm 1980) concerning a career woman who felt unable to bear the child of the man she loved. Following her decision to terminate her pregnancy the couple parted, the last scene of the film showing Vera alone, involved in her busy academic round yet clearly feeling the loss of her family life. It is surely significant that an actress who had recently been seen in such a role should be the first in this series of interviews. In discussing the film she observed:

A shortage of femininity has arisen. Why is there more and more talk about child rearing? Because women are less and less occupied with it. At one time, we would specially take the time to please men with our hairstyles, our dresses. Today a man of thirty wants to get married but there is no one to marry. People say 'Surely there's someone where you work?' But then we're all the same – trousers, boots, cigarettes, a profession. We are too much alike.[122]

Similar sentiments were expressed by the stage and film actress Lyudmila Chursina in an interview entitled 'Femininity is our Strength'. More directly, People's Artist of the USSR, Ada Rogovtseva, responded in the following words to the question 'What does being modern mean to you?': 'Being first and foremost an ordinary mum! Being a good wife, a loving daughter ... Our emancipation never liberated us from this great female duty and never took away these great joys. In my opinion the fear of having children and the neglect of family responsibilities are signs of social laziness.'[123]

The identification of femininity with motherhood and the encouragement of nurturant qualities in women is repeatedly reinforced in articles portraying women as home makers. The message is spelt out in interview after interview with women who have highly successful careers that, for a woman, achievements at work are not enough. As one female journalist expressed it, 'A woman remains a woman, and her great strength is probably that, whilst on a par with men at work, she reserves for herself that area of women's affairs which makes her the custodian of the family hearth.'[124] The theme is inevitably taken up by the women interviewed. 'Happiness in a home depends on the woman', declares a woman machine operator in a characteristic example. Her husband and six sons, we are told, are more efficient at work than those who do not have such a devoted and caring woman to look after them. Women who have full-time jobs themselves are thus urged to regard the creation of a secure home environment as their duty, almost indeed as a patriotic act: a 'strong home front', women are informed, turns a man into a good and responsible worker who can give his whole attention to the demands of production.[125]

This playing down of women's own contribution to the workforce and concentration on their role in the home is at its most explicit in articles advising young couples on the essential ingredients for a happy marriage. One such piece which appeared in the magazine *Sel'skya nov'* in 1979 warned young wives first and foremost not to nag and to restrain any feelings of jealousy or possessiveness: 'Men really value women's indulgence . . . their talent for forgiveness', the writer added. Displaying an interest in their husband's work was also considered of prime importance: 'Ask him about the new tractors or how the meeting of the collective farm management committee went.' At the same time 'however busy you are at work and around the house' wives were urged never to neglect their appearance or to forget a man's love for his stomach: 'There is of course no need to make a cult of cooking but to say you hate it is unnatural.'

Meanwhile, the writer informed young husbands that, although they were now the head of the family, they should be seen to take note of their wives' opinions. They were advised of the importance of buying their wives presents, paying compliments and thanking them for their help: 'When she gives you a clean shirt say "Thank you, Lenochka", when she notices an article in a magazine to do with your work say "Clever girl, Tamara, thank you!"'[126]

One might be forgiven for concluding on the basis of this article that young rural women in the USSR of today do little work outside the home, are emotionally unstable and probably not too bright. Certainly the piece offers a prescription for marital harmony which rests firmly on a foundation of male condescension and female deference and its entire tone is thoroughly patronising to women. Yet this emphasis on women as the servants of their husbands and their children is by no means unusual in Soviet journalism. Indeed, the implication in much of this writing on the home and marriage is that self-sacrifice should be the hallmark of the successful wife and mother. A lengthy piece in *Krest'yanka*, addressing women on their role in the home, spelled this out:

You expect neither praise nor reward. You are well acquainted with extreme physical stress, at times with severe emotional fatigue and with bitter disappointments when it seems that you have wasted yourself on trifles. But then who, if not you, also knows great, pure and unselfish joy! Joy from the knowledge that you are making a living fortress for those who are nearest and dearest to you, that you are helping them to live, even if they do not understand that now . . . And so once more you are on your feet at the crack of dawn; once more, as if in perpetual motion, you are keeping the home steady and moving it forward, the courageous captain of your family ship. And whatever your mood, however you feel, you give yourself the order, "smile, captain!" – because you know, if you are a good housewife, that your smile is worth a good deal, your mood is transmitted to the members of your household and you have no right to make life difficult for them.[127]

Writing such as this which, to the Western reader, is strongly reminiscent of advertisements aimed at female consumers – 'When a mother cares, it shows' – appears likewise to be expressly designed to induce a sense of inadequacy in those who fail to achieve such a level of self-denial. For the logical outcome of an ideology which makes women the source of harmony in the home is surely to place the burden of guilt upon women should discord arise. Soviet women are indeed told by the media that it is the wife's job to 'iron out the sharp corners so that quarrels can be avoided'.[128] Thus, if women have complaints, they are warned to take care in voicing them:

The demands of modern young women are, as a rule, justified, but the manner in which they are expressed is not always appropriate. Many wives do not understand that they should spare their husband's self-esteem, that they should not be too categorical or express their demands abruptly. Otherwise a husband may develop an inferiority or guilt complex towards his family and the whole thing may boil over from time to time in drunkenness and rows.[129]

Similarly, academics writing in the popular press hold women responsible for men's attitudes towards their children. A letter to *Krest'yanka* from a young woman, Nadya, describing her feelings after she and her baby had been deserted by her husband, received the following commentary: 'A man who has a child is still not a father. To become one he must take upon himself a father's functions. And in this a great deal depends upon the woman . . . Nadya didn't succeed in teaching her husband to be a father.'[130]

Through this mass of admonishments and exhortations to women men are, by implication, portrayed as astonishingly passive recipients of female care. In her role as 'the custodian of the family hearth' a woman is held to account for her husband's attitude to drink, to his children and to his work. Evidently, a woman is to be a mother not only to her children but also to her husband.

It is difficult to envisage how the image of womanhood promoted in the Soviet press in recent years could do anything but reinforce traditional rural notions of 'a woman's place'. Certainly the overwhelming emphasis that it is the woman who is primarily responsible for the home runs directly counter to attempts to interest men in sharing domestic tasks or in seeing child care as anything other than a woman's job. The preoccupation with femininity and the nature of womanhood as defined and expressed by the nation's propagandists is undoubtedly seen as a convenient means of encouraging women to perceive themselves primarily as mothers. Yet for women who are at the same time expected to be exemplary members of the workforce, the government's pronatalist stance makes extraordinarily complex demands of their time and energy. A typical piece in *Krest'yanka* concluded with a fine summary of the multiple roles to be undertaken by the 'mistress of the house'. She was to be 'its chief director and at the same time its chief servant, its healer and teacher, its brain centre, its heart and its soul'.[131] It is a prescription which provides little relief for women who are already grossly overburdened and gives scant hope of release from the stress which, as will be examined below, many women clearly feel.

CONFLICT IN THE RURAL FAMILY

The roots of conflict

The fact that Soviet women today still carry a double burden of work in the economy and in the home is recognised at the highest levels. Anxiety over the birthrate, however, not only hampers attempts to translate this recognition into remedial measures but actively reinforces the status quo. The result for women, as Soviet social scientists increasingly point out, is overwork leading to stress and fatigue. The situation provides fertile soil for the growth of conflict within the family.

A survey of women agricultural workers in Kiev Region in the late seventies found that the vast majority complained of tiredness at the end of their working day before beginning the second half of their 'double shift'. Of these women, 78% said that they found it difficult, and at times very difficult, to cope with their combined workload at home and work. Women who did not respond in this way were those either with no children or with grown-up children, or living in households where all the members of the family shared domestic tasks. A slightly earlier survey from the Ukraine had likewise discovered that two-thirds of the women who found their work difficult blamed this on the problems they were having 'fulfilling their functions in the family'.[132]

In her unpublished doctoral dissertation Nadezhda Shishkan, an eminent writer on women in the workforce, estimated that the work involved in carrying out all the nation's domestic labour and private agriculture could employ some 50 million full-time workers. In reality, however, between 70% and 80% of this work was performed by women who were already employed full-time in the labour force. In charting the effect of this burden of work on Soviet women she concluded that it led to increasing psychological strain which was one of the causes of the falling birthrate, marital breakdown and child neglect. Other social scientists have noted the link between female overwork and the rising divorce rate: 'Discord between spouses often results from placing on a woman full responsibilities at work and at the same time expecting her to be a good housewife', noted one writer on divorce. Viktor Perevedentsev recently observed that letters to the press on the subject of divorce show that problems connected with the division of domestic labour 'lie at the root of a significant proportion of all divorces'.[133] In a state which is attempting to increase its birthrate, the current high rate of marital breakdown is a cause of grave concern. The instability of the family is seen as a major element in women's reluctance to have more children. The growing recognition that female overwork leads to marital conflict has recently been reflected in sex education pamphlets aimed at a young male readership. Some of these pamphlets, which have as yet appeared only in small editions, include the advice that housework and child care should be shared with the aim of avoiding conflict and marital breakdown.[134]

Pamphlets such as this, however, represent no more than a drop in the ocean when viewed alongside the mass of pronatalist propaganda reinforcing traditional roles. Moreover, the advice which they present to adolescent boys has come too late to have any impact on the behaviour of the present generation of married couples. Occasionally, women's resentment at what they see as parasitic behaviour by many men appears in print in the rural press: 'Nowadays all the work and all the worry about the family lie in the main on women. Men have no sense of responsibility either towards their family, or towards their children or towards their work. And so they start to 'play around'', first they like one woman, then another', runs a characteristic outburst.[135]

In a recent series of correspondence on the theme of marriage and divorce in *Krest'yanka*, a particularly frank letter from a woman in Primorskii Territory showed precisely how overwork had in her case led to resentment and to marital difficulties. It is a letter which makes chastening reading when set alongside the view of female self-sacrifice propounded in current journalistic writing:

Many people think us a model family. My husband doesn't drink, there are no rows at home, the children are neat and polite. But nobody knows what this has cost me! Whilst my husband was studying – and I insisted on this myself – first of all in school, then at the institute, for twelve whole years I took all the housework upon myself. I ran around like a rat in a cage: from home to work, from work to home. I just waited, thinking that when my husband got his diploma we would do everything together – both work in the home and relax. I had good reason too, as there was nothing to teach my husband about it: he had lived for many years with his sick mother so he had learned how to wash and cook, not to mention any man's job such as repairing or making things. It's a long time now since my husband became an engineer and a respected man in our district, whilst I am a housewife as before with an incomplete secondary education. No, it's worse than that, I am a slave. I alone owe everything to everybody but no one owes me anything. My sons are already grown up and imitate him in every way. They think that it's all right, that that's how things should be in a family. Beside my husband in his brand new clothes – I always buy him all the latest things, after all he has a responsible job! – I feel old and ugly. I feel that love has gone. My husband is beginning to seem unpleasant to me, or even more than that, repugnant. I feel glad when he is away on a business trip. My husband evidently feels something: he has started to express his dissatisfaction.'You are not affectionate', he says 'You've become cold.' But where can I get warmth from when he has extinguished my love year by year?[136]

The prevalence of divorce

In 1965 divorce was made entirely a matter for the people's court. Three years later the 1968 Family Law replaced the 1944 legislation on marriage and divorce. Since 1968 a divorce has been once more obtainable at a registry office in cases where couples have no minor children and are divorcing by consent. Such a divorce is made absolute after a period of three months from registration. A divorce by registration only can also be obtained in cases where the whereabouts of the spouse is unknown, if a spouse is of unsound mind or sentenced to more than three years' imprisonment. In all other cases divorce may be granted only in court. The court is obliged to attempt reconciliation and may defer a case, usually for up to six months, to allow for this. Custody, maintenance and divisions of property are decided by the court in cases where couples have failed to reach agreement. Charges for the registration of divorce range from 50 to 200 roubles at the discretion of the court. The principal restriction on divorce now concerns men who are not permitted to petition for divorce without their wife's consent if she is pregnant, or for a period of one year after the birth of a child.[137]

Between 1959 and 1970 the annual Soviet divorce rate rose from 5.3 to 15.2 registered divorces per 1,000 registered marriages, the sharpest increase occurring in the mid-sixties following the relaxation of the law.[138] Marital breakdown in the USSR is no longer merely an urban phenomenon. Between 1962 and 1981, the proportion of divorces granted to rural couples rose from 14% to nearly 17%. Although this figure represents a small minority of all Soviet divorces, its significance lies in the fact that the rural population has declined considerably over the last twenty years. In 1962 rural inhabitants made up 50% of the Soviet population. By 1979 the rural population had shrunk to 38% of the total. It may be estimated that, whilst the urban divorce rate increased by one sixth during the 1970s, the rural divorce rate doubled in this same period.[139] The growth in rural divorce was reported to be particularly high amongst young couples and in regions in close proximity to large towns.[140]

The demographic structure of the Soviet population gives rise to a situation in which, in all areas, men have a higher rate of marriage than women. Hence, more women than men remain unmarried after divorce in both urban and rural areas and in all republics. Predictably, the 1979 census revealed that there were more divorced women in urban areas than in rural areas and in European republics than in Central Asian republics. Across the country, the number of divorced or separated women in rural areas was just over half the total in urban areas. The greatest discrepancy between numbers divorced in urban and rural areas was recorded in Central Asia, notably in Turkmenia, where women in the towns were eight times more likely to be divorced or separated than those in the countryside. At the other end of the scale the number of divorced or separated women in the Ukrainian countryside stood at two-thirds of the total recorded in the towns.[141]

Reasons for divorce

Alcohol abuse

In the majority of cases in both urban and rural areas it is the wife who petitions for divorce. A range of surveys on divorce carried out since 1960 has shown that a major cause of marital breakdown in the countryside is heavy drinking by men. In almost all these surveys over 40% of women's petitions cite their husbands' alcoholism as their reason for seeking a divorce, whilst one researcher concluded that in over 70% of cases divorce was in some way connected with the husband's drunkenness.[142]

A three-year survey of divorce cases brought by collective farmers in Belorussia in the early seventies provides an interesting example of the reasons given for requesting divorce. Under Soviet law the spouse is required to show that 'further cohabitation and the preservation of the family have become impossible'.[143] Table 15 indicates the proofs of breakdown presented by Belorussian couples and the reasons accepted by the court. Alcoholism was not only the most common reason for breakdown cited in women's petitions but also the proof most frequently accepted by the court.

Drunkenness is by no means a new phenomenon in the countryside, though it would appear that the pattern of drinking has changed considerably. Heavy drinking is no longer confined to public festivals or family celebrations but goes on throughout the year. For many men drinking is evidently a major leisure activity which they deem a legitimate part of rural culture. As one commentator observed in the mid-seventies, 'It is frequently not the drunkard who is censured but the sober man who "wants to be a saint".'[144] Surveys have shown that heavy drinking is most prevalent and creates most problems in the more urbanised villages and especially in those which are expanding. The phenomenon has been attributed to relatively high pay, an increase in free time and a lack of education amongst men in rural areas. Women are far less likely to drink than men, yet in recent years the press has not infrequently commented on the rise in alcoholism amongst rural women. On the basis of press comment it seems fair to say that women are far more heavily censured for drunkenness than

Table 15 *Reasons for divorce in petitions from collective farmers, Belorussia, 1972–3*

	court	Opinion of wife	husband
Alcoholism	38.7	44.3	10.6
Incompatibility	15.1	6.7	22.2
Adultery	9.4	12.6	15.3
Frivolous reasons for marriage	8.5	2.0	4.5
Prolonged unavoidable separation	5.4	3.8	3.1
Loss of affection	5.3	8.6	12.3
Cruelty	3.6	5.6	0.6
Imprisonment	3.3	2.6	2.1
Physical or mental illness	2.1	1.7	2.6
Interference by parents	1.5	4.4	11.3
Sterility	0.8	0.7	1.0
Physiological incompatibility	0.3	0.3	0.5

Source: V. T. Kolokol'nikov, 'Marital and Family Relations among the Collective Farm Peasantry', *Soviet Sociology*, Winter 1977–8, p. 27.

are men for whom heavy drinking has been, if not socially acceptable, then at least generally tolerated.[145]

Yet is is clear that drunkenness has been the cause of much distress in the countryside. Accidents or violence of any kind receive very little publicity in the Soviet press yet reports have appeared of serious accidents and fatalities (usually in connection with farm machinery) which have been caused by drunkenness at work. Vandalism and fights amongst young people have likewise been attributed to heavy drinking.[146] Other reported cases include incidents of assaults on women by drunken men. In one such case a sixteen-year-old girl wrote to a national newspaper asking for help as she was suffering continual abuse from a heavy drinker of twenty-three. The problem had begun when she refused to go out with him because of his drinking and he had punched her in the face in public. In another case, a young woman specialist had twice been the target of attempted rape by drunken men in the village to which she had been sent for her first job. In both cases the men involved had received prison sentences.[147]

Alcohol abuse may have a disastrous effect on relationships in the family. A survey of rural families in Estonia in 1974 found that 14% of respondents attributed problems in their family life to male drunkenness. Such a response appears far more typical of rural women than of urban women. Rural women seeking abortion for example, are, according to one survey, more likely than urban women to cite their husband's heavy drinking as a factor dissuading them from having a child.[148] Guzel Amalrik, writing in the mid-sixties, described the relationships with local women of men sentenced to exile in a remote Siberian village:

> They come to see us sometimes and each one starts shouting at the top of his voice about his old woman: 'She's this and she's that, she wouldn't let me drink, she hid the home brew, I'm going to give her a fright.' And yesterday one hopeless drunkard told us how he had ripped up her dress with his teeth and beat her with a poker: 'Let me drink', he said; 'if you don't, I'll burn the hut down, so there!'[149]

The occasional reports which do appear in the press make it plain that domestic violence is by no means confined to the most disaffected section of society. Indeed, journalists are often at pains to underline the high standing of women victims in the local community. In one case, for example, the report stated that the 'best dairy woman on the collective farm, a member of the management committee' had received a fractured skull from a hammer blow delivered by her 'blind drunk husband'. In another case, investigated at length by *Krest'yanka*, the wife was described as 'a leading dairy woman, with stately good looks, an excellent housewife who could turn her hand to anything'. The years of domestic violence from which she and her children had suffered were common knowledge in the village yet she had never asked for help and, as a result, no one had offered to intervene. The attention of the press was attracted to the case by a letter to *Krest'yanka* from the two, now grown-up, daughters which they had written before leaving home:

> We have no life because of our father's drunkenness. Every day he drinks and makes a scene, throws knives, a hatchet or scissors at her with the foulest of words and is always threatening to kill her and us too. Mother is afraid to complain about him ... it's unbearable to go on living like this. He's a monster not a man; we don't want a father like this! Help us, please.[150]

Fear of reprisals clearly haunts women who have drunken husbands to contend with. A group of women writing anonymously to the press to complain of illegal alcohol sales in their village explained their fear of signing their names as 'there might be family rows or other sorts of unpleasantness'. The scale of the problem has been underlined throughout the 1970s and early 1980s by the importance attached by women activists to combating drunkenness. Irina Fedorina, agricultural machine operator and delegate to the 26th Party Congress, writing in *Krest'yanka* in 1981, mentioned the disastrous results of alcohol abuse and asked, 'Is there a greater evil in our country than drunkenness?'[151] Other women, active in the Party or women's councils, would appear to agree that there is not. As will be examined in Chapter 3 below, women activists are particularly concerned at the effect of drunkenness and domestic violence on children and spend much of their time attempting to tackle the problem.

Women such as these who are most concerned about the drink problem have, until recently, consistently reported a lack of co-operation and support for their efforts on the part of local officials. It is by no means a new complaint. The eminent sociologist, A. G. Kharchev, writing in 1965, noted the failure of those in authority to take alcohol abuse seriously:

An especially large amount of criticism has been levelled at social organisations and at the police by women divorcing because of their husband's drunkenness. Almost all of them pointed out that if certain employees had not regarded drunkenness as some sort of childish prank but had really tackled it and its consequences then there would have been no need for many divorces.[152]

Women activists and journalists alike have frequently reported an unwillingness to intervene in domestic affairs on the part of those in authority. Thus a vicious circle develops in which officials fail to act unless invited by one of the parties involved, whilst the victims fail to request assistance through fear.[153]

The failure of the authorities to tackle alcohol abuse has nowhere been more graphically displayed than over the question of the sale of alcohol. Though sales have long been strictly controlled by law in the Soviet Union it is evident that supply has rarely been a problem in rural areas. Complaints from women across the country make it clear that in many villages there is no need to resort to home distilling to ensure a supply of spirits around the clock. Complaints to the press from women have described rural shops where an extensive range of wines and spirits can be purchased on credit at any hour of the day or night in direct contravention of the law. The disastrous consequences of selling alcohol on credit become only too apparent each monthly pay day when accounts are settled. Women have complained of their husbands immediately forfeiting half of their month's wages in this way at the village store. In the words of a typical letter, 'Some of the men acquire 80 or 90 roubles-worth of vodka, liqueurs or strong wine a month. But it's us – the wives and children who suffer. We can't pay debts like this for our husbands.'*[154] The tone of women's letters and journalists' reports give the impression that rural women in these circumstances are perpetually at war with their local women shop-keepers. In one account, for example, it was reported: 'Tarantsova holds the men of Tyunikovo firmly in her hands. Sometimes women beg or demand that she stop selling their husbands vodka. If a wife proves too persistent Tarantsova merely suggests to the woman's husband at an opportune moment that his wife is trying to order him around, and swift vengeance is often visited upon the stubborn wife.' In another case a woman who asked a shop manageress to stop selling alcohol on credit reported, 'She told me I needed a good dressing down. She had to fulfil the plan.'[155]

As plan targets for shop trading are set by monetary value it is far easier to fulfil the plan by selling expensive items such as alcohol rather than the cheaper commodities required in the running of the home. Journalists sent from Moscow to investigate local conditions re-gularly find that officials turn a blind eye to the results of this state of affairs provided that the figures for plan fulfilment look good. The usual result of press intervention is the dismissal of the woman shopkeeper from her job, whilst those who have tacitly condoned her activities rarely suffer similar reprisals.[156]

When the failure of local officials to take the drink problem seriously has been coupled with a lack of response to women's own needs, women's sense of grievance is plain in their complaints to the press. A letter to *Krest'yanka* about the effects of the opening of a new public bar, 'The Little Aurochs', in a rural community in Belorussia is typical:

Until this drinking establishment appeared it was a bit quieter in our village. What did they build it for? Was it to make drunkards of our husbands? If that was it, then it has successfully achieved its mission. For ages in our village we've been calling it not 'The Little Aurochs' but 'Women's Tears'. The bar is flourishing but the money can't be found to build a nursery, and many women who would like to go to work are obliged to sit at home with the children.[157]

The tone of women's letters to the press since the mid-1970s suggests that they were becoming increasingly aggrieved at what they saw as official insensitivity to the misery caused by heavy drinking.

With the accession to power of Mikhail Gorbachev it certainly

---

*When this letter was written the average wage of a collective farmer was 92 roubles per month, of a state farmer, 127 roubles and of an industrial worker 162 roubles.

cannot be said that the Soviet government at national level remains indifferent to alcohol abuse. The anti-alcohol campaign has involved not merely propaganda but an extension of the criminal law with clear directions on enforcement to the appropriate agencies. The measures aim to eradicate drinking at work and in public places and to tackle questions of supply. This includes enforcement of regulations on alcohol sales and the laws on home brewing. There will also be planned reductions in the production of alcohol. It remains to be seen whether these measures will be translated into action on a sufficient scale to relieve the distress which alcohol abuse has caused rural women.

Infidelity

In June 1981 a lengthy letter was published in *Krest'yanka* from a married man of forty who had fallen hopelessly in love with a woman in his village who was also married and apparently did not share his feelings. His letter to the magazine was a cry for help which the editor referred to the readers.[158] Since then, several thousand letters have been received by the magazine in response to this and subsequent articles on the subject of divorce and the avoidance of marital breakdown. Those which have been published have often been remarkably frank in recounting their authors' own experiences. They provide a valuable insight into prevailing rural attitudes in an area which has been very little researched by Soviet rural sociologists.

Initial reactions to this first letter were extremely varied. Some correspondents, particularly the men, offered sympathy and encouragement, informing the magazine that they had experienced a similar predicament themselves. Others, notably women, reacted with hostility and exasperation to the man's letter:

I can't stand men who can't control themselves. You could lose your family, if you haven't already lost it. But I assure you that you won't find happiness. And you won't bring happiness to anyone because you're a weak-willed person. Remember that you have a son. You'll break up your own family and someone else's. You really do need a dressing down, and a good one at that.[159]

At another level there were women who had found the letter upsetting: 'I have been married for nine years, my little boy is about to start school. I read your letter and it frightened me. How can years spent together be empty, whilst a fleeting love for someone else's wife eclipses everything in the world? How can that be fair?'[160] The fear expressed in this letter would appear to be by no means unique. Other correspondents to *Krest'yanka* have written of the misery caused by jealousy and possessiveness arising from the fear of losing a spouse's affection. Surveys have shown that such chronic insecurity is most likely to cause marital difficulties in rapidly urbanising villages, precisely those rural areas in which divorce is most common. Fear of this sort, fuelled by an environment in which divorce is no longer a rarity, may well be most acutely felt by those who have remarried, as in this letter from a dairy women in Khar'kov Region of the Ukraine:

I separated from my first husband because he found another woman. I took it all very badly. But then I met a good man and we got married. Sergei is a machine operator and it often happens that he has to work from morning until late at night. He comes home tired but he is always joking and laughing – that's the kind of person he is. But I always think there's more to it, that he has got someone else. And I can't do anything with myself. After all, I really trusted my first husband and he deceived me. And so I get irritated at the least little thing. Either I reproach Sergei or I cry. At first he used to laugh it off but now my tears annoy him . . . I am afraid that our happiness won't last long.[161]

In response to the initial letter of the forty-year-old man came appeals for the avoidance of divorce by others who saw themselves as the victims of marital breakdown. Amongst these were teenage girls who wrote of their distress when their own parents separated.[162] Their view that the children should come first is supported by occasional surveys of rural opinion. Respondents to a survey carried out in Estonia in 1974, for example, were asked whether a married person who falls in love with someone else should leave their family so as to avoid insincere relationships, or remain in the interests of their children. The responses given are shown in Table 16. Most respondents in all groups were against the breakdown of the family in these circumstances. In the countryside, however, the majority in favour of remaining for the sake of the children was considerably higher than in the towns. It is also notable that few rural respondents saw the issue as a delicate one demanding no outside interference. Doubtless the closeness of relationships in the countryside leads many rural men and women to expect the involvement of family and friends in their personal affairs.

Letters received by *Krest'yanka* support the view that a marriage should not be dissolved because one of the partners has fallen in love with someone else. The notion that the welfare of the children should take precedence over a search for personal happiness is, most significantly, expressed by those who have themselves experienced the dilemma. For many correspondents who wrote in this vein, it is clear that their decision to maintain a marriage for the sake of the children is adhered to despite their obvious distress,

Table 16 *Opinions of urban and rural inhabitants in Estonia on marital breakdown, 1974*

	Rural inhabitants		Urban inhabitants (Estonian origin)		Urban inhabitants (Russian origin)	
	Women	Men	Women	Men	Women	Men
Response A[a]	71.6	67.0	53.4	48.2	48.1	51.3
Response B[b]	11.8	13.4	14.2	11.8	22.5	17.6
Response C[c]	14.9	15.8	30.9	36.5	27.0	28.8

[a] The person should not break up the family and leave the children.
[b] It is acceptable for a person to leave their family in these circumstances.
[c] This is a delicate question. The person involved should not be subject to pressure or advice from others.
Source: Yu. V. Arutyunyan and Yu. Kakhk, *Sotsiologicheskie ocherki o Sovetskoi Estonii,* Tallin, 1979, p. 51.

I am thirty with a family. I have lived with my husband for ten years but I have never loved him. It is not that I am unhappy, we get on well, my husband doesn't drink, he is affectionate and kind. I respect him as a person and as the father of my children. But I don't love him. I love someone else. I love him so much that I can't put it into words. How my heart aches and my whole being pines from words left unspoken! He has a family too. I know that I have to think of the children and I feel sorry for my husband too: why have scenes, why hurt a person who is in no way to blame? I don't criticise the author of the letter because he has fallen in love. I am in love too and torment myself with it. I criticise him because he doesn't know how to love. There is no need to 'give up the whole of your life'. Live. But don't think only of yourself. Above all think of those whom you live with and whom you love. There's only one of you but there's three of them. It's hard to restrain your feelings, very hard, but it is possible.[163]

Clearly, a decision of this kind demands both courage and resolution, and from the contents of other letters published in the magazine, it is apparent that some have greater success than others in overcoming their personal desires. The writer of the following extract, for example, appears far less firm in her resolve. The letter is also interesting in suggesting the role played by village society in a situation of this kind:

We met in the fields. A middle-aged man got down from a tractor and asked me for a drink of water. That was all. But he fell in love with me and started to follow me around. We both have families. The whole village began to talk about it. I won't pretend that I love my husband. It probably wasn't love at all but just pity when we decided to unite our lives. Now there's no escape for me. I have to live for my children. My friends tell me 'You'll live, you'll get used to it, you'll love.' No! My heart aches and loves someone else. How can this have happened? Who's to blame? Can it really be that hot July day and that glass of water?[164]

The majority of the letters published in *Krest'yanka* reflect the view that the children must come first. As this falls in line with government plans to promote a more stable family it may be that the printed letters support an editorial bias, rather than the opinion of the mass of correspondents. However, it must be said that press support for maintaining an existing family is by no means unqualified. Journalists commenting on the correspondence have shown themselves sensitive to the degree of self-sacrifice which a marriage endured for the sake of the children may demand. It has also been noted that children are themselves not always best served by the maintenance of a marriage at all costs, as in this chilling example:

A year after our wedding I realised that I didn't love my wife. I was honest with her about this but I didn't desert my family. We have a son who is dearer to me than anyone else in the world. He is in the second form at school now. He is a sickly and reserved little boy and is not doing very well at school. If I left my family, what would happen to him? I am trying to bring him up to be bold and courageous, a real man. It is my duty. That is what I think.

A psychologist's commentary which followed this letter was sharply critical of those who 'think themselves, if not heroes, then at least highly moral people' whilst apparently traumatising the very children in whose interests they claim to act.[165]

In close-knit rural communities, those who are unable or unwilling to endure an unhappy marriage are liable to find separation a particularly painful and public business. Where neighbours and workmates are not infrequently also relatives or friends, individuals enjoy far less privacy than in the city. Fear of public censure undoubtedly remains a major deterrent to anyone on the verge of divorce. The story of her experiences recounted by a woman schoolteacher in a letter to *Krest'yanka* provides an example of the pressures imposed by rural society. As a young woman she had refused to marry the man she loved, in the knowledge that another girl in her village was expecting his child:

They got married and I went away. At first I was very upset, later I got married without love to a man who promised me care, concern and devotion. The years went by, my family grew, I had a lot more work, but there was no love. For many years I cared for my family's welfare as best I could, hoping that everything would change in time. But I knew that there was no family, and never had been. But then we moved to another village. And one day I met by accident a man who had a wife and child. For three years that was all there was to it – we just looked at each other. But then he couldn't stand any more ... He and I have had to put up with a lot of unpleasantness. People look askance at us at work, there's no way to avoid it in our village – this is where you really envy townspeople! His wife is ready to pounce on me like a tigress, after all we work together. My husband calls me obscene names and of course my children and pupils are all around ... How do you endure this sort of thing![166]

Difficulties such as these are not the only ones faced by rural divorcees. Financial as well as psychological pressures are commonly encountered by single parents after divorce. In the majority of cases women retain custody of the children and their ex-husbands become liable for the payment of maintenance. In practice, only a small minority of men make adequate maintenance voluntarily. In most cases maintenance is made the subject of a court order. Although Soviet law provides for the deduction at source of maintenance payments from a spouse's income, it seems clear that the enforcement of court orders is often inefficient. Cases receiving publicity in the press provide examples of men dodging payment by constantly moving around the country and of both employers and police who are less than zealous in their treatment of persistent non-payers.[167]

Prospects for re-marriage provide a further disincentive to rural women contemplating divorce. As described above, in almost all areas in 1979 the number of divorced women who had not re-married was considerably higher than the number of men in this position; a phenomenon resulting from a national demographic structure unfavourable to women. Statistics on re-marriage from the Ukraine and Moldavia in the mid-seventies support this finding. In addition, these surveys show the disparity between male and female rates of re-marriage to be considerably greater in rural areas than in the towns. A survey carried out in rural Belorussia in the early seventies found that men were twice as likely as women to establish a new relationship soon after separation. In this study it was discovered that, at the time of divorce, 23.2% of men but only 11.6% of women had permanent ties. The author of this study concluded, 'many divorced collective farm women face a very real prospect of spending the rest of their lives alone – "neither bride nor widow"', as the folk saying has it'.[168]

Nevertheless, women continue to be the majority of petitioners in rural divorce cases. It seems unlikely that there will be any reversal of this trend in the near future. Indeed, divorce may well increase as educated young women today entertain higher expectations of marriage. The Estonian survey quoted above in Table 16, found that young people in these more developed rural areas were more sympathetic to those facing difficult personal decisions and less likely to adopt hard and fast moral rules than were their parents' generation.[169]

The spread of urban culture and, in particular, the emphasis on emotional fulfilment in personal relationships is, however, by no means confined to the youth of the villages. The schoolteacher whose letter is quoted above described how she had written to her aunt, her closest relative, explaining her situation. Expecting a moral lecture in reply, she had been stunned by her aunt's conclusion, 'My dear, don't be a bluestocking. If you feel a love like that and he returns it, cherish it; don't insult it, don't break down. Hold your head high and go on through everything, only don't renounce love!'[170] Such an unexpected response is characteristic of the concern expressed by many rural women today for the quality of personal relationships. As women's expectations of marriage grow and as the level of urbanisation increases, there is every indication that the rate of divorce in rural areas will continue to rise.

SOME CONCLUDING OBSERVATIONS

Rural women's attitudes towards marriage and the family have changed radically since the 1950s. They are no longer submissive to their elders or deferential to their husbands. They look for emotional fulfilment in their personal relationships, have fewer children and are more likely than men to initiate divorce if a marriage breaks down. They write to the press expressing their grievances and demand nurseries and consumer services.

Yet despite these changes in women's attitudes brought about by increased educational opportunities and the influence of urban culture, the activities which absorb much of women's time outside paid employment have changed very little. In rural areas the combined burden of housework, child care and private farming is particularly heavy on women. Most men make only a minimal contribution to domestic labour, even when their wives have demanding jobs in the socialised sector. The essential, unpaid work on the plots continues to be viewed largely as an extension of women's housework, its low status bearing little relation to its enormous contribution to the rural economy. The time and energy which women are still constrained to expend on servicing their families in the home and on the allotments severely limits both their leisure time and their advancement in paid employment. It is into this situation that the state has stepped with its pronatalist policies, emphasising the primacy of women's domestic responsibilities. In a socialist society which has failed to implement the classical Marxist prescription for women's emancipation, however flawed it might be, anxiety over the birthrate has now produced policies which seem likely only to reinforce women's 'double shift'.

There is an undoubted tension between the new, urban-influenced attitudes of women towards the family and the maintenance of the traditional division of labour within the rural domestic economy. In these circumstances it seems probable that the changes in women's attitudes will serve to increase their alienation. The continuing demands of the family, acting as one of the barriers to women gaining skilled and responsible jobs, appear likely to contribute to women's growing disenchantment with rural life.

3

Women's roles in rural culture

EDUCATION

Since 1960 the improvement in the educational attainment of the Soviet population has been considerable. Even in the countryside, which has throughout the period suffered the loss of many of its ablest young people to the towns, attainment has increased significantly. By 1979, almost half the rural population over the age of ten had received some form of secondary education: nearly double the proportion in 1959.[1]

An analysis of the structure of the rural workforce in terms of educational attainment (Figure 8) demonstrates most clearly the pattern of change during the 1970s. In 1970 more than half the women employed in rural areas of the USSR had received no more than primary education, whilst almost a fifth had not received even this amount of schooling. Figures recorded for rural men in this same year were not a great deal better. At the other end of the spectrum, however, the proportion of employed men and women who had completed their secondary education was roughly equal, whilst more women than men had received a higher or special secondary education. By 1979 the number of employed men and women with primary education or less had fallen significantly. At the same time the proportion of those with complete secondary education had doubled, reaching approximately 40% of the workforce. In 1979, 16.4% of employed rural women had received higher or special secondary education; the gap between male and female attainment at this level increasing considerably.

The data from Estonia and Tadzhikistan give an indication of the extent of regional variation concealed in these national averages. They

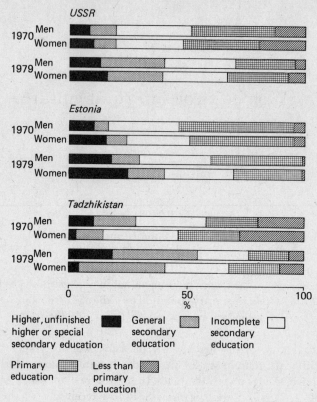

Figure 8   Educational attainment of the employed rural population, USSR
and selected republics, 1970–9

Sources: Itogi ... 1970, Vol. III, Table 6, Vestnik statistiki, 2, 1981, pp. 63–78.

illustrate the effect of migration, of cultural factors and of rural
development. Estonia had experienced a relatively high level of
migration from the villages to the towns, resulting in a lower than
average proportion of young people in the rural population: the age
groups which have most benefited from increasing access to secondary
education. With a rapidly developing rural infrastructure, however,
Estonia employs a large number of rural specialists, the majority of
them women. At the other end of the scale, migration to urban areas
remains at a very low level in Tadzhikistan. In consequence, the
villages of the republic have a young population and a higher overall
level of educational attainment in the rural workforce than that of

Estonia. The impact of cultural factors, however, means that rural women in Tadzhikistan continue to be considerably less well educated than rural men. Though both republics experienced a marked improvement in education during the 1970s, the attainment of employed rural women by 1979 was very different, reflecting the pattern of development of each republic.

The right to secondary education was enshrined in the new Soviet Constitution of 1977. Four years earlier eight-year education was made compulsory across the country. Throughout the 1970s concern was expressed for the quality of education in the countryside and huge sums earmarked for capital investment in rural schools.[2] The problems which beset rural education in the Soviet Union are considerable. Vast distances, the pattern of small, scattered settlements across much of the country, together with a lack of good roads and transport, have been major obstacles to the development of secondary education in the countryside. In 1970, for example, more than half of all rural primary schools had less than thirty pupils; a sixth had less than sixteen pupils. Similarly, around 60% of rural eight-year schools had less than 200 pupils, whilst only 5% of urban eight-year schools were so small. Eight-year schools commonly serve an area within a 6 or 7 kilometre radius, whilst secondary (ten-year) schools regularly attract pupils from a 12 to 15 kilometre radius. In such a situation an efficient transport service is essential, yet press reports indicate that the problem of poor roads and disappearing school buses is regularly faced in many rural areas.[3] Rural depopulation and, in particular, the ageing of the population have created additional headaches for planners. As young people have left the countryside, the rural birthrate has fallen dramatically in many areas. In consequence, schools have been faced with the problem of falling rolls leading to many closures. In the early seventies, for example, in Novosibirsk Region it was reported that between fifty and seventy rural primary schools were closed down each year.[4]

Rural education compares unfavourably with urban education in the first instance because of a relative lack of nursery schooling. Rural schoolchildren are further disadvantaged by the quality of both staff and facilities in primary and secondary schools. The standard of living of the rural teacher does not attract well-qualified graduates to make a career in rural schools. As a result, fewer teachers have higher education in the countryside than in the towns, whilst the quality of their work is further impeded by falling rolls which oblige many

teachers to tackle subjects outside their specialism. Rural schools have
been reported to be afflicted by equipment shortages, from insufficient
books or televisions and tape recorders to a lack of science laboratories
in secondary schools. In the 1969–70 academic year, for example, 61%
of rural secondary schools had a physics laboratory and 38% had a
chemistry laboratory. Comparable figures for urban schools stood at
90% and 76% respectively.[5] A further hindrance to the education of
rural children was revealed in a letter to *Pravda* by the head of a
secondary school in Osh Region of Kirgizia. He complained that every
year children were kept away from school by farm managers who
insisted that they were needed for potato and cotton picking. Between
1977 and 1981, the head reported, children had never begun the
academic year in his school before November.*[6]

Since 1973 a concerted effort has been made to tackle the many
problems posed by rural education.[7] Data provided by the census of
1979 suggest that measures taken have already had a significant effect
on the educational attainment of rural women. As Table 17 illustrates,
female educational attainment has improved in both urban and rural
areas over the period. The improvement has, however, been most
marked in rural areas during the 1970s, significantly narrowing the
gap between the educational attainment of urban and rural women.
What remains to be seen is whether the girls and young women who
form the chief beneficiaries of this improvement in rural secondary
education will, in fact, remain in rural areas. Their decision to stay in
the village or to move to the town depends largely on rural
employment prospects. As has been demonstrated in Chapter 1 above,
occupational segregation in the rural workforce severely limits
women's opportunities to find well-paid and interesting work in the
countryside. As a result, education, employment opportunities and
migration are closely connected for rural women. Traditional spheres
of female employment in agriculture provide little or no stimulus to
women to obtain better educational qualifications. In dairying, for
example, the grading system in operation is in no way connected with
educational attainment. The underdevelopment of the service sector
in the countryside means that there is as yet little demand for skilled
women workers in this area. At the same time, the major area of
demand for skilled workers in the countryside is that of agricultural
machine operation, a field of employment which is effectively closed to

* The school year in the USSR begins on 1 September.

Table 17 *Educational attainment of rural and urban women, USSR, 1959–79*

	1959	1970	1979
Women with higher or secondary education (per 1,000 women over age 10)			
rural women	255	296	436
urban women	455	568	693
Number of rural women per 100 urban women with higher or secondary education	56	52	63
Increase in number of rural women with higher or secondary education (1959 = 100%)	100	116	171

Source: Vestnik statistiki, 6, 1980, pp. 47, 51.

women. Rural areas, therefore, provide few suitable opportunities for women with general secondary education. Whilst men are able to obtain well-paid work as operators or mechanics through attending courses or vocational-technical schools, there are few job prospects at an equivalent educational level for rural women. Women in the rural workforce are therefore polarised into unskilled manual labour or highly skilled work demanding higher education. The manner in which employment opportunities have developed for women may act as a spur to their gaining further or higher education. On the other hand, women with secondary education who are unable to gain higher qualifications are generally presented with a clear choice: a move to the city or a job which makes few demands of their talents.[8]

Figure 9 illustrates the relative educational attainment of rural men and women across the USSR. Although the national rural average stood at 81 women per 100 men with higher or complete secondary education in 1970, it can be seen that, over large areas of the Soviet Union, women with this level of education out-numbered men. This was particularly true of those areas of the northern European USSR and Siberia which had borne the brunt of rural depopulation. In these areas the fact that a higher proportion of women than men had higher or secondary education reflects the pattern of rural employment described above. These data on comparative educational attainment also add weight to the observation by rural sociologists that young women in the countryside today are often better educated than their husbands.

Table 18 shows the educational attainment of women aged twenty

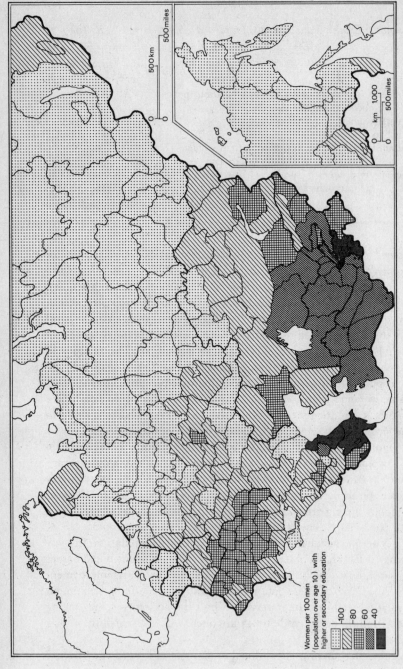

Women per 100 men
(population over age 10) with
higher or secondary education

100
80
60
40

500 km
500 miles

km 1000
500 miles

Figure 9   Female educational attainment, rural areas of the USSR, 1970

Source: *Itogi . . . 1970*, Vol. III, Table 3. Projection based on Dewdney, p. 144.

Table 18 *Rural women aged twenty to twenty-nine with higher or secondary education, selected republics, 1970*

	% women in the twenty to twenty-nine age group in rural areas	% women of all rural people in this age group with secondary education	% women of all rural people in this age group with higher education
RSFSR	48.3	56.9	60.7
Belorussia	48.7	54.4	62.8
Latvia	52.3	61.8	64.1
Lithuania	49.2	65.3	63.6
Estonia	45.3	60.2	60.4

Source: Itogi ... 1970, Vol. III, Table 1.

to twenty-nine in 1970 in those republics where women were over-represented amongst people with higher or secondary education.

Though women formed a minority of this age group in almost all these republics, they nevertheless formed a clear majority of those with secondary education. Women were particularly over-represented amongst those with higher education, reflecting the fact that members of the highly feminised teaching profession form the largest sector of the rural intelligentsia. It must be said that in 1970 the proportion of women with this level of education stood at no more than a fifth of the twenty to twenty-nine age group in any of these republics. Nevertheless, the appearance of a stratum of well-educated women to out-number men marks a decisive break with the traditional patterns of educational attainment in rural areas.

The structure of the rural workforce and the attitudes of young women towards current employment opportunities in the countryside are reflected in surveys of the career and educational aspirations of secondary school students. These surveys make it clear that work in the village, and especially in manual agricultural jobs, finds little favour with young people in the countryside. A survey of 4,000 school students in four regions of the RSFSR in the early seventies, for example, found that no more than a quarter had any desire to work in the village. The majority of school leavers in a variety of surveys from this period indicated the wish to continue their studies after school, yet only a minority of this group intended to pursue agricultural specialisms. Rural school students, it would appear, regard agricultural occupations as having low prestige. The RSFSR survey cited above, for example, found that the students gave the highest evaluation to the professions of doctor, soldier, driver, teacher, artist and engineer. The lowest evaluations were given to the jobs of livestock worker, fieldworker, shop-worker, zootechnician and accountant; an assessment which appears the more significant for its inclusion of two specialisms commonly encountered in farming.[9]

This same survey showed that twice as many girls as boys aspired both to a higher education and to work in the city on graduation. Of those who intended to qualify as agricultural specialists and return to the village there were one and a half times more boys than girls. Amongst school students planning to become skilled farm workers boys out-numbered girls by ten to one. The disinclination of girls to consider work in agriculture has been confirmed by other surveys which also show them to be highly attracted to teaching and medicine. With such a strong orientation towards non-agricultural work girls have little choice but to look to the towns to continue their education. Rural educational institutions offer little besides agricultural specialisms and rural girls are clearly not enthralled by the choice of employment offered by contemporary agriculture.[10]

Not surprisingly, when a large proportion of school leavers seek a higher education, many fail to attain their goal. Not only do educational institutions have insufficient places for all those wishing to attend, but the quality of rural education puts rural students at a considerable disadvantage when in competition for places with students from urban schools. Less qualified teaching staff, inadequate equipment and the lack of sufficient science or foreign language teaching closes the doors of many higher educational institutions to rural students. Preferential treatment is now given to rural students applying for entry to agricultural institutes and colleges of education in the hope that they will remain in their native region and return to work in the village on completing their course. As a result of this policy, by 1977, rural students made up 54% of students in colleges of education in the RSFSR.[11]

It has been observed, however, that rural students often become urbanised during their period of training. A survey of students at Nizhnii Tagil College of Education from 1974 to 1976 found that 70% of first-year students of rural origin planned to return to the village on graduation. By the final year only 13% still intended to make a career

Table 19 *Plans and attainment of 10th-form students, Novosibirsk Region, 1975 (in % of sample)*

	Rural		Urban	
	Boys	Girls	Boys	Girls
Plan				
Work	12.9	3.1	7.9	3.0
Vocational-technical institute or courses	15.3	14.6	4.0	6.0
Special secondary education	41.2	52.3	17.5	38.0
Higher education	30.6	30.0	70.6	53.0
Attainment				
Work	45.8	37.7	34.1	40.0
Vocational-technical institute or courses	23.5	23.9	5.5	12.5
Special secondary education	11.8	26.9	15.2	17.5
Higher education	16.5	11.6	42.8	29.0

Source: D. L. Konstantinovskii, *Dinamika professional'nykh orientatsii molodezhi Sibiri*, Novosibirsk, 1977, pp. 127, 144.

in rural education. As the overwhelming majority of students were women, this change of plan was said to be primarily due to family reasons: by the final year around half of them were married and intended to avoid rural employment as far as possible.[12]

A large-scale survey of rural and urban school students in Western Siberia in 1973–5 compared their aspirations and achievements during and after their final year at school (Table 19). In rural areas 10% more girls than boys aimed to receive higher or special secondary education. In the towns the proportion of both boys and girls aiming for this level of education was rather higher than in the countryside, yet the gap between the plans of boys and girls was not so wide. In practice, urban boys were the most successful group in entering higher or special secondary education, two-thirds of them achieving their stated goal. Approximately a half of urban and rural girls aspiring to this level of education actually gained entry to such courses. Rural boys were the least successful group, with only two-fifths achieving their aim. Rural and urban girls aiming for special secondary education had a similar rate of success, yet rural girls did especially poorly when seeking higher education: only two-fifths of such girls achieved their aim, compared with well over a half of all other groups.

Rural students of both sexes did not aim as high as urban students, yet they still saw lower level courses as preferable to immediate employment. In the event, those moving directly into a job formed the largest group of all school leavers, with the exception of urban boys. Well over a third of urban girls and rural students of both sexes who had planned to continue their education had found themselves joining the workforce on leaving school.

Despite preferential treatment for rural students, therefore, village girls may still experience difficulty in continuing their education. In view of the present nature of much agricultural work, a rejection by an educational institution can be a bitter disappointment, as the following letter shows. As a school leaver and leading Komsomol member, its author had urged her whole class to stay and work in animal husbandry before applying for higher education. She had subsequently become the leading dairy woman on her state farm for a period of three years. The farm then sent her to the preparatory department of a medical institute to help her fulfil her ambition to become a doctor. When the institute rejected her she wrote the following letter to the District Party committee (*raikom*) secretary who had encouraged her to stay on the farm:

I went to be a dairy woman even though I had never milked a cow before – my parents had kept me from it. But all the same I had faith in myself. Every morning at four o'clock I walked the 2 kilometres to the unit through rain, mud, snow, frost and gales. Dawn would break as I finished milking nineteen cows by hand. Then it was feeding time – silage, mixed feed, hay, straw, mucking-out – and you had to hump the lot yourself ... There was no Saturday, no Sunday, no New Year, no 8 March ... I always thought that the preparatory department was for those who worked wholeheartedly, who didn't have time for extra lessons. It seems I was mistaken. It seems that the preparatory department is for those who have easy jobs and receive coaching. It's not surprising that they do better at interview ... Since all this happened I've lost my faith in work.[13]

In this case the sympathetic attitude of the *raikom* secretary secured a second interview and entry into the institute. Yet for most women who fail to gain entry to further education and are unhappy with the work offered to them in the countryside, the alternatives include a move to the city or part-time study in the hope of continuing their full-time education at a later date.

For rural women, however, the prospects for academic success as external students whilst in full-time employment become far less bright with age. Sociological surveys indicate that those who desire a higher education but are unable to enter an institute as a full-time student view part-time study as a matter of some urgency. A survey of sixteen-to nineteen-year-olds in villages of Orel Region in the 1960s found that almost twice as many young working women as men wanted to continue their education, and in this way to move out of the sphere of manual labour. As the author of the study commented, 'They know perfectly well that if they do not acquire a specialism before they get married then they will have no such opportunity in the future. For the conditions of village life make it very difficult for rural women to gain external or evening education, not to mention full-time education.'[14] Other surveys have observed this same phenomenon and noted how women who already have a reasonable standard of general education are the group most likely to continue their studies part-time. Surveys of Novosibirsk Region in the early seventies further analysed this trend. It was found that, after the age of twenty-four, women became less likely than men to consider continuing their education, and indeed, after this age, men formed the majority of external students. In the age group twenty to twenty-four, however, women significantly out-numbered men amongst external students. Moreover, twice as many women as men of this age were studying for a higher or special secondary education. For both sexes opportunities for part-time study at any level were far more restricted than in the towns.[15]

Despite problems such as these, and the continuing difficulties faced by rural education, the improvement in the educational attainment of rural women over the past two decades has been impressive. Though there remains in the countryside a considerable proportion of predominantly elderly women with very low levels of educational attainment, the period has seen the emergence of a growing body of young, well-educated women in rural areas. On the basis of evidence from sociological surveys the attraction of rural girls towards higher and further education is undeniable. What is considerably less certain is whether appropriate employment can be found in the countryside for the growing numbers of young women who are able to benefit from increased access to education.

LEISURE

In the USSR the manner in which people use their leisure is not seen simply as a matter of individual choice. As non-working time has increased in recent years for many groups of workers with the introduction of the five-day week, official concern has grown that people should use their leisure 'rationally'. This concern is expressed not merely at the anti-social use of leisure but also at the waste of free time on pursuits which are not considered to lead to personal development.[16]

In the countryside, people enjoy considerably less free time than those who live in the towns. It remains common for agricultural workers to work extremely long hours during the summer months with few days off. With the introduction of the five-day week it was found in the early seventies that the average urban worker enjoyed more than three hours leisure time on working days and over six hours on days off. A survey of agricultural workers in Belorussia from this same period found that in the winter just over half had three or more hours free time on working days. In summer only a fifth of those surveyed enjoyed this amount of free time whilst over 40% had none at all. In consequence many see their lack of free time, rather than the lack of cultural facilities in rural areas as the major problem which prevents them from pursuing the activities they would like.[17]

The leisure time of rural women

Lack of free time is a problem from which women suffer far more than men. As women are far more heavily involved than men in housework, child care and private agriculture, they inevitably enjoy less leisure. Figure 7 in Chapter 2 illustrates not only the use of working time but also the relative amounts of free time available to men and women collective farmers in the Kuban'. The men machine operators had more than double the amount of leisure enjoyed by the dairy women on working days in both summer and winter. On days off throughout the year the dairy women had no more than 55% of the free time enjoyed by the men. A survey of Belorussian collective farmers in 1971–2 found that twice as many men as women had over three hours free time per day. At the other end of the scale, 8% of the men but 21% of the women said they had no free time whatsoever. In Rostov Region, where a 1973–4 survey found a far greater degree of similarity between the leisure time available to men and women, women on state farms nevertheless enjoyed 400 hours per year less free time than did the men.[18]

Despite the difficulties involved in quantifying leisure time, due not least to seasonal patterns of employment in the countryside, surveys show a surprising degree of agreement as to the average amount of free

UNUSUAL SITUATIONS
'You go and watch the television and I'll wash the floors.'
(*Krest'yanka*, 3, 1975, p. 29)

time enjoyed by rural women. From the Ukraine to Tadzhikistan, surveys from the early seventies report an average for collective farm women of two to two and a half hours free time per day.[19] This average does, however, conceal a great deal of variation according to type of employment, marital status and family size. In addition, free time may vary considerably within any given district according to the quality of essential services supplied to rural homes and the availability of consumer services on individual farms. On Stavropol' Territory collective farms in 1974, for example, women livestock workers had an average of one and a half hours free time per day throughout the year, whilst women working in the service sector had two and a half hours per day. Women fieldworkers had a pattern of employment showing considerable seasonal variation, yet overall they had more free time than other groups of women: two and three-quarter hours per day in summer and three and a half hours per day in winter. On Rostov Region collective farms in this same year unmarried women enjoyed just under two and three-quarter hours free time per day whilst women with children had only one and a half hours leisure per day.

The author of the Stavropol' Territory study put forward a five-point plan for increasing the leisure time available to rural women:[20]

1) The working day should be reduced by increased automation especially in animal husbandry;

2) Work organisation should be improved; more women should be trained to operate machinery and two-shift working should be universally introduced;

3) Child care facilities should be open for longer than parents' working hours;

4) Time spent in private agriculture should be reduced
   a) by more help being given by farms, e.g. in the preparation of animal feed;
   b) by the promotion of greater equality between men and women;

5) Time spent on housework should be reduced
   a) by extending the provision of essential services;
   b) by the provision of more labour saving devices for the home;
   c) by the provision of more consumer services.[21]

Urban women, who have already reaped the benefits of many such improvements in work organisation and consumer services, enjoy considerably more free time than do rural women. A mass statistical survey carried out in the RSFSR in the late seventies found that rural women had less than half the leisure time of urban women.[22] Nevertheless, urban women continue to enjoy far less leisure than urban men. The promotion of greater equality between men and women in domestic labour, a recommendation which the author of the five-point plan confines to private agriculture, appears essential if real strides are to be made in increasing the free time available to rural women. As one commentator has observed, when people feel that their free time is insufficient for their needs, they will attempt to reduce the amount of time which they spend on obligations outside work and leave these to others to fulfil. In this way, men try, and evidently succeed, in gaining free time at the expense of women.[23]

Patterns of leisure use

Increased educational attainment and the influence of the mass media have brought about significant changes in rural culture since 1960. As would be expected, the demand for improved cultural facilities on the urban model has come from the young and educated. Thus, patterns of leisure use vary widely according to age and education and also according to sex, marital status and the amount of free time available. The pattern of leisure use for both sexes changes significantly on marriage and still further after the birth of children. Single men and women spend a minority of their leisure time at home and a good deal of time visiting friends and relatives and in social

Table 20 *Leisure activities of rural women, Stavropol' Territory, 1974, by age and education (% respondents in each age or educational group)*

		Educational attainment			
			Classes completed		
	Semi-literate	Primary education	5–7	8–9	10
Read novels	—	12	85	91	100
Read newspapers, magazines	—	12	80	90	90
Listen to radio	10	10	50	100	100
Watch television	5	35	100	100	100
Go to cinema	—	—	41	98	100
Go to concerts, theatres museums	—	—	10	20	50
Go for walks	100	100	100	100	100

	Age groups			
	16–25	26–35	36–45	46–55
Read novels	100	80	50	12
Read newspapers, magazines	100	100	90	13
Listen to radio	100	90	50	50
Watch television	100	100	100	50
Go to cinema	90	81	20	—
Go to concerts, theatres, museums	30	10	10	10
Go for walks	100	100	100	100

Source: G. G. Markova, 'Svobodnoe vremya i razvitie lichnosti zhenshchin-kolkoznits na sovremennom etape stroitel'stva kommunizma', candidate degree dissertation, Rostov on Don, 1977, p. 97.

activities. On marriage, people spend more than three-quarters of their leisure time at home, a trend which increases significantly when children are born.[24]

Table 20 illustrates the activities engaged in by rural women according to age and educational attainment. The sole activity shared by all groups of women in this study was walking or, as some writers have expressed it, simply spending time in the open air. This represents the only activity in the Table characteristic of traditional peasant behaviour. In the oldest and least educated groups, women had relatively little contact with the mass media whilst the adoption of reading as a pastime demands a level of literacy which many older rural women simply do not possess. Regular cinema-going was the preserve of the young and educated whilst visits to concerts, theatres and museums was a minority activity for all women. The apparent unpopularity of concerts and drama no doubt reflects the lack of opportunity to attend performances in the countryside. It is significant that the proportion of those attending falls sharply over the age of twenty-five; for women with children time becomes a major factor in the use of leisure and attending plays and concerts may necessitate a trip to town. The leisure activities commonly engaged in by rural women are considered in greater detail below.

Leisure activities and the interests of rural women

Television and rural clubs

Watching television has been described by one Soviet writer as 'the basic form of leisure for rural dwellers'. On average people in the countryside watch seven hours more television a week than people in the towns. The majority of young people in the villages say that watching television is their favourite leisure activity. Surveys consistently show television viewing to be the largest single activity in leisure time budgets of both rural women and men.[25]

The use made of village clubs varies enormously with the quality of facilities. Clubs are used primarily by people under thirty, by skilled manual and white-collar workers and by men more than by women. The disparity between male and female club attendance is caused not only by women's domestic commitments but also by such factors as unsocial hours worked by many women in dairying. However, the quality of buildings, equipment and staff appear to be the decisive factor in the attendance of village clubs by rural women. Press reports and sociological surveys make it clear that the state of rural cultural facilities leaves much to be desired. In 1978 it was reported that some 5,000 large and expanding rural settlements had no club building of any kind, whilst 20% of existing club buildings needed major repairs. The situation appears to be particularly bad in the Non-Black Earth Zone and especially in villages officially considered as having no viable future (*besperspektivnye*). The high turnover of staff in rural clubs exacerbates the problems caused by poor facilities. In many villages it is clear that such provision as exists is both scant and intermittent.[26]

Drama and music

Where club facilities are well organised, amateur drama and music groups are often extremely popular. In Vinnitsa Region of the Ukraine, for example, it was reported in the early seventies that some 200,000 people, most of them under thirty, were involved in activities of this kind. Judging by recent letters to the press, however, the participation of young people today would appear to be largely confined to drama and pop groups. Elderly rural women are clearly the guardians of the country's folk music traditions. In Belorussia, for example, I was told that an enormous number of requests are received by the press from older rural women for help in locating the words of little known folk songs and that the interest of this group of women in amateur folk concerts and festivals is extremely high.[27] A woman pensioner from Kustanai Region in Northern Kazakhstan wrote recently to *Krest'yanka* in 1983 expressing her regret at the lack of interest of the young in folk culture:

I often wonder whether we used to sing too much and our children got tired of it? It is clear that people don't like amateur music now, I heard that from my own granddaughter. You only have to look at our marvellous district Palace of Culture. Out of the thirty-five people in the choir most of them have something to do with the cultural department or they are teachers who I think do amateur music because they feel they have to. Perhaps I'm not quite right about that but I don't think I'm very far wrong. I really feel sorry for people who won't sing because they think they won't be as good as Alla Pugacheva.* And as for folk singing . . . Alright, I've said enough! Don't misunderstand me I really don't mean that it was better in the old days. Things are a thousand times better today. Only why do people today give themselves airs?[28]

Reading

As educational attainment in rural areas has increased, reading has become an important aspect of leisure for increasing numbers of rural people. The network of libraries has expanded and rural people are far more likely than they were twenty years ago to purchase books for themselves. Novels, especially the classics, are said to be popular purchases, as are well-produced children's books. As the manager of a rural book shop in the Ukraine commented, 'I can still remember a time when book-lovers from the city would come to small village shops like this one to get hold of books in short supply. Now we can't always satisfy the demands of the local population.'[29] Library use, however,

* The most celebrated Soviet pop singer of the period.

still appears to be largely confined to the most educated sectors of rural society. In Stavropol' Territory between 1971 and 1975, library use by rural women increased steadily yet varied enormously according to the quality of facilities. On five collective farms in the region libraries were used by between 7% and 20% of rural women, each borrower reading an average of seven to ten books a year. Rural women are said to be particularly interested in literature on the themes of personal relationships and moral issues, whilst men prefer war novels or stories about acts of heroism. Women also like to read novels and stories on everyday themes, including the factual accounts of incidents in the lives of rural people printed in magazines such as *Krest'yanka* and newspapers such as *Sel'skaya zhizn'*. Such articles are said to be widely discussed, especially by women.[30]

It is clear, however, that many rural women never or rarely read and that this is particularly true of the older age groups. Less fluent in reading, many women in these age groups, if they read at all, are more likely to read short stories or magazine articles than novels. A 1976 survey of the Chuvash Autonomous Republic found that 70% of women pensioners in the sample were functionally illiterate: small wonder then that only one in five women in this age group ever read a newspaper, compared with two-thirds of the men.[31]

Sport

In many sociological surveys of the leisure pursuits of rural people, sport is often conspicuous by its absence. Where sport is included in surveys it is apparent that very few rural women regularly participate. On Orel Region farms in the mid-1960s, for example, less than 10% of sixteen- to nineteen-year-old women took part in sport. By the age of thirty the proportion had fallen to around 2%. By contrast, some 29% of men under thirty were involved in some form of sporting activity. The reasons for the lack of female participation were found by the author of this survey to be twofold: a lack of time, and the pressure of public opinion. In sports clubs organised in these villages the stress was on provision for the men, as one young woman complained, 'There are skis and skates for the boys, albeit not many, and there are weights and a football, dominoes and billiards. But for us girls in the winter there are only skis. It would be good to skate but there are no boots smaller than size forty-one. And there's no gymnastic club either.' For married women, especially those with children, the lack of free time became the major obstacle to their involvement in sport. Yet the view was also

UNUSUAL SITUATIONS
'It was that big!'
(*Krest'yanka*, 3, 1975, p. 29)

expressed that sport was still considered to be a male activity and that
women should be spending their free time doing something useful in
the home. When asked if she would like to do more sport if she had the
time, a woman of twenty-eight replied, 'Yes, I'd love to. But, you
know, I sometimes have some free time now, especially in winter, but
I'd feel ashamed to go skiing. People would say "There's no end of
things to do at home but there she is off skiing." '[32] Prejudice against
women taking part in sport has evidently by no means died out. A
letter to *Krest'yanka* in 1978, for example, from a stable man on a state
farm complained that few girls had joined the newly established riding
club:

It seems that the idea is instilled into many girls at home that horse-riding is
not for women, that it's indecent and bad for their health. So this is what
happens: the girls can't bring themselves to break with these superstitions
openly but they come to the stables on their own in the evenings and ask to be
allowed to ride a horse. I don't refuse them because I can see that they love
horses, that they treat them well and don't ride at all badly.[33]

Rural men and women in Rostov Region in 1973–4 were asked
which sports, games and pastimes they knew how to do. The responses
showed that women had a far narrower range of sporting interests or
opportunities than men. On state farms, over half the men could swim
or ride a bicycle compared with around a third of the women. Nearly a

fifth of the men could ski, skate, dance and play football and volleyball, yet no more than 9% of the women could do any of these except dance. Amongst schoolchildren in the sample a far higher proportion of girls was involved in sport of all kinds, yet the gap between male and female activity remained very wide. Over 90% of boys could swim, cycle, skate and play football and volleyball. Amongst the girls, 87% could cycle and 74% could swim whilst 53% could play volleyball. Yet only a quarter of girls could skate and a mere 8% took part in the characteristically 'male' game of football. Only in dance did the proportion of girls outstrip that of boys.[34]

In recent years the rural press has made attempts to combat traditional prejudices against women's participation in sport. *Krest-'yanka* has included features on successful sportswomen, especially women riders, and on regions or farms which have taken pains to develop sport for women. In a characteristic example from a collective farm in Kazakhstan the feature described the humble beginnings of the women's sport movement on the farm. In the mid-1970s two school leavers started work as dairy women and began to play ball games at the end of their working day. Later they were joined by a third, an older woman who had been good at volleyball at school but had never played since because 'there was work on the unit, marriage, the first child, the second. What kind of games can there be there?' Gradually more women joined in until their interest was noticed by the Komsomol secretary who acquired nets and balls for them. In winter they transferred their enthusiasm to skiing and began to take part in competitions. By 1981, regular sporting events were being held on the kolkhoz with eighty women, 40% of the competitors, taking part.[35]

Farm managers are often quoted in these articles on sport for women, setting their seal of approval on the activity. In an attempt to encourage others, they stress the positive effects of sport on the life of the farm. 'Mass involvement in physical culture is one of the major factors in our success in production', runs a typical comment, whilst for women themselves sport is recommended as a source of health, strength and youthfulness.[36] Though rural sport is developing rapidly it continues to play only a tiny part in the lives of most rural women. Though prejudice may be overcome by the efforts of the press and local organisers, the time factor remains a major barrier to increased female participation.

Women's attitudes to leisure

The observation is often made of rural people by Soviet researchers that they have an 'inadequate culture of leisure'. In other words, rural dwellers, in their opinion, spend too much of their free time doing very little which might 'lead to their personal development'. A Belorussian survey from the early seventies found that collective farmers spent three-quarters of their free time resting 'without doing anything in particular'.[37] In part this certainly results from a lack of education for many rural inhabitants. Many villagers have little interest in or understanding of certain elements of urban culture such as music or art appreciation which meet with the approval of urban-based sociologists.

Rural women in Stavropol' Territory in 1974 were asked how they would spend their free time if they had more of it. The majority, 60% of those questioned, said they would read, knit, sew, play with their children or watch television, i.e. they would spend more time on the activities which they already enjoyed. The remainder, however, said that they did not know what they would do; they had little idea how to use their leisure time and no demand to try something new.[38] On average, surveys from a wide range of areas of the USSR have found that rural men in all age groups are more likely than women to read, watch television and listen to the radio. Women are more likely to spend their free time visiting friends and relatives or entertaining. Rural women are also more likely than men to do nothing in particular with their leisure time. This phenomenon cannot be explained simply as a result of lower levels of educational attainment. Though Soviet sociologists are in the habit of censuring such a use of free time, at least one has pointed out that, under present conditions, rest at the end of the working day is essential for those employed in agriculture.[39] For most rural women, however, work does not stop at the end of the shift on the farm. The heavy burden of work borne by women with children makes fatigue a major factor in their use of leisure time. In rural conditions it seems probable that women with young children, in particular, may lack not the education or the desire, but simply the energy to use their leisure as those observing them would wish.

Whilst the majority of older women make few demands of organised leisure facilities, and many younger women with families lack the time to enjoy them, it is clear that there are groups of women in the

countryside, particularly the young and unmarried, who are far from
satisfied with rural leisure provision. Whilst elderly people in the
village rarely use rural clubs and have relatively little contact with the
mass media, young people feel acutely the lack of urban-style
entertainment and cultural activities. In the early seventies, for
example, 72% of young rural specialists on Chelyabinsk Region state
farms said that they found village culture boring. Even amongst
unskilled workers of the same age, 40% gave this response.[40]

Amongst collective farm women in Stavropol' Territory in 1974,
representing all ages and occupations, 38% said they were not entirely
satisfied with the work of rural clubs and 25% said they were
completely dissatisfied. The state of rural clubs and lack of facilities for
young people has become a regular source of debate in the rural press.
A letter from a young woman in Ryazan' Region contains a typical list
of complaints:

It's boring in our village, especially in the evenings. There's nowhere to go
dancing or meet people of your own age even though we do have a club with a
tape recorder, two radios and a television set. Everything except the television
is locked up. They bring a film show once a month and we have to be thankful
for that. In neighbouring villages there are dances, concerts and new films
nearly every week but you often can't get there, especially in the evenings, as
they're 7 or 8 kilometres away. So that's how we live![41]

Letters to the press suggest that parents are very keen that young
people should not be left with idle hands and it is evidently an urban
leisure style which is in demand. In developed areas such as Estonia
where distance and transport between town and country present fewer
problems, the gulf between urban and rural culture is less significant;
around 40% of theatre-goers in Estonia, for example, live in the
village.[42] Yet across much of the country the gap between expectations
and available facilities for young people is enormous. Young women
who are dissatisfied with what the village has to offer may find in the
sphere of leisure, as in work, a further potent reason for moving to the
towns.

RELIGION

Religion and the state

Since 1917, religion, an important element of traditional rural culture,
has repeatedly come under attack from the Soviet authorities.
Following the militant atheist campaigns of the 1930s, a period of

detente in church–state relations began on the eve of the Second World War and continued until the death of Stalin in 1953. A harsh but short-lived campaign against religion was waged in 1954 but it was not until the end of the decade that a major offensive against the influence of the church was renewed. The 1959–64 campaign, directed primarily against the Christian and Jewish faiths, produced an enormous upsurge in both atheist propaganda and the use of legal sanctions. Thousands of churches were closed down and congregations refused permission to register. As registration with the state authorities was required of groups of worshippers by law, such a refusal obliged congregations either to disband or to continue illegally. During the period of the campaign the Russian Orthodox, Lutherans, Catholics and Baptists were estimated to have lost half of their churches, whilst the Jews lost three-quarters of their synagogues.[43]

Since 1965 the struggle against religion has continued, though in a less overt manner. The 1977 Constitution reiterated the state's commitment to freedom of conscience: 'Citizens of the USSR are guaranteed freedom of conscience, that is, the right to profess or not to profess any religion, and to conduct religious worship or atheist propaganda. Incitement of hostility or hatred on religious grounds is prohibited.'[44] In practice, however, freedom of worship continues to be constrained by the compulsory registration of congregations and by the provisions of the Criminal Codes. Directing religious ceremonies or activities, for example, which may cause harm to a person's health, which involve minor children or lead people to refuse to perform civic duties is a criminal offence under Soviet law. Similarly, whilst the right to conduct atheist propaganda is enshrined in the Constitution, the right to evangelise is not. Thus, ceremonies and activities such as baptism, fasting and the religious instruction of children may be deemed illegal under the law. Unlike Christians and Jews, Moslems have been treated relatively leniently in the post-war period. It would appear, however, that this situation has been changing since the Afghan coup of April 1978. Soviet writers have referred to the existence in Soviet Central Asia of an Islamic revival, and concern has led to new propaganda campaigns against Islam since late 1980.[45]

Rural women and religious belief

Against such a background, Soviet data on religious belief and observance should be treated with some caution. In view of the sanctions available to the authorities the possibility cannot be ruled out that responses to questions put by sociologists may not entirely reflect the truth. The data presented below are concerned primarily with the prevalence of Christian belief in the countryside and the forms of religious observance practised by rural women.

Surveys from the 1960s and 1970s indicate the number of believers to be far larger in the countryside than in the towns, ranging from around one and a half to three times more. The proportion of committed Christians and agnostics amongst sample populations in Penza, Kaluga and Voronezh regions and in Belorussia in the 1960s ranged from 12% to 24% of urban inhabitants and from 24% to 35% of rural inhabitants. A survey of Leningrad Region in 1975–6 found that 3.4% of workers in three Leningrad factories described themselves as committed Christians whilst 13% of collective and state farmers in the region did so.[46]

Women form the majority of Christians in both urban and rural areas. The Leningrad survey quoted above found that across all social groups an average of 3% of men and 14% of women described themselves as committed Christians. Amongst the Russian Orthodox, the most widespread denomination in the countryside, surveys from the late 1960s found between 76% and 80% to be women. The evidence of Soviet surveys indicates that the overwhelming majority of these women are both elderly and poorly educated. A survey carried out on three collective farms in Orel Region between 1963 and 1969 provides a characteristic portrait of rural Christians. Of the 3,600 people questioned, 16% of the men and 57% of the women said they believed in God. Of believers of both sexes, 69% were pensioners.[47] The proportion of women believers of working age was, however, considerably higher than that of men, as Table 21 shows. The gap between male and female believers was at its greatest amongst the youngest age groups. Whilst men in all age groups were more likely to declare themselves agnostic than convinced believers the opposite was true for women over the age of thirty.

Table 22 shows the occupational and educational background of believers and non-believers in this same survey. In line with the age structure of Christian women, the greatest proportion of believers was discovered amongst those with little or no education and amongst unskilled or non-working women. Of the sample with a complete secondary education, however, women were three times more likely than men to be committed Christians and six times more likely to be agnostic. Similarly, women in management were between two and a

Table 21 *Religious belief amongst collective farmers, Orel Region, 1963–9*
(as % of each age group, by sex)

| | Women | | Men | |
Age	Believers	Agnostics	Believers	Agnostics
20–4	24	26	2	13
25–9	26	33	6	12
30–4	43	26	8	20
35–9	42	31	12	15
40–4	48	28	8	22
45–9	60	24	9	13
50–4	65	24	21	31
55–9	71	17	18	32

Source: V. N. Kolbanovskii (ed.), *Kollektiv kolkhoznikov*, Moscow, 1970, pp. 230–1.

Table 22 *Education, occupation and religious belief of women collective farmers, Orel Region, 1963–9 (as % of each educational or occupational group)*

	Believers	Agnostics	Non-believers
Edcation			
No formal education	79.3	13.1	7.6
Semi-literate	65.0	23.5	11.5
Primary education	50.7	28.1	21.2
Incomplete secondary education	30.8	27.7	41.5
Secondary education	5.6	24.0	70.4
Occupation			
Housewives and pensioners	77.1	13.7	9.2
Unskilled labourers	50.3	28.1	21.6
Livestock workers	35.7	28.1	36.2
Service workers	33.3	21.1	45.6
Management	14.3	14.3	71.4

Source: Kolbanovskii, pp. 239, 241.

half and three times more likely than men in these posts to be either believers or agnostics.

Religious observance

Soviet researchers employ a variety of indicators of religious belief, such as church attendance, participation in religious rituals and acceptance of the basic tenets of the Christian or other faith. Participation in religious services and rites of passage may, however, not necessarily be an expression of religious conviction but rather of local tradition or custom. Similarly, the tenets of faith understood and accepted by those declaring themselves believers may reflect the strengths and weaknesses of various denominations. Thus, amongst Orthodox believers it is reported that only a minority pray at home and very few read the Bible. Though Bibles are a scarce commodity in the USSR and levels of literacy amongst the elderly women who form the majority of Orthodox believers are low, these twin handicaps do not appear to hinder Bible study amongst other denominations. It would appear that the level of knowledge about the fundamentals of Christian faith amongst Orthodox believers is very low and reflects the traditional preoccupation of Orthodoxy with ritual rather than teaching. Such factors help to explain the large proportion of self-confessed rural Christians who deny the possibility of life after death.[48]

As Christel Lane has pointed out, the importance of ritual and the weakness of the Orthodox Church in teaching may contribute directly to a loss of belief in areas where churches have been closed. Data from the Orel Region survey are strongly suggestive of such a correlation between church attendance and the persistence of religious belief. Other surveys have indicated that, as churches are closed, women come to dominate the remaining congregations. In areas where no churches are functioning, unregistered groups of Christians have formed themselves into house churches and women are reported as playing an important role in Orthodox groups of this type. They are said to perform services and rites of passage and to see that religious customs and festivals are observed.[49]

The importance of women's role in disseminating religious information is reflected in the concern of Soviet commentators to develop atheist work with women. The authority of women within the family, it has been noted, means that religion cannot be expected to die with the older generation. Women, especially those belonging to Protestant sects, teach their children, particularly their daughters, about Christ and in some cases may prevent them wearing Young Pioneer scarves or taking part in school activities.[50]

As churches have closed and acceptable secular rituals have become more widely available, participation in religious ceremonies marking births, marriages and deaths has declined significantly. One recent source stated that in both urban and rural areas 3% of Soviet marriages were solemnised in church in 1961, compared with 0.5% in 1972. Of children born in 1961, 40% were baptised compared with 20% in 1972, whilst the proportion of deaths marked by religious funerals fell from 60% to 32% between these two dates. In many areas, however, it has been noted that the use of religious ceremonies may be far higher than the national average. This is the case, for example, in Moslem Central Asia and Catholic Lithuania, where it is common for people to mark important events in their lives with both secular and religious ceremonies.[51]

Elderly women in the countryside are said by Soviet commentators to be particularly influential in ensuring that infants are baptised. Given the shortage of rural nurseries, young women are often dependent on their mothers to care for their children while they go out to work. In such circumstances a grandmother is often able to persuade non-religious parents to have their child baptised, or may arrange for the ceremony to be performed without their knowledge. Women Orthodox believers are also largely responsible for keeping icons hanging in rural homes. In Orel Region in the 1960s over 90% of rural schoolchildren said that they had icons at home, compared with only 14% of children questioned in the city. It appeared that women were often unwilling to remove icons even if they no longer had a religious significance for them through fear of censure by friends and relatives. Some even kept icons for superstitious reasons, as a source of protection for their homes.[52]

The persistence of superstition

The Orel Region survey found superstitious beliefs to be remarkably widespread amongst collective farmers. Half the women and a fifth of the men questioned believed that dreams could reveal the future and over a third of the women believed in the 'evil eye' and the healing abilities of wise men and women. Though far fewer men than women held superstitious beliefs it is interesting that more men believed in dreams and the 'evil eye' than believed in God. Significantly, superstition has been found to be considerably more widespread in areas with no working church.[53]

Although superstition is generally regarded by Soviet researchers as dying out, it can still exert a powerful influence over people's thinking, given fertile ground. A curious case from a village in Lipetsk Region appeared in the rural press as recently as 1980. The matter came to light when a national newspaper received a letter from a girl whose mother had been accused of witchcraft. The affair had begun when their neighbour's cow became ill and the local vet was unable to treat the animal successfully. The cow's owner then turned to the local 'wise man' who diagnosed the presence of 'bad neighbours'. From this it was concluded that the woman at the centre of this story had the 'evil eye'. The rumours of witchcraft grew and were fed when first the 'wise man's' daughter and then his cow were also taken ill. Such was the reaction to this turn of events that, as the author of the letter wrote, 'Now, whatever happens to anyone is mother's fault: she's bewitched them or put a spell on them. It's dreadful to watch her suffering. She's stopped going visiting and no one comes to see her. Our house has become empty and lonely.' When the woman first heard the rumours she went to the village Soviet for help but the local officials considered the whole affair a joke and took no action. The pressure of public opinion on the woman concerned, however, turned her into an insomniac and heavy drinker and even led her to come to blows with one of her neighbours. The intervention of the press led to concerted action to quash the rumours and to support the woman involved. A journalist sent to the village, however, reported the unpromising attitudes which she found amongst local people. Though some thought the matter nonsensical there were plenty who recounted the story in all seriousness and were clearly prepared to believe that witchcraft might have been involved. Soviet researchers have noted with concern how little atheist propaganda is aimed at the eradication of superstition and occult practices in rural areas.[54]

Atheist propaganda

The acknowledged importance of women as transmitters of religious information, especially to children, makes them a prime target group for atheist propaganda. Religious belief is attacked on the grounds that it 'forms in a woman an incorrect, anti-scientific world view, distorts her spiritual life and moral ideals, reduces her interest in social activity and deflects her from participation in communist construction'. The elderly, unskilled and ill-educated rural women who form the majority of Orthodox worshippers are taken as the model for all Christian women who are typically viewed as ill-informed and out of touch with modern society. The methods and aims of atheist propaganda are defined as 'waking Christian women up from their religious sleep, setting alight their curiosity and a genuine interest in science and culture'.[55]

It has, however, been noted by Soviet writers that the greatest discrepancy between the proportion of rural men and women who believe in God occurs in the age group twenty-six to forty-five. Though the elderly may predominate amongst rural Christians, in the younger age group women are far more likely than men to profess a religious belief. Marx described adherence to religion as 'the sigh of an oppressed creature'. It provides an interesting comment on the lives of rural women that it is precisely this view of religious faith which is reflected in the recommendations of sociologists of religion and atheist propagandists in the USSR. It is repeatedly stated that women will not be freed from religion until they are able to participate equally with men in social activities and further education. For this to be made possible, it is argued, men must take upon themselves a share of the domestic responsibilities now left to women.[56] Other writers have related religious faith in rural women to their position in society as a whole:

The overcoming of religiosity in women is linked to the problem of eliminating the vestiges of authoritarianism in family organisation, of low-skilled female work, semi-literacy and exhausting primitive domestic labour. It is essential that we solve the problems of how to improve consumer services, extend child care facilities, increase women's free time and use it to develop and exhibit their intellectual abilities; in short, the factual elimination of the vestiges of women's inequality in daily life.[57]

To meet these differing perceptions of the reasons why women believe in God, atheist work takes on a variety of forms. Lecturers and propagandists are trained by the Communist Party to conduct atheist work in the villages. Although the numbers involved in the work are said to be increasing, it is admitted that a shortage of skilled organisers and propagandists still exists in rural areas. As a result the Party not infrequently relies on teams of touring propagandists, mobile libraries and clubs to bring the atheist message to the countryside. A recent article in *Krest'yanka* magazine described the flourishing atheist work conducted by women librarians permanently based in a village in Vladimir Region. Much of their work was based on their conviction of the need to alert rural women to the achievements of science and technology. A club for young people was set up, for example, to provide a forum for talks and discussions on science and medicine with titles such as 'From the Fantastic to the Real', or 'With Faith, but without Illusions'. Members of the club were encouraged to further their interest by borrowing or subscribing to popular scientific magazines. Exhibitions of atheist books on themes such as 'Life: its Origin and Development', 'How People Created God' and 'Medicine in the Struggle against Religious Ideas and Folk Remedies' were also said to have been a great success. By way of a comment on the appropriateness of such an approach one woman, described as a believer, was quoted as saying, 'I always leave here in a good mood, wanting to live and work . . . The people and the books have helped me to experience the joy of existence here, on earth, and not in heaven, to see the world around me with new eyes.'[58]

Attempts to reach women on matters specific to them, though often stressed by atheist propagandists, appear to have made little headway in the countryside. Women's clubs, formed with a view to combating religion, appear to be a largely urban phenomenon. Although the view that a link exists between female emancipation and the elimination of religious faith is often propounded by writers on Christian communities in the European USSR, atheist propaganda based on this assumption appears to be largely confined to Islamic areas. Work of this type in Central Asia and parts of Transcaucasia not only concentrates on customary practices such as marriage by *shariat*, polygamy, and the payment of *kalym* (bride price), but also attempts to change male attitudes towards women. In Dagestan during the 1960s, for example, the Party organised conferences for young men on the theme of 'Love and Respect for Our Mothers, Sisters, Wives and Women Friends'. At some of these, housekeeping competitions were held to discover which of the men were best at cooking, cleaning, washing and other traditionally female concerns.[59] Agitation on these lines has been notably absent from atheist work in European areas.

Whilst it remains official Soviet policy to combat religion without causing offence to believers, the form of propaganda regularly employed in the press cannot be said to comply with this rule. Committed Christians, in particular those who attempt to evangelise, are habitually characterised by the media as 'fanatics'. Anti-religious stories printed in national newspapers and magazines frequently focus on the bizarre and the unpleasant, the implication being that such activities are typical of believers. In cases describing Protestant sects religion is often depicted as a phenomenon from which sect members themselves, as well as the public at large, need protection.

A characteristic example of the genre appeared in *Krest'yanka* in 1980. Entitled 'The Girl and the Cross', it concerned a divorced woman of thirty with a young daughter. On the death of her elderly mother the woman had been left without any close relatives. Described as 'weak by nature', she received no support from anyone in the village except 'stern and reserved women in black headscarves' – local Christians. The article laid the blame for the ensuing development of the woman's mental illness firmly upon religion. In a horrific climax, she attempted 'to sacrifice her daughter in the name of Christ', was committed to a mental hospital and the child was taken in by foster parents. The message of the article, spelled out clearly in its conclusion, was that children must be protected from religion and atheist work must be increased.[60] Lurid material of this type which attacks believers rather than presents reasoned arguments against religion forms a major element in the atheist propaganda conducted by the press.

On a less strident note, former believers are seen as potentially highly effective atheist propagandists and, where possible, are recruited as lecturers by the Party. Their attacks on religion are given coverage in the press as a means of weakening the faith of others. In an edition marking International Women's Day 1981, the republic newspaper *Pravda Ukrainy* published the opinions of a woman pensioner who was formerly a collective farm team leader and now worked as an atheist propagandist. As a young woman she had been an Orthodox believer, had then become a Baptist and finally joined the Jehovah's Witnesses before renouncing religion entirely. Addressing herself to rural women, she announced:

In order to have power over your souls the clergy use religion to darken your consciousness with the words of the Christ they have invented. They teach you, 'Be like children, consider yourselves sheep in Christ's flock.' In our wonderful age when people have flown into space, religion still goes on telling people, 'you are a child, you are a sheep, be submissive, obey'. No, we are not sheep! We are the creators of the new and most rational society – Communism![61]

Although lectures and articles are seen as vital tools in the fight against religion, the most effective form of atheist propaganda is generally regarded as being individual work with believers. Not only do many believers fail to attend public meetings and lectures but, it is pointed out, the reasons for the persistence of religious belief are highly specific to individuals: 'the environment in which people live, their level of education, their problems in life'.[62] The prevailing official view is that a skilled propagandist will gradually make contact with a believer, engage the person in discussion about religion and, in the process, become a close friend, someone the believer will come to rely on. As the American political scientist, David Powell, has pointed out, the logic of such a plan of campaign is not without its faults. To discover that they have been chosen as objects for propaganda or 're-education' is of itself likely to alienate and infuriate believers, making them less receptive to arguments put to them. Nevertheless, enormous resources of time and energy are employed in this approach and, wherever possible, a propagandist is matched to someone of his or her own sex and of similar age and background. Thus, rural women are to be found attempting the tricky task of converting their religious peers to atheism. It is work for which many, it has been admitted, are ill-equipped. 'An atheist must have a knowledge of psychology and educational theory, must know how to influence people emotionally', one recent commentator noted, yet conceded that in practice those involved often had insufficient expertise to produce the desired result.[63]

In recent years the effectiveness of atheist propaganda has increasingly been called into question. The tendency to view believers as ignorant and cut off from society has been challenged as an 'outdated assumption'. It has been admitted that many believers do take a live interest in current affairs, science and culture. Similarly a need has been seen to forsake the superficial and crude treatment of religious topics in the press in favour of a deeper appraisal of responses to human problems such as 'loneliness, suffering and the need for consolation'.[64] Clearly the Communist Party feels that religion is far from defeated in the USSR and that greater efforts are needed to combat its influence.

Women continue to be the mainstay of the church in rural areas. Though the mass of female Christians are elderly and have little education, a significant proportion of younger women also profess a belief in God. With the closure of churches the role of women has been extended in the unofficial church. At the same time women believers continue to play an important part in preserving religious belief in their own families. Though contemporary data on rural women and religion are sparse and may well be unreliable, the comments of atheist propagandists indicate that women in the countryside are viewed as important communicators of religious faith to the rising generation. It may perhaps provide some evidence of the success which women have had in this role that propagandists are being obliged to reconsider their traditional view of believers in response to the appearance amongst them of the young and educated.

POLITICS

Female participation in formal political activity

The extent of participation by rural women in political activity is largely determined by the amount of free time at their disposal. Data suggest that, for young women at least, family responsibilities rather than education or tradition are now the decisive factor in their involvement. Surveys have found that rural schoolgirls are considerably more active in Young Pioneer and Komsomol activities than are boys. Until marriage, young women often form the majority of activists in social and political work (*obshchestvenno-politicheskaya rabota*) and predominate in leadership positions in, for example, rural Soviet and Komsomol committees. On marriage, however, the rate of female participation begins to decline, whilst in leadership positions women's influence falls dramatically. By the time women have two children or enter their thirties, their rate of participation in political work is no more than half that of men. Although it was noted by rural sociologists in the 1960s that vestiges of prejudice against women's involvement in politics had not entirely died out, this factor today is undoubtedly far less significant than the distribution of domestic responsibilities between husband and wife. The importance of the time factor has been underlined by the fact that, where rural women work industrial hours and nursery facilities are well developed, rates of participation in politics increase considerably.[65]

Social and political work in the Soviet context covers a wide range of activities. It includes not only membership of the Party, Komsomol and local Soviets, but also involvement in trade union work, production councils, women's councils, the people's courts or work as propagandists and lecturers. Surveys suggest that between 25% and 30% of women collective farmers engage in social and political work. For the majority, however, participation is very limited, perhaps no more than once a year. Around 9% of women are involved on a regular basis once or twice a month, whilst up to 2% have commitments which occupy them once or twice a week. In one survey from the Ukraine in the mid-seventies, of all the women involved just over half said they did this work out of a sense of duty, the remainder through 'a desire for contact with people'.[66]

Women in local politics

Table 23 shows the involvement of women in social and political work in one rural district of the Ukraine in the mid-seventies. Only on parents' committees did women form more than half those involved. The low participation of women in trade unions was due to the fact that most members in this region were machine operators or agricultural specialists, work in which women were poorly represented. Few collective farm women were engaged in propaganda work as this demands substantial theoretical knowledge and a high level of general education which most of them lacked. Women involved in this work were usually teachers, medical workers or in other professions demanding a higher or special secondary education.

Across the country as a whole women formed 48.3% of all rural Soviet deputies in 1975, a figure which remains roughly constant year by year. By 1981 over 4.5 million Soviet women were members of the Communist Party: 26.5% of the membership. Since 1960 the proportion of Party members who are women has risen steadily from 19%. Between 1960 and 1975 the proportion of Komsomol members who are women rose from 44% to 52%. Unfortunately, published figures give no indication as to the proportion of rural women amongst female Party members. As the composition of Party Congress delegates closely matches the composition of national membership, however, it may be estimated that some 8% of Party members are women in rural professions, comprising some 34% of the female membership (see below, Table 26). On one collective farm in Shchors District which was said to have particularly favourable conditions for women to participate in politics, 12% of Party members and 53% of Komsomol members were women. These figures appear to support the estimate given above as well as national figures on Komsomol membership. Rural Komsomol membership in this survey mirrored the national rate for women whilst Party membership by this group of rural women was less than half the national female average.[67]

Table 23 *Women's participation in social and political work, Shchors District, Chernigov Region, Ukraine*

	Total number of people involved	% women	% women who are collective farmers
Rural Soviet deputies	704	46.9	49.1
Members of rural Soviet committees	562	43.1	50.0
Members of trade unions	1,868	15.7	100.0
Members of trade union committees	151	16.6	100.0
Members of women's councils	186	100.0	60.2
Members of people's control groups	1,262	40.4	100.0
Propagandists and lecturers	488	34.2	17.4
Agitators and political information conveyors	742	45.4	37.4
Members of comrades courts	148	45.3	68.7
Members of parents' committees	172	57.0	73.5
Members of editorial boards of collective farm newspapers	110	42.7	61.7
Members of collective farm management committees	180	12.2	100.0

Source: V. P. Zagrebel'nyi, 'Formirovanie otnoshenii sotsial'nogo ravenstva zhenshchin i muzhchin-kolkhoznikov v usloviyakh razvitogo sotsializma', candidate degree dessertation, Kiev, 1977, pp. 108–9.

As Party membership demands both greater maturity and a considerably higher degree of personal commitment than Komsomol membership these data lend weight to the contention that older rural women are hampered by domestic responsibilities from participating fully in politics. The low representation of rural women, however, also reflects the method of recruitment into the CPSU and the concentration of rural women in low-skilled work. As Mervyn Matthews has pointed out, Party membership confers elite status on individuals who already hold key positions in the economy. Thus, in the mid-sixties, 94% of kolkhoz chairpersons, 50% of agricultural specialists, 23% of machine operators but only 4% of 'peasants', i.e. unskilled agricultural workers, were Party members. As few women hold positions of responsibility in rural areas, a far higher proportion of men are therefore recruited into the Party.[68]

Although fewer women than men take part in political activity, Soviet rural sociologists are generally of the opinion that those who do participate play an influential role in decision making and are not slow to express their views. Committees and local Soviets with women in the chair are said to be particularly efficient and effective. One sociologist made the following observations on the basis of Soviet and Party records and of personal attendance at collective farm meetings over a ten-year period. Rural women, in his opinion, were more active than men and reacted more sharply to shortcomings. They had less patience than men with those who broke labour discipline, got drunk or behaved without consideration for others. At the same time, they were more likely than men to take offence at a lack of consultation or rudeness from those in management. In conclusion this author stated, 'The successful outcome of matters considered at collective farm meetings depends as a rule on their approval in principle by the women.'[69]

The women's councils (zhensovety)

In addition to the formal channels of political activity described above women may also be drawn into the work of the women's councils (*zhensovety*). These bodies began to appear in the late fifties and early sixties 'to lead work with women', primarily in areas with large non-Russian populations and in the countryside. The women's councils have been developed on an ad hoc basis as a local need for them has been perceived. As a result, their distribution and effectiveness vary considerably from one region to another; they are, for example, particularly strong in Moldavia and Central Asia.[70]

In Central Asia and Islamic areas of the Caucasus, the work of the women's councils in many respects reflects that of the Zhenotdel in Russian villages in the 1920s. In the least urbanised villages of these areas women's lives remain constrained by tradition and their participation in social activities may be severely limited. It is still by no means unknown for a girl to be removed from school at the age of sixteen in order to be married to the man of her parents' choice. Since the 1960s the women's councils have been involved in the arrangement of 'family evenings' in rural areas to which men are invited only if they bring their wives. By tradition in many of these communities it is considered degrading for a man to be seen with his wife in public. These evenings have been deliberately organised, therefore, to counter such prejudices and are said to have been most successful in areas with a local Russian population. In these regions the Russian practice of dancing after a concert or discussion has been introduced and young Central Asian couples have, it seems, begun to dance together at these functions.[71]

Women's councils in these areas see their role not only as drawing women into social life but, more fundamentally, as developing women's self-confidence and helping them to enter the workforce. Women's clubs have been developed through the councils to provide a meeting place for rural women where they can also receive basic education in areas such as health or child care or meet successful women workers. Women's council activists are also involved in developing work with families preparing arranged marriages and withdrawing girls from school.[72]

In European areas the women's councils today are relatively little concerned with developing women's self-confidence or drawing them into the labour force. In line with the women's councils of Central Asia, however, they are concerned to transmit the aims and priorities of the Party to rural women. Though women's councils have not until recently had a formalised role or centrally issued instructions as to their functions it is clear that, where these bodies flourish, they do so with both the support and control of local Party organisations. Press articles describing highly active women's councils underline their close links with local Communist Party organisations. In Moldavia, for example, a women's council chairperson, herself a Party member, explained:

In our district we try to teach the most active members and work to stabilise the membership. With the help of the propaganda and agitation department of the Party district committee we gather the leading women's council activists together twice a year for study and to share their experiences ... What do we teach them? How to plan their work, how to provide the organisation for every undertaking, not to get carried away with lots of different schemes – some of them have that fault! We teach them to help Party and Soviet organs to put their decisions into practice, carefully choosing their methods and their area of activity.[73]

In Moldavia, over half the activists in women's councils are said to be Party members. In some cases the plan of women's council activities is worked out not by the women themselves on the basis of such guidelines, but in joint discussion with local Party officials and farm management. Consequently, women's councils cannot be said to act as a forum for women's issues except where these are in line with Party policy. The press provides numerous examples of the ways in which women's councils act as an agent of the Party, especially in the sphere of production. On one collective farm in Tula Region, for example, the fifteen activists of the women's council resolved to improve the productivity of the farm's dairy unit. This was achieved mainly through constant checks on labour discipline and honours for those raising productivity. In a similar example from Omsk Region in 1981 the women's council insisted that those breaking labour discipline be moved further down the waiting list for collective farm housing. In other areas it is reported that local Party secretaries regularly attend meetings arranged by women's councils to discuss the Party's aims in relation to improving both productivity and working conditions for women on the farms.[74]

The improvement of women's working conditions is a major area of activity for the women's councils and, in this, they take on a similar role to that of a trade union. On certain farms women's councils have been responsible for the implementation of shift work in dairying and for the support of women machine operators. In other cases women's councils have ensured that health and safety at work is improved, that hot meals are provided and mobile shops organised to assist women working unsocial hours. Examples have been given where the councils have not restricted themselves to the more prestigious aspects of agricultural work but have improved conditions for women labourers, often the most neglected group of workers in farming. On one collective farm in Bashkiria for example, women preparing beet after harvesting usually worked outdoors in the wet and windy weather of late autumn. As a result, many of them suffered from colds and influenza each year. The women's council put pressure on the farm's management and trade union committee to erect a temporary shelter for the women, to organise a hot meals service and provide field vans with washing and rest facilities. It must be said, however, that not all women's councils see these areas of need and complaints have been published from women in districts with poor conditions for women's work and councils which do little or nothing to tackle the problem.[75]

Women's councils not infrequently act as a pressure group to improve living conditions and consumer services in rural areas. A prime target for such work is the improvement of nursery facilities and the establishment of extended day schools for the supervision of children whose parents are still at work when the school day ends. Reports have also appeared of villages in which women's councils have

helped accelerate the introduction of new shopping facilities and
essential services such as gas and water supplies. In many areas
women's councils organise clubs for women as a centre both for
recreation and for education. Most appear to include meetings with
local personalities on their agenda as well as talks by doctors, lawyers,
teachers and writers. Many include craft activities and advice on
fashion, housework and gardening; others include discussions of
literature or attempt to encourage women to complete their secondary
education at evening classes. In some cases, men are invited to round
table discussions on moral themes.[76]

It is in the sphere of morality that women's councils may have a
distinctive role to play. Much of the effort of the councils appears in
places to be directed towards combating alcoholism and overseeing
child welfare. The ways in which local activists carry out this function
varies enormously from place to place and, once again, appears most
effective where Party support is enlisted. In one village of Belorussia for
example, women's council members successfully petitioned the local
Party to close down a bar and open a food store in its place. In other
examples women have conducted 'raids' on shops to ensure that the
law on alcohol sales is being observed. In one case, on a sugar beet farm
where illegal distilling flourished, women activists worked together
with the local police to carry out 'raids' on those suspected of the home
production of spirits. As a result, two local women distillers and sellers
of home brew were brought to trial and the practice was reported to
have ceased.[77]

On the initiative of women's councils meetings are regularly held in
some districts at which those whose families suffer from their heavy
drinking are called to account. Warnings may be issued at such
meetings of the possibility of their compulsory treatment for alcoholism. The degree of effectiveness of this type of work appears to depend
largely on the amount of support which the women's councils receive
from other local organisations. Whilst some complain that they receive
no support whatsoever, even in cases where children are clearly at risk,
others receive a great deal of assistance. In one case which, it was
admitted, was very rare, women's council activists in the Chechen
Ingush Autonomous Republic made use of a provision of the RSFSR
Civil Code to combat alcoholism. The article in question allowed the
court to declare a person incapable of managing his or her own affairs if
his or her family were placed in a difficult financial position owing to
heavy drinking. The women's councils in this case obtained court

orders against three men whose wives were then given the right to collect the men's wages and control all the family finances.[78]

The measures taken by women's councils are, however, not only directed at men. Women with drink problems are also the target of their efforts to safeguard children. Visits to what are described as 'difficult' families are a major concern of women's councils in certain areas. Activists may endeavour to help parents or to 'arouse their conscience' with regard to the well-being of their children before taking more sweeping measures. In one case in Lipetsk Region, women activists were in the habit of calling on such families at eight or nine o'clock in the evening to see whether the children had done their homework and the parents had checked it, or simply to see whether the parents knew where their children were. In at least one case women's council members would bring pressure to bear on women who, it was felt, were failing to fulfil their role as mothers: 'They sometimes have to have a talk with women who do not want or do not know how to create comfort and peace at home for their children and their families, who take no care over tidiness and cleanliness.'[79]

Finally, women's councils may undertake propaganda work reflecting the current priorities of the Party. They are, for example, frequently involved in the establishment of new Soviet rituals to counter religious festivals and ceremonies and may be involved in individual atheist work with believers. In the late seventies, as concern over the birthrate grew, women's councils in some areas were drawn into the propaganda effort to encourage births. One council in North Kazakhstan, for example, formed a club for mothers of large families with the slogan 'Happiness is a Big Family', and planned to help these women run their homes and raise their children successfully. In Moldavia, women's councils in one district were urged 'to raise the status of the heroine-mother'. As a result, 237 heroine-mothers were publicly honoured and given priority in the allocation of building materials, fuel and theatre tickets as well as free travel and birthday celebrations organised by women's council activists.[80] In short, women's councils across the country have been involved in a wide range of projects, some of them in response to women's needs at work or at home, others in response to the Party's goals in the economy and in society at large.

Yet rural sociologists have reported that in the majority of rural areas the work of women's councils has little impact. Sociologists with whom I discussed the role of women's councils in 1980 were unanimous in their view that they represented a form of organisation for women which had outlived its usefulness. It was felt that rural women no longer needed separate bodies to take care of their interests as they were now just as able and willing as men to take their complaints to the unions, the Soviets or the courts. The view was categorically expressed that women's councils no longer have any political significance.[81]

Such an opinion does not explain the depth of coverage of the work of women's councils in the rural press. It seems likely that in most cases their work has indeed been restricted to developing handicrafts and traditional female pursuits such as cooking and flower-arranging. The gulf between the view of sociologists and the wealth of references to the councils in the press suggests that the publicised examples represent the tip of an iceberg and are atypical of women's councils as a whole. It seems probable that the regular publicity given to their initiatives has been a reflection of Party approval for the principle of mobilising women in this way. In early 1986, this approval found formal expression in Mikhail Gorbachev's speech to the 27th Party Congress. Speaking on methods of 'strengthening the family', he called for the revival and expansion of women's councils into a unified system under the Committee for Soviet Women. The guidelines for their development which have since been published make it clear that the new women's councils will be placed firmly under Party control.[82]

Rural women in national politics

It is the frequent boast of Soviet writers that women play a prominent role in national politics in the USSR. Whilst it is undoubtedly true that female representation in legislative bodies is far greater than in Western countries, women nevertheless remain absent from key positions of political power at national level. Small numbers of rural women are involved in national politics; their participation in the USSR Supreme Soviet and at Communist Party Congresses since the mid-seventies is examined below.

Table 24 provides a profile of deputies elected to the 9th and 10th Convocations of the USSR Supreme Soviet in 1974 and 1979. Despite the fact that more than half the deputies were elected for the first time at each Convocation, the pattern of representation of different social groups remained strikingly similar. Though forming nearly a third of all deputies, women were under-represented by comparison with their share in the Soviet population. Almost three-quarters of Soviet

Table 24 *Profile of USSR Supreme Soviet deputies at the 9th and 10th Convocations (1974 and 1979), representation of rural women*[a]

	9th Convocation		10th Convocation	
	Number	%	Number	%
Total deputies	1,517	100.0	1,500	100.0
Deputies elected for the first time	846	55.8	831	55.4
Women deputies	475	31.3	487	32.5
Deputies under 30	279	18.4	317	21.1
Party members (full and candidate)	1,096	72.2	1,075	71.7
Non-Party and non-Komsomol deputies	247	16.3	218	14.5
Workers and peasants	769	50.7	766	51.1
Career politicians[b]	473	31.2	465	31.0
Representation of rural women				
amongst all deputies	235	15.5	232	15.5
amongst all women deputies		49.5		47.6
amongst all non-Party deputies		32.8		30.3
amongst all with rural occupations		54.1		57.0
Rural women deputies	235	100.0	232	100.0
under 30	88	37.4	77	33.2
Party members	100	42.6	100	43.1

[a] 'Rural women' in this case denotes deputies with identifiable rural occupations.

[b] 'Career politicians' denotes Party secretaries, trade union officials, members of the KGB and others in senior administrative positions in the state apparatus.

Sources: *Deputaty Verkhovnogo Soveta SSSR. Devyatyi sozyv*, Moscow, 1974; *Deputaty Verkhovnogo Soveta SSSR. Desyatyi sozyv*, Moscow, 1979.

deputies were Party members and nearly a third were career politicians, almost all this latter group being men.

Almost half the women deputies had rural, primarily agricultural occupations; a remarkably high proportion in view of agriculture's declining role in providing work for women. The composition of rural women deputies to the USSR Supreme Soviet suggests that they are unlikely to play an influential role in its operation. Not only are they concentrated in manual, non-managerial occupations but, when compared with the body of deputies as a whole, they are disproportionately young and non-Party. Table 25 examines their chances of re-election and compares them with men in rural occupations. Although women form the majority of deputies with rural occupations, men are more likely to be re-elected. This fact undoubtedly reflects the higher occupational status of the men in this group, their concentration in managerial posts or the more prestigious technical professions. Amongst women elected for a first term, managers and Party members are in the minority. Amongst the small group of women re-elected to the USSR Soviet Supreme, however, work in management or Party membership clearly becomes an increasingly important criterion for re-election. The sharply increasing proportion of women with outstanding achievements in production is also a striking feature of deputies serving a second or subsequent term.

The make up of delegates to Party Congresses closely reflects the structure of Party membership across the country. Thus, in 1976, women formed 24.3% of Party members nationally and made up 24.5% of delegates to the 25th Party Congress in that same year.[83] As Table 26 illustrates, the representation of women in rural occupations amongst Congress delegates remained almost static from 1976 to 1981. The occupational structure of rural women delegates is illustrative of the way in which Party membership and key positions in the economy are inextricably linked: managers and specialists make up approximately 2% of the agricultural workforce yet form around half the rural women delegates to Party Congresses. Only twenty rural women, 2% of their number, were present at both Congresses.

At the highest levels within the Communist Party women are conspicuous by their absence. Only one women, Ekaterina Furtseva, who became Minister of Culture in 1960 under Khrushchev, has ever been a member of the Politbureau. Between 2% and 3% of Central Committee members are women, their proportion amongst candidate members being slightly higher and reaching 7% in 1981. No rural woman has ever been a full member of the Central Committee and, until 1981, only four had ever been elected as candidate members.[84] At the 26th Party Congress in 1981, five of the eleven women candidate members of the Central Committee had rural occupations. Two of these women, Valentina Parshina, a brigade leader from Leningrad Region, and Nina Pereverzeva, a machine operator and team leader

Table 25 *Re-election of rural women*[a] *to USSR Supreme Soviet Convocations*

	At 9th Convocation		At 10th Convocation	
	Number	%	Number	%
Total rural women elected	235	100.0	232	100.0
Rural women elected for a second term	34	14.5	25	10.8
Rural women elected for a third term or more	11	4.7	11	4.7
Total rural men elected	199	100.0	174	100.0
Rural men elected for a second term	32	16.1	37	21.3
Rural men elected for a third term or more	17	8.5	23	13.2
Rural women elected for the first time	190	100.0	196	100.0
Of these:				
in management posts	57	30.0	51	26.0
Party members	71	37.4	77	39.3
Heroes of Socialist Labour	13	6.8	9	4.6
Rural women elected for a second term	34	100.0	25	100.0
Of these:				
in management posts	18	52.9	17	68.0
Party members	20	58.8	14	56.0
Heroes of Socialist Labour	10	29.4	6	24.0
Rural women elected for a third term or more	11	100.0	11	100.0
Of these:				
in management posts	6	54.5	9	81.8
Party members	9	81.8	8	72.7
Heroes of Socialist Labour	9	81.8	10	90.6

[a] 'Rural women' denotes deputies with identifiable rural occupations.
Sources: *Deputaty ... Devyatyi sozyv; Deputaty ... Desyatyi sozyv.*

from Rostov Region, had previously been delegates at the 25th Congress. The other three were delegates for the first time and were as follows: Maria Golubeva, a dairy women from the Altai Territory of the RSFSR, Kholbuvi Rustamova, a brigade leader from Uzbekistan and Maria Zasukha, a dairy woman from Kiev Region in the Ukraine. At this same Congress, four women with rural occupations were

Table 26 *Rural women*[a] *delegates to the 25th and 26th Party Congresses (1976 and 1981)*

	25th Congress		26th Congress	
	Number	%	Number	%
Rural women as % all delegates		8.3		8.4
Rural women delegates	416	100.0	420	100.0
Of these:				
sovkhoz managers/kolkhoz chairpersons	20	4.8	20	4.8
brigade leaders	107	25.7	110	26.2
heads of livestock units	44	10.6	29	6.9
team leaders	34	8.2	35	8.3
specialists	18	4.3	11	2.6
machine operators	22	5.3	19	4.5
other occupations	171	41.1	196	46.7

[a] 'Rural women' denotes delegates with identifiable rural occupations.
Sources: *XXV s″ezd Kommunisticheskoi partii Sovetskogo Soyuza. Stenograficheskii otchet*, Moscow, 1976, Vol. II, pp. 329–596; *XXVI s″ezd Kommunisticheskoi partii Sovetskogo Soyuza. Stenograficheskii otchet*, Moscow, 1981, Vol. III, pp. 289–523.

amongst the seventeen who formed 23% of members of the Central Auditing Commission of the CPSU.[85]

The role played by these women on such bodies is a matter for conjecture. It seems improbable, however, that women who continue in full-time agricultural employment would also play an influential part in decision making at such a level alongside career politicians of national stature. What is certain is that very few rural women gain extensive political experience at national level. Table 27 provides profiles of twelve women who have been prominent in Party and government activity during the 1970s. The Table is restricted to those present at the 25th or 26th Party Congresses and at the 9th or 10th Convocations of the USSR Supreme Soviet. Women have been included only if they have twice been Congress delegates and Supreme Soviet deputies or if they have been present at one Party Congress but at three or more Supreme Soviet Convocations.

Table 27 *Rural women in national politics*

Name	Party Congresses 25th	26th	USSR Supreme Soviet Convocations	Year of birth	Nationality	Education	Occupation	Heroes of Socialist Labour
Annamukhamedova, Gyzylgul			6th, 9th, 10th	1921	Turkmen	Secondary	Kolkhoz chairperson	*
Donenbaeva, Kamshat Baigazinovna	*		9th, 10th	1943	Kazakh	Incomplete secondary	Tractor driver	*
Formanyuk, Alexandra Mikhailovna	*		7th, 8th, 9th	1930	Ukrainian	Secondary	Pig rearer	*
Gasanova, Shamama Makhmudaly kyzy	*		4th to 10th	1926	Azerbaidzhan	Higher	Kolkhoz chairperson	**
Gasanova, Zalkhai Makhmud kyzy	*		8th, 9th, 10th	1941	Azerbaidzhan	Higher	Team leader	*
Lyubchenko, Lyubov' Andreevna	*		6th to 10th	1922	Ukrainian	Higher	Kolkhoz chairperson	*
Marina, Nina Evdokimovna	*		9th, 10th	1929	Russian	Special secondary	Head of pig unit	*

Name		Convocation	Year	Nationality	Education	Occupation	
Novruzova, Gyulushan Garib kyzy	*	7th, 8th, 9th	1930	Lezgin (Azerbaidzhan)	Special secondary	Dairy woman	
Rakhmonova, Sanobar Abduazizovna	*	9th, 10th	1947	Tadzhik	Secondary	Brigade leader	
Serbin, Lidya Spiridonovna	*	7th, 8th, 9th	1923	Ukrainian	Incomplete secondary	Team leader	*
Verenikina, Valentina Grigor'evna	*	8th, 9th, 10th	1939	Ukrainian	Special secondary	Leader of tractor brigade	
Vishtak, Stepanida Demidovna	*	4th to 9th	1918	Ukrainian	Primary	Team leader	**

Sources: *Deputaty . . . Desyatyi sozyv*; *Deputaty . . . Desyatyi sozyv*; *XXV s"ezd*, pp. 329–596; *XXVI s"ezd*, pp. 289–523.

The youngest of these women was thirty-four in 1981 whilst eight of them were over fifty. The majority of the older women were recruited into the Party before 1961, four of them in the immediate post-war period following distinguished or courageous service during the war. Lidya Serbin, for example, was a partisan in the Ukraine whilst Stepanida Vishtak was deported from her collective farm in the Ukraine to Leipzig where she worked in forced labour from 1942 to 1945. All but two of these women are in leadership positions in agriculture and half have higher or special secondary education. Nine are Heroes of Socialist Labour, whilst Shamama Gasanova and Stepanida Vishtak have been awarded this medal twice. It is notable that only one Russian is featured in this Table whilst no less than six are from Central Asia or Azerbaidzhan. This suggests a deliberate policy of promoting women from these areas into prominent positions in public life.

The involvement of rural women in formal politics mirrors their activity in paid employment. At the lowest levels, women are reasonably active and said to participate conscientiously and effectively. At the top of the pyramid, in politics as in management, women are few and, in politics at least, appear to lack influence. Although rural women are highly visible in certain spheres of Soviet political life, their access to positions of power cannot be said to match their massive contribution to the Soviet economy and society.

Political responses by rural women

It is this contribution to national life which indisputedly gives women enormous potential social and economic power in the Soviet Union. Yet there is little evidence of women working collectively to achieve significant improvements in their domestic or working lives. As we have seen, the women's councils operate more as an informal arm of the Party than as a focus for 'women's issues'. At national level this trend is even more apparent. The Committee for Soviet Women often appears far less interested in the problems of women in the USSR than in the promotion of the CPSU's foreign policy objectives as translated by the International Democratic Federation of Women, a body which it helped to found in 1945. In pursuit of these international goals, the committee is heir to that element of Bolshevik thought which, in the 1920s, viewed women's issues as diversionary. Statements by leading Soviet women illustrate this viewpoint. Lidya Lykova, deputy chairperson of the RSFSR Council of Ministers, made the following comment about the UN Conference on Women held in Copenhagen in 1980:

Some Western delegations tried to turn the discussion to so-called 'women's issues', and to emasculate the political essence of the question. The democratic forces of the international women's movement and especially the International Democratic Federation of Women countered these attempts. They strove to direct the measures taken by the forum ... towards the major problems facing humanity and exposed those who are pushing the world to the brink of war. The progressive forces were completely victorious. The participants of the forum called on the women of the world to fight the threat of a new war, the arms race, imperialism, neocolonialism, apartheid and zionism.[86]

As the American political scientist, Barbara Wolfe Jancar, has observed, 'As long as women view their own interests as secondary, and revolution, universal suffrage, world peace or democracy as primary, they may gain legal and economic recognition, but the achievement of equal status will be continually postponed.' Thus, she continues, in authoritarian states such as the Soviet Union, which have 'commanded equality' from above, the process may go no further than those in control desire. The development of full equality may imply too great a challenge to established patriarchal authority. It is a contention which has been given support by the treatment of the independent women's group which emerged in the USSR in 1979. The unofficial publication of the group's journal in December of that year, its rapid suppression and the arrests and deportations of its authors led one of them to conclude: 'No other regime is so afraid of its own women!'[87]

In the absence of an autonomous women's movement, Soviet women lack the support of a feminist ideology with which to counter sexual stereotyping. They appear to internalise traditional myths about women and to blame themselves for their lack of formal success in work or politics. Conversations with women from a wide range of backgrounds during a research visit to Minsk in 1980–1 left me with the impression that women see their failure to gain leadership positions as the result of innate female characteristics. Even highly educated women with successful careers made comments such as 'Women seem to lack something', 'We're too emotional. We don't see things on a large scale like men do', thereby interpreting the question in psychological rather than sociological terms. Limited survey data and the comments of sociologists tend to confirm this impression.[88]

Though a 'feminist consciousness', as the term is understood in the West, cannot be said to have developed in the Soviet Union, it should not be concluded that women are therefore satisfied with the measures taken by the state on their behalf. There is no evidence that the embryonic women's movement described above has in any way touched the countryside. It may, however, be possible to describe certain problems as women's issues in rural areas even though they are not dealt with through collective political action. It is the intention of this section to analyse the issues which concern rural women as they are expressed through the medium of complaints to the press. It will also examine women's behaviour in order to identify responses which may be described as political or which have brought about a change in government policy.

Women's complaints to the press

The following analysis of rural women's letters of complaint to the press is based on letters published in *Krest'yanka* over a four-year period from August 1979 to July 1983. *Krest'yanka* is a popular women's magazine which has had an increasingly broad circulation over the past twenty years despite the decline in the rural population. During the period of this survey alone the print run increased from 6.5 to 9.5 million copies, the majority of these being on subscription. A recent readership survey found that copies are passed round several families in the villages, making the total readership considerably larger than the circulation. *Krest'yanka* is read by women of all ages, though the majority of respondents to the readership survey were under thirty. The magazine is also read by men who sometimes write to the magazine requesting advice or assistance with personal or employment problems. The fact that men use *Krest'yanka* in this way suggests that sending such a letter is widely seen as an effective course of action in rural areas.[89]

It must be said, however, that this analysis of complaints is based on an extremely small sample. *Krest'yanka* receives some 40,000 letters each year, though what proportion of these are complaints is unknown. In the four-year period surveyed, 239 complaints received publicity through two regular features in this magazine. The first, *Krapiva* (stinging nettle), is the main forum for consumer problems in *Krest'yanka*. The second, entitled 'The letter is not published but measures have been taken', gives readers a broad outline of specific complaints received by the magazine with details of the action which resulted from press intervention. The complaints cover an extremely wide range of subjects and not infrequently include a whole catalogue of misdemeanours by local officials and managers. As the 'measures taken' often include disciplinary action, dismissals and even criminal proceedings it is apparent that the letters themselves would have made interesting reading. Clearly this view is shared by *Krest'yanka*'s Soviet readers who declared their interest in this feature during the readership survey and asked that the letters be published. In all cases the claims made in the complaints covered by these features have been substantiated by those investigating them.[90]

Table 28 provides a breakdown of these letters of complaint by subject. Over half the complaints related to consumer problems of all kinds, in particular the low standard of shopping facilities in rural areas. Nearly a third of complaints concerned employment, the majority of these relating to poor management. It is notable that the proportion of published complaints about dishonesty in management increased significantly towards the end of the survey period. Though no complaints of this type were published during the latter half of 1979, poor management had become the target of a quarter of all published letters of complaint by 1983, perhaps reflecting the concerns of the Soviet administration since the death of Leonid Brezhnev. In every case complaints about working conditions related to the operation of livestock units. This clearly is a major area of concern for women employed in the countryside. *Krest'yanka*'s readership survey found that readers wanted the magazine to print more examples of farms with modern systems of work organisation and the use of technology so that such methods might be put into practice in their own areas. Evidently, women see such articles as a means of bringing pressure to bear on managements to implement less oppressive and strenuous work regimes, especially in dairying.[91] Complaints about rural culture featured in no more than 11% of published letters whilst 'other complaints' largely involved cases of unfair dismissal or the non-payment of maintenance.

The survey of published letters thus suggests that rural women are most anxious to air their views as consumers and, secondly, as employees. This may, however, reflect only the fact that *Krapiva* is predominantly a consumer feature and the bulk of published complaints are therefore of this type. Occasionally articles are published on the basis of a recurrent theme in readers' letters; for example, illegal

Table 28 *Analysis of letters of complaint to* Krest'yanka *magazine, August 1979–July 1983*

	Number	%	%
Total	239	100.0	100.0
Work			
Poor management (includes drunkenness at work, rudeness or indifference to workers, dishonesty)	45	18.8	
Working conditions (includes poor organisation, pay)	27	11.3	30.1
Consumer affairs			
Shops and services (includes erratic opening hours, delays, rudeness, dishonesty, poor workmanship)	72	30.2	
Child care facilities (includes shortage of places, poor conditions)	20	8.4	55.2
Living conditions (includes essential services, housing, roads and transport)	40	16.7	
Culture			
Shortage or quality of cultural facilities	19	7.9	
Drunkenness and illegal alcohol sales	7	2.9	10.9
Other complaints	9	3.8	3.8

alcohol sales or the lack of child care facilities. Such articles confirm the impression that the regular letter features do no more than scratch the surface of the correspondence received by the magazine. Certainly, the reluctance to publish the letters themselves ensures that these major features do little to shed light on women's attitudes to the matters which concern them.

Limitation of family size

The fall in the Soviet birthrate has been due, as we have seen, to a variety of factors, the most significant being a general move by Soviet women to restrict the size of their families. Though rural women continue to have more children than urban women, the two-child rural family is now characteristic of much of the USSR. Surveys demonstrate that women in European areas almost invariably have fewer children than the number they see as ideal. In addition, it has been found that, on average, husbands want more children than their wives do; a fact which women tend to regard as evidence of male irresponsibility.[92] The evidence presented in these surveys indicates that both urban and rural women have not only fewer children than the Soviet government considers acceptable, but also fewer than they themselves would like. It is a phenomenon which has been seen by some Soviet sociologists as a response by women to the unreasonable burdens placed upon them. At least one Soviet commentator, Yuri Ryurikov, writing in the journal *Voprosy filosofii* in 1977, has interpreted women's actions as a political response:

The current decline in the birthrate ... also has some positive aspects. It can be viewed, in part, as a spontaneous response by women to their excessive workload and lack of equality with men – a response which consists of eliminating the single factor over which they have the greatest control. The falling birthrate is an important – in fact, indispensable – lever that women can use in their effort to achieve full equality with men ... The new lower birthrate is an essential factor in an enormous social revolution – the transition from a patriarchate to a 'biarchate' in which the two sexes are equally sovereign.[93]

It is an indisputable fact that the operation of this 'lever' by Soviet women has created enormous government concern and has obliged the state to reconsider its policies. What is considerably less certain is whether women's actions are in fact producing the 'social revolution' which Ryurikov foresaw. When political responses are spontaneous and unorganised and when criticisms are implied rather than articulated, policy-makers remain free to diagnose the problem and prescribe the treatment of their own choice. The recent measures taken by the Soviet government to boost the birthrate, together with the pronatalist propaganda appearing in the press, do not appear promising for the development of a 'biarchate', to use Ryurikov's term, in the USSR. Increased maternity leave on reduced or no pay with no attempt to introduce the concept of paternity leave, an increase in part-time and home working for women with children and the reinforcement of traditional sex-role stereotypes by the media all serve to perpetuate women's inferiority in the labour force and the notion that child care is an exclusively female concern. The restriction of family size is the hallmark of women's response to overwork and, in particular, to the failure of men to take on their share of domestic responsibilities. It is a response, made by rural and urban women alike, which is frequently regarded with sympathy by Soviet academics. Yet, though the 'double burden' has become the subject of much rhetoric by Soviet politicians, the reluctance of government to tackle the root causes of the problem has produced an official reaction which seems likely to have negative rather than positive results for the status of Soviet women.

Migration to the cities

The standard pattern of migration from the countryside to the cities of the Soviet Union has traditionally been one in which men formed the majority of migrants. Young men, drawn away from the village for national service in the armed forces, would regularly be recruited into the industrial workforce on demobilisation and would never return to work in their native villages. Young women, unable to find a husband, would be 'driven' out of the villages, as one writer put it, in order to establish a family of their own. It is a pattern which may still be observed in the less developed areas of the Soviet Union.[94]

As the mechanisation of agricultural production has increased, however, the pattern has been reversed. The major reason for the growing intensity of female migration to the cities in the more developed regions of the USSR is the shortage of skilled work for women in rural areas. The prevailing division of labour in agriculture lies at the root of the problem. With increasing automation agriculture demands proportionately greater numbers of workers with technical skills. As the handling of machinery in the countryside remains essentially a male preserve, however, the need for female labour falls year by year. A paradoxical situation thus arises in which the most modern and highly automated farms may offer the poorest employment prospects to rural women. This pattern, observed by growing numbers of Soviet sociologists, was succinctly expressed by one writer thus: 'the higher the level of mechanisation and specialisation in the countryside, the greater the demand for male labour and the less for female labour'.[95] As farms modernise, the prevailing patterns of occupational segregation make women ever more marginal to agricultural production.

An example of how this operates at the local level is provided by a survey of trends in one rural district of Kostroma Region in 1973. The planned capital investment in agriculture in the region for the period to 1980 led to the following prognosis for the structure of the labour force. Increased automation would, over this seven-year period, reduce the total workforce by 2.8%. This overall reduction would, however, be achieved through an increase in male workers of 16.9% and a decrease in female workers of 20.2%. Among the reasons for such a development would be a sharp increase in the number of machine operators required in arable farming. It was assumed that all these extra workers would be men. In addition, as livestock units became automated, there would be a sixfold increase in the number of men required to service machinery, thereby considerably reducing women's predominance in animal husbandry. Increased automation in arable farming would, at the same time, put a great many women labourers out of work. During this same period it was estimated that the service sector in the region would expand only very slowly and would in no way compensate for the loss of agricultural employment.[96]

For young women with secondary education the employment opportunities provided by the contemporary countryside hold few attractions. The options presented to the majority were recently summed up by one leading economist as:

1 work in a livestock unit, frequently in appalling conditions
2 an office job, of which there are very few
3 work as a field labourer, which is subject to bad weather and fluctuating earnings.[97]

For increasing numbers of women the lack of skilled work available to them in the countryside leaves little choice but to seek employment or further education in the towns.

Sociological surveys of the plans of school leavers show that rural girls regard work in agricultural machine operation as closed to them and are highly motivated to leave the village. Since the early sixties, surveys have consistently shown that over 80% of rural girls plan to leave the village on finishing school. In the 1960s data suggested that boys were similarly motivated. By the mid-seventies, however, with the increase in automation, boys showed far greater inclination to remain in the countryside. In Belorussia, for example, one survey found that only 13% of girls but 40% of boys in the eighth form intended to remain in the village. Rural girls in this survey were characterised by an extreme lack of interest in agricultural work.[98]

It is the attitude of rural young women to the agricultural work available to them which forms the major factor in their decision to migrate to the cities. Consequently, observers of the phenomenon often regard female migration as a negative rather than a positive response: girls reject rural employment yet often have little better awaiting them in the cities. Low wages and hostel life are the frequent results of a move to the city for young women newly recruited into the industrial workforce. As one recent article pointed out, the consequences for a woman's personal life may not always be happy. Describing the 'pile of letters' received by *Krest'yanka* magazine from recent migrants to the cities, all of them women with unhappy marriages, this writer observed how inauspicious the start of married life could be for women from the village:

And so a life begins in which he may be living in one hostel and she in another. And this can go on for some years. A child is born: after all they can't always wait until they have a place of their own. And there's always the simple consideration that a young family with a child will get somewhere quicker than a couple without children: quicker it's true, but still not tomorrow.[99]

The strains of urban life for young women from the countryside have led some observers to express astonishment at the singlemindedness with which many pursue their chosen path away from the village. One writer described how he had seen beautifully modernised villages in the Kuban' where girls still left school and moved straight to town: 'the girls go to the Krasnodar worsted mills and live six to a room. There are no comforts in the hostel, no romance.'[100]

Surveys make it clear that the decision of young women to leave the village is often not simply the result of an appraisal of employment prospects, especially at a time when schools and Komsomol alike are at pains to persuade them to remain. A vital factor in the migration of young women is the attitude of their parents to rural life. It appears to be a widespread belief amongst older rural dwellers that the city promises a better life for their children. It is a view born largely of their own experiences, as one Ukrainian Party secretary explained:

Life was hard for parents of today's young people during the post-war years and the 1950s. Wages were low, there were shortages, the labour-day didn't always provide for the family. And so the conviction grew in the mothers and fathers that, well, we've worked so let our children live a bit. And so young people leave, they are drawn to the city, even though everything changed a long time ago.[101]

It is evident, however, that older rural women do not necessarily share the view that 'everything has changed'. Women have been found to be far more likely than men to dislike rural life or to see city life as offering more. Soviet social scientists are agreed that mothers are the principal influence on the decision of young women to leave the village and that only a minority try to persuade their daughters to remain. Most rural women, surveys indicate, want their children to become specialists in non-agricultural professions. Women's opinions of the prevailing conditions in agriculture, and especially in livestock units, lead them to encourage their daughters to look elsewhere. Comments printed in the press suggest that older women are unimpressed by official efforts to retain young women on the land: 'Her father and I have spent our whole lives in muck and filth, let Zina do some other work. There's nothing for her to do in the country ... But, if she wants to then we're not against it. She can sit in an office, she can learn book-keeping by all means.'[102] In similar fashion the head teacher of a rural school in Voroshilovgrad Region of the Ukraine complained that mothers and grandmothers undid all the school's careers advice work. Whilst the school did all it could to urge girls to seek work in dairying, their mothers did just the opposite. 'They say "you can make for anywhere you like, daughter, even if it's a thousand miles from home, but I'll not let you go into a dairy unit – I'll lie down in the road first!".'[103]

The negative impact of development on women's employment opportunities, coupled with higher educational attainment and increasing disenchantment with rural life have produced high rates of female migration across much of the USSR. Figure 10, showing rural sex-ratios in 1970, illustrates the effect of differential patterns of migration in four republics of the Soviet Union. Traditional patterns of migration in which men form the majority of migrants remained characteristic of Tadzhikistan and Armenia. In the RSFSR and Estonia, however, fewer young women than men were to be found in the village. In Estonia especially rural men out-numbered women in all age groups under forty. The concern expressed in both scholarly and popular publications at the rate of female migration from the countryside indicates that this pattern of development has intensified since 1970. Social scientists have pointed out that, given the prevailing division of labour in the countryside, demographic imbalance is the inevitable consequence of technological progress.[104]

The immediate social consequences of intense female migration have provided the phenomenon with its popular title: the 'bride problem'. A survey of Kalinin Region in the mid-seventies gives a characteristic example of its effect on rural men. In the area of twelve rural Soviets surveyed over a two-year period eighty-seven men returned to their native villages after completing their army service. A

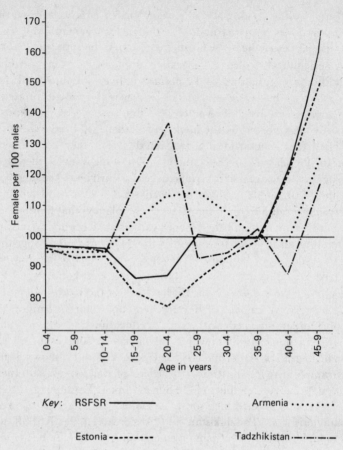

Figure 10   Rural sex-ratios, selected republics, 1970
Source: Itogi ... 1970, Vol. ii, Table 3.

Key: RSFSR ————————   Armenia · · · · · · · ·

        Estonia - - - - - - -   Tadzhikistan ·—·—·—·—

total of forty-four of the men got married, a third of these to urban
women, in which case they moved to the city. The remaining forty-
three were still unmarried after two years in the countryside. Where
the chances of finding a wife are slim, young men are unwilling to
settle. Sociologists have noted that, in areas where the young are
predominantly male, agriculture suffers from an extremely high
turnover of workers and the villages from an increase in 'anti-social
behaviour'. Sooner or later, most unmarried rural men find their way
to the towns, a fact which creates enormous headaches for farm

managers. One who had employed eleven young men on their return from the army commented, 'There are no brides for five of them. There's no sign of one in the whole district. And I shudder when I think that they'll stay single for a year or so and then they'll be off.'[105]

As the young men follow the women to the towns farms suffer not only from a rapid turnover of staff but often from a chronic shortage of skilled labour. The 'bride problem' exacerbates the difficulties which farms face in maintaining a stable workforce of machine operators. At the same time, female migration leads to staff shortages in livestock units and delays the implementation of the more attractive shift systems. Social scientists and farm managers alike are increasingly coming to realise that capital investment will remain ineffective as long as a stable, skilled labour force cannot be established on the land. It is being recognised that a positive response to the demands of young rural women is a critical factor in resolving the problems of agricultural production in the USSR. As one state farm manager in Vologda Region expressed his view of the disappearance of young women from the land, 'This is now the number one problem . . . and we won't get it off the agenda until we create good working and living conditions for women.'[106]

The reactions of women of all ages to the drudgery which rural life continues to impose has resulted in an enormous movement of the young away from the villages. The attitudes and demands of rural women have not been coherently expressed through formal political channels, yet their unorganised and unco-ordinated action has had an enormous impact on the structure of rural society across much of the USSR. In places, the effect of female migration has been such as to jeopardise plans for rural development. The social and economic consequences of women's actions have brought issues affecting rural women to the forefront of debates on the future of the agriculture.[107]

Just as women's response to their situation has been unco-ordinated, so methods of tackling the resulting problems have, as yet, been highly diverse and localised. As we have seen, in areas which have been particularly hard hit by labour shortages, whole classes of school leavers have been persuaded to remain on the farms for a limited period at the instigation of the Komsomol. There have also been attempts to retain young people on the farms in these areas through increased investment in housing, consumer services, roads and nurseries.[108] Farms which have an adequate female workforce in animal husbandry and see female migration primarily as a 'bride problem' have adopted a different approach to the question. Where a farm's principal concern is to retain a stable male workforce in agriculture, the problem becomes one of creating acceptable employment for women. Some farms have diversified, introducing new forms of agricultural production such as fur-farming, soft fruit production or beekeeping.[109] Other farms have introduced or expanded subsidiary industries. Industrial processes, often closely linked to agricultural production, have been introduced in many areas since 1960 in an attempt to combat the effects of pronounced seasonality in agricultural employment. Now, however, industry is being specifically developed on many farms for the employment of rural women. Examples of concerns opened for this purpose include food processing plants, radio assembly shops, clothing factories and workshops reviving traditional peasant crafts to provide souvenirs for the tourist trade. As yet, however, relatively few farms can offer industrial conditions attractive enough to dissuade young women from moving to the cities. It has been pointed out by at least one Soviet economist that such developments should not in any case be seen as the solution to female migration as subsidiary industries would become considerably less profitable if every farm were to have them.[110]

These varied local approaches are at one in their assumption that men are the central figures in agriculture. It is an assumption which has received support from certain Soviet social scientists during the 1970s. The response of these commentators to the arduous nature of agricultural work as performed by many rural women is to suggest that women should be moved out of agriculture altogether and concentrated in the service sector or light industry. Indeed, one economist has gone so far as to suggest that women's participation in all sectors of the rural workforce should be restricted in view of the underdevelopment of the service sector and government concern to raise the birthrate. From the opposite end of the spectrum warning voices have observed that opinions such as these ignore one of the fundamental tenets of Marxism–Leninism that only the active involvement of women in production can ensure economic and social equality between the sexes.[111]

Though the intense migration of women to the cities has developed in response to diminishing job opportunities few commentators propose a radical change in the prevailing division of labour which has brought this about. Tursunoi Akhunova, a celebrated Uzbek machine operator, explaining the support given by the Party to Central Asian women in the 1950s, observed: 'There were people who understood that if you banned women from machines then, in the future you would have to ban them from agricultural work altogether.'[112] It is a comment which has significance for the whole of Soviet agriculture today. Though women have never been formally barred from operating agricultural machinery, the recruitment of women into work on machines is not viewed by farm managements as a serious option.

In the absence of attempts to tackle the sexual division of labour on the land or of initiatives to develop acceptable non-agricultural employment opportunities for women, the problems posed by female migration are likely to increase as agriculture is modernised. It is clear that love of the countryside or an attachment to one's native district are no longer sufficient for young women to accept low-skilled, poorly paid work in difficult conditions. The negative attitudes of many young rural women towards agriculture are not simply the result of an infatuation with the novelties of city life but are endorsed by older women with many years experience of agricultural work. The reaction of young women to the future which is offered them on the land mirrors the inequality of opportunity which is becoming an increasingly striking feature of modern Soviet agriculture. Though expressed in actions rather than words, it may be said that access to skilled work is very much a women's issue in the Soviet countryside, and indeed recognised as such by a small group of Soviet academics. As one of their number has concluded:

The prevailing division of labour between men and women in agriculture limits the productive activity of women collective farmers, fosters dissatisfaction with their work, lowers their productivity and opposes the interests of society... The aspiration of young women to move from village to town can be regarded as an aspiration by women to achieve equality with men in their choice of profession.[113]

Conclusions

On the eve of the socialist Revolution of 1917, the vast majority of Russia's population, its peasantry, had been free from the bonds of feudalism for less than sixty years. The mass of rural women lived out their lives under male authority within the hierarchical structures of the peasant family. Arranged marriage, difficult divorce and regular pregnancies were characteristic features of their personal lives. The primitive nature of peasant agriculture and the poverty of the former serf households placed heavy burdens on women whose work in subsistence farming and whose domestic labour were a major source of support for their families.

In the contemporary USSR the rural environment in which the descendants of these women live is very different. The world's first socialist state is now a major industrial power. Its agriculture is collectivised or state-run with many of its essential processes mechanised. Rural living standards have improved considerably, especially during the last twenty years. As the countryside has changed, rural women have themselves been transformed from the illiterate and downtrodden masses described by the activists and commentators of the 1920s. The old peasant family has vanished, and in the rural family of today, women are often better educated than their husbands and are regularly to be found taking the lead in decision making. In limiting the size of their families and as the principal initiators of divorce, rural women demonstrate that they are not prepared to tolerate the standards of family life experienced by their mothers and grandmothers. As independent wage-earners, economic necessity no longer obliges them to accept the dictates of other family members.

Yet the process of modernisation through which these changes have been brought about is one over which rural women themselves have had little control. Development planning has remained firmly in the hands of the Communist Party in which rural women have always been poorly represented. Though Soviet women were, from the first, urged to take part in political activity, the leading and guiding role of the Party was invariably emphasised. The mistrust of autonomous political action by women which led to the demise of the Zhenotdel ensured that women's activities from 1930 were harnessed to the promotion of the Party's economic goals. Since that time, the participation of rural women in the process of development planning has been very largely restricted to an involvement in the implementation of decisions already taken.

Throughout the process of development, women's control over the day to day decisions affecting their working lives has likewise been limited. With collectivisation, most rural women for the first time came under the authority of men from outside their own families. Few women were promoted to management positions with greater responsibility than that of team leader. The pattern of employment of women in management which characterised agriculture in the 1930s remains in evidence to this day. Though women have made some progress at middle-management levels on the farms, their representation remains disproportionately low. At the highest levels of farm management women fare little better than they did in the early years of the collectives.

Through their labour, rural women have made a massive contribution to the process of modernisation in the USSR. Yet this lack of equal involvement in decision making, both locally and nationally, has led to a neglect of women's issues. In the first instance, in the face of the country's parlous economic and strategic position Soviet leaders saw recovery and growth as paramount. In the longer term, Soviet planners have continued to give priority to defence expenditure and industrial development. The allocation of resources to the service sector which would assist women to combine their multiple roles in employment and in the home has remained a low priority. At the local level, the demands of plan fulfilment on the farms may lead managers to delay the implementation of schemes and policies which could benefit women. In consequence, rural women are likely to identify many of the problems which they still face as originating in the disinterest, inertia or lack of vision of male managers and officials. From attitudes such as these, they feel, stem the lack of support for women facing discrimination in employment, the want of consideration given to introducing less arduous work schedules or the failure to implement investment programmes for child care facilities.

Yet the roots of many of the unsolved problems which beset rural women's lives go far deeper than local apathy, obstruction, or short-term economic imperatives. In a state which pledged itself to promoting the emancipation of women, sexual inequality undoubtedly persists. The reasons for continuing prejudice and discrimination against rural women stem in part from the course of development chosen by the Soviet Union's leaders and the resulting inadequate implementation of socialist policies on women's emancipation. At the same time, the crude economic determinism which characterised Soviet theory on relations between the sexes assumed a change in male attitudes under socialism which has evidently failed to take place. In the absence of specific attempts at re-socialisation, traditional patterns of male behaviour towards women have been little changed. Finally, the persistence of inequality can be linked to the changing demands of the Soviet state on women, particularly in the area of population policy. The major elements in the persistence of inequality in the lives of rural women today are discussed in greater detail below.

Education and training

In the realm of education, major advances have been made since the 1920s when the campaign for universal literacy was the Soviet government's prime concern. By the 1950s the development of rural education had begun to open up work in teaching, medicine and agricultural specialisms to rural women. Women have greatly benefited from the advance in rural secondary education which has taken place in the 1970s and, across much of the USSR, now form a majority of the rural population with higher or secondary education. The achievements of Soviet education in the countryside have been substantial and impressive. Nevertheless, the improvement in female education has not had such a significant impact on women's access to skilled work in rural areas as might have been expected. Furthermore, the sex-specific vocational training characteristic of the school curriculum, and the attitudes towards women and technology displayed in rural schools, are themselves an important factor in the unequal access of rural women to technical further education. The effect of technological advance on female employment in the countryside is becoming a major problem both for women and for agricultural planners. It is one which rural education is certainly doing little to alleviate and may, indeed, be further compounding.

Technological advance and the sexual division of labour

With the appearance of tractors on the fields of the USSR during the 1st Five-Year Plan, considerable efforts were made to ensure that women took their place amongst the vanguard of agricultural workers using the new technology. Yet throughout the 1930s the needs of defence provided the justification for the training and employment of women in this work. Women were, from the very beginnings of the movement, viewed as a reserve army which would ensure the continuation of food supplies should war threaten the country. Indeed, during the struggle for survival in which the USSR was soon engaged, women played an invaluable role in driving the machines which kept production moving. Yet despite the attempts at positive discrimination embodied in recent legislation, women machine operators today are fewer, both in number and in relation to men, than before the Nazi invasion of 1941. Encouragement at national level has been insufficient to combat discriminatory practices on farms across the country.

The rural bias against entrusting women with machinery is not confined to tractor and combine driving but extends to specialist level where agriculture is notable for its extremely low rate of employment of female engineers. As the mechanisation of agriculture increases, the results of effectively excluding women from technical jobs become ever more visible. In fatstock production, in certain areas of arable farming such as sugar beet production and even in dairying, male labour is increasingly employed to operate or service machinery as it is introduced. Men entering these areas of production, often for the first time, do so as an elite workforce. As women are frequently not retrained to operate the new machinery, their work becomes devalued as they are left to perform by hand the tasks which the machines cannot do.

The establishment of collective farming in the USSR and the campaigns to promote women's work with machines have failed to present a serious challenge to the traditional division of labour on the land. Under the old system of peasant agriculture, men were responsible for the principal tasks of arable farming, from ploughing to threshing, calling on women's assistance at peak times and with routine work such as weeding. As tractors replaced horse-drawn ploughs and harrows, men learnt to operate the machines which, from the late twenties, began to modernise their traditional sphere of work. On the private peasant farms, women had produced chiefly for subsistence in the family's vegetable garden as well as carrying out almost all the household's domestic labour. With collectivisation, subsistence farming continued on the private plots and women's unpaid labour formed the major contribution to this area of production. As a result, women spent less time than men in waged work on the collective fields. As men were, therefore, viewed as the mainstay of the workforce in the socialised sector of agricultural production, women predominated in unskilled, manual labour, receiving a limited share of the rewards and of the recognition which collectivised farming had to offer.

Since the 1930s, then, the traditional division of labour has ensured that men have controlled technology on Soviet farms. Except in wartime, women have experienced great difficulty in entering this male sphere of employment. As mechanisation increases, however, men are not experiencing the same degree of difficulty in entering traditionally female occupations. Their entry into these areas is, however, entirely conditional on the advent of a high degree of automation and the more prestigious employment prospects which accompany it. In recent years it would appear that the long-established forms of occupational segregation in agriculture, notably in arable and livestock farming, have been modified by a new division of labour: one in which men operate and service machinery whilst women predominate in manual work using only simple hand tools. The considerable improvement in female educational attainment has not of itself been sufficient to challenge the concentration of women in low-status occupations: over 70% of agricultural labourers in the USSR today are women.

The results of such a division of labour have meant that, as agriculture modernises, the demand for male labour grows whilst that for female labour declines. In a socialised economy, women who fail to gain access to mechanised work are unlikely to face the degree of impoverishment experienced by women in many Third World countries where technological advance has led to a loss of female income. Nevertheless, the concentration of women in low-paid manual work with its seasonal unemployment does serve to depress their earnings and reduce their economic independence. The high proportion of single parents and mothers of large families who are prepared to endure the prevailing conditions in dairying for the sake of a constant income underlines the economic consequences for women of their exclusion from skilled, mechanised work.

With few acceptable alternatives to agricultural employment in the countryside, young women increasingly find themselves presented with a choice between heavy manual labour in fields and livestock units or a move to the town. It seems probable that this pattern will intensify as agriculture becomes increasingly automated. The very name popularly given to the difficulties posed by female migration from the villages – the 'bride problem' – in itself sums up how marginal women have become to modern agricultural production in the USSR.

Domestic labour and child care

The concentration of women in seasonal manual labour, their low representation amongst machine operators and their failure to gain promotion are all frequently attributed to the family commitments which they continue to shoulder. The ideas of communal living and socialised child care which were commonly mooted in the 1920s were never implemented. The mass of the rural population was certainly both uncomprehending and antagonistic towards such communes as were set up in the countryside, whilst the Party was fundamentally hostile to their autonomy. By the mid-1930s all such experimentation had been superseded by the Party's decision to strengthen the nuclear family. With its emphasis on urban industrial development, the Soviet government has concentrated on providing consumer services and child care facilities for the expanding population of the towns. In the rural areas, the shortage of services makes domestic labour both arduous and time consuming, whilst the necessity for private agriculture makes still further demands on women's energies.

As classical Marxism assumed that male domination would disappear with the abolition of private property, so Soviet theory has continued to ignore the existence of patriarchy in Soviet families. In consequence, there has been little attempt to tackle the division of labour within the family. Comments in the popular press on male roles within the home generally confine themselves to the suggestion that men should help their wives. The assumption is commonly made both by journalists and academics, that, because women bear children, they should automatically take prime responsibility for their upbringing and, by extension, for the care of the home. Whilst male roles have been little challenged in the course of the USSR's modernisation, the extension of female employment has led to an intensification of women's work. The conflict between maternity and employment has been a constant topic for discussion by Soviet academics during the last two decades. The reluctance to contemplate a change in male roles had led a substantial body of academic opinion to consider reducing women's involvement in employment to enable them to fulfil their obligations in the home. So well established is the view that the male career pattern represents the norm that, even amongst writers sympathetic to women's advancement in employment, there is a tendency to view the female half of the labour force as 'a special category of workers'.[1]

In the countryside, the 'double shift' which women face undoubtedly limits their employment opportunities. Where child care facilities are few, women with young families may choose employment in seasonal manual labour to enable them to look after their children. Skilled women workers may opt for unskilled and low-paid work in the service sector in order to gain a standard working day. Women with successful careers may turn down offers of promotion or give up work in management as the demands made of their time and energy both at work and in the home may be too great. The symptoms of strain exhibited in women's lives, the unwillingness of men to take an equal share in domestic labour and child care and the effect which this has both on female employment and on marital stability have been viewed with concern by some social scientists in the USSR. Amongst this group of academics, sexual equality is seen as unobtainable without the highest possible degree of employment of women in waged work. These writers, moreover, do not regard the roles which women currently perform within the home as an inevitable consequence of maternity. As Nadezhda Shishkan has pointed out: 'If the function of childbearing is a natural function of the female labour force, then the care of children, their upbringing and domestic labour are, under socialism, a function of both society and the family, and in the family, of both parents.'[2]

The habitual confusion of women's biological and social roles which characterises the bulk of academic writing and journalism can, however, no longer be regarded as accidental or the product of insufficient thought. With the growth of concern over the falling birthrate, biological determinism has been granted academic respectability by Soviet educational theory.

Pronatalism and rural women

As anxiety over the falling birthrate and rising divorce rate has increased, certain sectors of Soviet academic opinion have demonstrated that the classic Marxist prescription for sexual equality – the full participation of women in social production – is by no means unassailable. Though recent shifts in policy have in no way been as radical as some economists might have liked, the legislative changes of 1981 nevertheless represent a reduction in women's involvement in the workforce. The Soviet government has shown itself to be currently more preoccupied with encouraging births in European areas than with promoting equal opportunities for women in employment.

Yet an appraisal of the new legislation alone does not convey the tenor of the change which took place in official policies and attitudes towards women during the 1970s. In the pronatalist climate which has developed in the Soviet Union, the promotion of traditional concepts of femininity and masculinity and of stereotypical patterns of behaviour has been elevated into a science by educational theorists. Thus, no less a figure than Vice-President of the USSR Academy of Pedagogy, A. Khripkova, is able to comment, 'I am convinced that if we succeed in instilling femininity and gentleness in girls from an early age, if we can raise boys to be genuine knights, then society will benefit and the family will grow stronger.'[3] It is a line of argument which the popular press has not been slow to endorse or to elaborate upon.

Media encouragement of women to see themselves as mothers and home makers is unlikely to ease the domestic burdens already placed upon them. It seems highly improbable that men could be encouraged to share domestic responsibilities in such a climate. Male unwillingness to share domestic labour evidently already obliges many rural women to settle for work which makes few demands of their talents. Media emphasis on motherhood and domesticity will surely not assist women to achieve their full potential in the workforce. Rural women already experience far greater difficulty than do urban women in obtaining work demanding technical knowledge. The sex-role stereotyping which characterises Soviet pronatalism today will, in all probability, serve to strengthen rural conservatism and complicate further women's access to work with technology.

The responses of rural women

In conclusion, it remains only to summarise the responses of rural women to the problems outlined above. How do they regard these issues and what are, for them, the major areas of concern, their principal preoccupations?

First and foremost, surveys consistently make it clear that rural women do want to work and show little interest in leading domestic lives. Though many view work as a matter of financial necessity, many more value the opportunity to work for the social contact, self-respect and independence which it brings. If there were no economic necessity to work, only a small minority of rural women would view full-time child care and domesticity as an attractive proposition. As some observers have pointed out, those who advocate the withdrawal of mothers with young children from the labour force are guilty of a signal lack of consideration for women's own views on the subject.[4] If a highly automated form of agriculture with a small and predominantly male workforce were to develop in the USSR as it has in Britain and North America, it seems clear that Soviet women would expect to be rather more than 'brides' for the agricultural workers of the future.

Young women in the countryside today are considerably more selective than previous generations in their choice of employment. Women with a good, general education for whom there is no lack of opportunities in the towns expect skilled work in reasonable conditions. Evidently, much of the work in which women are currently employed in the countryside cannot be said to answer this description. As a result, increasing numbers of young women leave the villages each year. It says much for the prevailing view of agricultural employment amongst older women that this exodus of the young from the villages is actively encouraged by mothers who have spent their working lives on the farms.

A growing concern for the quality of personal relationships is characteristic of women in the Soviet countryside today. Articles in the press on the themes of marriage and family life receive an enormous response from rural women. Though the old standards of peasant family life have been consigned to history, relations within marriage clearly remain far from egalitarian. In response to the burdens placed upon them, women have become vocal in their complaints about the standards of rural shops and services and the shortage of child care facilities. Evidence suggests that they would like to see greater efforts made by men in the domestic economy. In the absence of a significant male contribution or state assistance, women have resorted to a reduction in the size of their families in order to obtain a manageable workload. Where marital difficulties cannot be resolved, rural women are displaying a growing willingness to petition for divorce rather than tolerate an oppressive relationship: it is a trend which appears particularly significant in view of the poor prospects for re-marriage which face many women in the countryside.

It cannot be said, however, that a feminist consciousness, in the Western sense, has developed amongst Soviet rural women. Their complaints are articulated chiefly through the medium of letters to the state-controlled press and in unco-ordinated, spontaneous action, most evident in the declining birthrate and female migration. There is no autonomous women's movement in the USSR and little prospect that one will develop in the near future. In the absence of such a movement, Soviet women are unable to make a coherent response to pronatalism. Lacking both a feminist analysis and an independent voice they have little with which to counter the threat to women's emancipation posed by current propaganda.

For most rural women, inequality remains a fact of life both in employment and at home. Unless radical measures are taken to lighten women's domestic workload and to provide acceptable hours and conditions in the workplace, women's responses to the rural way of life seem unlikely to change. For thousands of young women each year, a move to the city will continue to seem the only way to obtain the lifestyle they desire. Unorganised and inarticulate though women's expression of dissatisfaction may be, across much of the country already it cannot be ignored. The lack of recognition of women's contribution to the rural economy and the failure to tackle the sexual division of labour on the land which have characterised Soviet development strategies have produced considerable problems in the contemporary Soviet countryside. The reactions of young women to the results of the years of neglect seem likely to create increasing headaches for those concerned with the future of Soviet agriculture.

Notes

INTRODUCTION

1 Ken Laidlaw and Roy Laishley, *Crisis Decade*, London, 1980, p. 24.
2 *WCARRD: A Turning Point for Rural Women*, Rome, 1980, p. 6.
3 Ester Boserup, *Woman's Role in Economic Development*, London, 1970. See also Zubeida Ahmad, 'The Plight of Rural Women: Alternatives for Action', *International Labour Review*, July–August 1980, pp. 426, 429–30; Martha F. Loutfi, *Rural Women: Unequal Partners in Development*, Geneva, 1980, p. 9; Audrey Bronstein, *The Triple Struggle: Latin American Peasant Women*, London 1982, pp. 267–8.
4 Clio Presvelou, 'The Invisible Woman', *Ceres*, 8, no. 2, 1975, p. 53; Marilee Karl, 'Women, Land and Food Production', in ISIS, *Women in Development*, Geneva, 1983, pp. 77–8.
5 Nici Nelson, *Why Has Development Neglected Rural Women? A Review of the South Asian Literature*, Oxford, 1979, p. 49.
6 Ahmad, pp. 430–1; Wellesley Editorial Committee, *Women and National Development: The Complexities of Change*, Chicago, 1977, p. xii.
7 Ahmad, pp. 425–6.
8 Nelson, p. 2
9 Hanna Papanek, 'Development Planning for Women', in Wellesley Editorial Committee, p. 15; Anita Anand, 'Rethinking Women and Development', in ISIS, p. 7.
10 Karl, p. 78; Mary Roodkowsky, 'Women and Development: A Survey of the Literature', in ISIS, p. 20–1.
11 Elise Boulding, *Women: The Fifth World*, New York, 1980, pp. 48 and 52.
12 Anand, pp. 6–7.
13 See Maxine Molyneux, 'Women's Emancipation under Socialism: A Model for the Third World?', *World Development*, 9, no. 9/10, 1981, pp. 1019–37.
14 John C. Dewdney, *A Geography of the Soviet Union*, Oxford, 1979, p. 135.
15 *Narodnoe khozyaistvo SSSR v 1975 g.*, Moscow, 1976, p. 7: Dewdney, p. 110.
16 M. V. Dovnar-Zapol'skii, *Issledovaniya i stat'i*, Kiev, 1909, Vol. i, p. 13.
17 *Ibid.*, p. 20.
18 *Itogi vsesoyuznoi perepisi naseleniya 1970 goda*, Moscow 1972–4, Vol. iii, Table 8.

19 Richard Stites, *The Women's Liberation Movement in Russia: Feminism, Nihilism and Bolshevism, 1860–1930*, Princeton, 1978, p. 242.
20 Frederick Engels, *The Origin of the Family, Private Property and the State*, New York, 1972, p. 82.
21 *Ibid.*, p. 79.
22 *Ibid.*, p. 152.
23 *Ibid.*, pp. 83 and 88.
24 See Alexandra Kollontai, *Selected Writings*, London, 1977.
25 H. M. Christman (ed.), *Communism in Action: A Documentary History*, New York, 1969, p. 8.
26 N. Rosnitskii, *Litso derevni*, Moscow–Leningrad, 1926, p. 113.
27 Stefan Hedlund, *Crisis in Soviet Agriculture*, Beckenham, 1984, p. 48; *Sputnik organizatora krest'yanok*, 2nd edn, Moscow, 1927, p. 39.
28 *Sputnik ...*, pp. 176–7; Jessica Smith, *Women in Soviet Russia*, New York, 1928, pp. 26–7; *Problemy sotsial'nogo razvitiya derevni Sovetskoi Sibiri*, Novosibirsk, 1979, p. 49.
29 S. G. Strumilin, *Problemy ekonomiki truda*, Moscow, 1957, p. 259.
30 Rudolf Schlesinger, *Changing Attitudes in Soviet Russia: The Family in the USSR*, London, 1949, pp. 107, 140.
31 *Ibid.*, p. 99; *Sputnik ...*, pp. 173–4.
32 *Sputnik ...*, p. 83.
33 Dewdney, p. 82.
34 *Itogi vsesoyuznoi perepisi naseleniya 1959 goda. SSSR (svodnyi tom)*, Moscow, 1962, Tables 47 and 48.
35 G. Novikov, *Zhenskii trud v kolkhozakh*, Leningrad, 1934, p. 22; *Narodnoe khozyaistvo SSSR v 1979g.*, Moscow, 1980, p. 411.
36 *Zhenshchina v SSSR*, Moscow, 1937, p. 170.
37 Yu. V. Arutyunyan, *Mekhanizatory sel'skogo khozyaistva SSSR v 1929–1957gg.*, Moscow, 1960, pp. 59–60; Novikov, pp. 33–4, 80.
38 Khudzhume Shukurova, *Sotsializm i zhenshchina Uzbekistana*, Tashkent, 1970, pp. 259–60; *O zhenskikh sel'skokhozyaistvennykh proizvodstvennykh soveshchaniyakh*, Baku, 1932, pp. 17–18. See also Gregory J. Massell, *The Surrogate Proletariat: Moslem Women and Revolutionary Strategies in Central Asia: 1919–1929*, Princeton, 1974.
39 *Itogi ... 1959*, Table 26; *Zhenshchina v SSSR* (1937), p. 118; *Itogi ... 1970*, Vol. III, Table 5.
40 Schlesinger, p. 278.
41 E. A. Sadvokasova, *Sotsial'no-gigienicheskie aspekty regulirovaniya razmerov sem'i*, Moscow, 1969, p. 31.
42 Yu. V. Arutyunyan, *Sovetskoe krest'yanstvo v gody Velikoi Otechestvennoi voiny*, Moscow, 1970, pp. 75 and 111; L. A. Anokhina and M. N. Shmeleva, *Kul'tura i byt kolkhoznikov Kalininskoi oblasti*, Moscow, 1964, pp. 283–5.
43 Arutyunyan (1960), p. 69; *Sovetskaya derevnya v pervye poslevoennye gody 1946–50gg.*, Moscow, 1978, pp. 42, 47; Arutyunyan (1970), pp. 408–11; V. S. Murmantseva, *Sovetskie zhenshchiny v Velikoi Otechestvennoi voine*, Moscow, 1979, pp. 132, 233–5.
44 L. M. Volynkina, 'Ispol'zovanie zhenskogo truda v kolkhozakh Kostromskoi oblasti', candidate degree dissertation, Moscow, 1976, p. 23; *Itogi ...*

1959, Table 13; *Sovetskaya derevnya* ..., pp. 111, 114.
45 Schlesinger, pp. 367–73.
46 F. Belov, *The History of a Soviet Collective Farm*, London, 1956, p. 189.
47 *Itogi* ... *1970*, Vol. III, Table 3; P. I. Kushner (ed.), *Selo Viryatino v proshlom i nastoyashchem*, Moscow, 1958, p. 213.
48 Kushner, pp. 226–7; Anokhina and Shmeleva, p. 313; Sadvokasova, pp. 141–8.
49 *Itogi* ... *1959*, Table 46.
50 *Ibid.*, Tables 46 and 48; N. I. Shishkin (ed.), *Trudovye resursy SSSR*, Moscow, 1961, p. 140.
51 Arutyunyan (1960), pp. 296–302; *Itogi* ... *1959*, Table 46.
52 *Itogi* ... *1959*, Tables 32 and 46.
53 Robert Conquest (ed.), *Agricultural Workers in the USSR*, London 1968, p. 71.
54 Hedlund, p. 60; International Labour Office, *1981 Yearbook of Labour Statistics*, Geneva, 1981, Table 3B. Figures for Britain are from 1978.

I. WOMEN IN THE RURAL WORKFORCE

1 *Narodnoe khozyaistvo SSSR v 1980g.*, Moscow, 1981, p. 7.
2 V. Perevedentsev, *270 millionov*, Moscow, 1982, p. 62; I. M. Slepenkov, 'Sel'skaya molodezh' kak sotsial'naya gruppa', in *Sotsial'naya struktura sel'skogo naseleniya*, Moscow, 1976, p. 138; *Sel'skaya nov'*, 3, 1979, pp. 22–3.
3 See below, Chapter 1, 'Women in dairying' and Chapter 3, 'Politics (Migration to the cities)'. See also B. S. Sultanova, 'Voprosy uluchsheniya ispol'zovaniya zhenskogo truda v kolkhozakh Yuga Kirgizii', candidate degree dissertation, Tashkent, 1972, p. 51.
4 *Itogi* ... *1959*, Table 33; *Itogi* ... *1970*, Vol. v, Table 12; *Vestnik statistiki*, 1, 1981, p. 63.
5 *Itogi* ... *1970*, Vol. v, Table 12.
6 *Narodnoe khozyaistvo SSSR v 1960g.*, Moscow, 1961, p. 361; *Narodnoe khozyaistvo (1975)*, p. 309; *Vestnik statistiki*, 1, 1976, p. 87; M. Fedorova, 'Ispol'zovanie zhenskogo truda v sel'skom khozyaistve', *Voprosy ekonomiki*, 12, 1975, p. 55; I. M. Sal'nikova, 'Sel'skie zhenshchiny kak sotsial'no-demograficheskaya gruppa', in *Sotsial'naya struktura* ..., p. 145.
7 R. K. Ivanova, *Sblizhenie sotsial'no-ekonomicheskikh uslovii zhizni trudyashchikhsya goroda i sela*, Moscow, 1980, p. 55; Yu. V. Arutyunyan and Yu. Kakhk, *Sotsiologicheskie ocherki o Sovetskoi Estonii*, Tallin, 1979, p. 30; V. I. Staroverov, *Sotsial'naya struktura sel'skogo naseleniya SSSR na etape razvitogo sotsializma*, Moscow, 1978, pp. 220, 245. See also Chapter 1 below, 'Women machine operators'.
8 V. P. Zagrebel'nyi, 'Formirovanie otnoshenii sotsial'nogo ravenstva zhenshchin i muzhchin-kolkhoznikov v usloviyakh razvitogo sotsializma', candidate degree dissertation, Kiev, 1977, p. 97; G. G. Markova, 'Svobodnoe vremya i razvitie lichnosti zhenshchin-kolkhoznits na sovremennom etape stroitel'stva kommunizma', candidate degree dissertation, Rostov on Don, 1977, p. 41. See also Chapters 1 and 2 below on private subsidiary agriculture.

9 *Narodnoe khozyaistvo (1980)*, p. 289; Ivanova, pp. 24, 27.

10 Ivanova, p. 27; N. M. Sapozhnikov, 'Selo segodnya: demograficheskie protsessy, resursy truda, kadry', unpublished typescript, Saratov, 1978, p. 38; T. F. Logvinova, 'Sotsial'nye i sotsial'no-psikhologicheskie faktory razvitiya professional'noi orientatsii sel'skoi molodezhi', candidate degree dissertation, Moscow, 1976, p. 18; *Krest'yanka*, 10, 1980, p. 8.

11 Z. F. Belikova, 'Kharakter i usloviya agrarnogo truda i zakreplenie kadrov v sel'skom khozyaistve', in *Problemy derevni i goroda*, Tallin, 1979, Vol. II, p. 80; Fedorova, p. 58; *Krest'yanka*, 7, 1976, p. 24.

12 V. I. Staroverov, *Gorod ili derevnya*, Moscow, 1972, p. 81; *Izvestiya*, 27 May 1975, p. 2; *Krest'yanka*, 4, 1977, p. 16.

13 *Krest'yanka*, 8, 1977, p. 23; 5, 1982, p. 18; 10, 1977, p. 8; and 6; 1976, p. 23.

14 *Ibid.*, 3, 1978, p. 8; and 4, 1975, p. 7.

15 *Ibid.*, 3, 1976, p. 2.

16 Fedorova, p. 60; *Sel'skaya nov'*, 8, 1979, p. 6.

17 Zagrebel'nyi, p. 87.

18 Interviews with editorial board of *Rabotnitsa i syalyanka*, Minsk, 20 January 1981, and with officials of 'Gastello' collective farm, Minsk Region, 19 December 1980.

19 See, for example, *Krest'yanka*, 6, 1976, p. 15; *Sel'skaya zhizn'*, 15 August 1979, p. 2, and 20 November 1979, p. 4: I. A. Argunov and N. V. Isakova, 'O professional'noi orientatsii vypusknikov sel'skikh srednikh shkol', in *Sel'skaya molodezh' Yakutii*, Yakutsk, 1979, p. 61; *Soviet Union*, 1, 1979, p. 29.

20 *Krest'yanka*, 7, 1980, p. 2; and 10, 1982, p. 16; *Sel'skaya zhizn'*, 26 August 1979, p. 4.

21 T. D. Ermolenkova, 'O 'zhenskikh' professiyakh', *Sel'skoe khozyaistvo Belorussii*, 6, 1972, p. 42; *Pravda*, 21 February 1975, p. 2.

22 *Sel'skaya nov'*, 5, 1981, pp. 3–4; *Krest'yanka*, 4, 1980, p. 26; and 12, 1978, p. 5.

23 *Molodoi kommunist*, 12, 1975, p. 13; *Krest'yanka*, 5, 1978, p. 6; and 1, 1983, p. 4.

24 *Krest'yanka*, 1, 1977, p. 16.

25 *Ibid.*, 7, 1980, p. 12.

26 *Sel'skaya nov'*, 8, 1979, p. 7. See also *Krest'yanka*, 2, 1978, p. 5.

27 *Sel'skaya nov'*, 8, 1979, p. 7.

28 *Krest'yanka*, 5, 1982, p. 18.

29 *Zhenshchiny-mekhanizatory (ocherki o zhenshchinakh udostoennykh v 1977 godu priza imeni Pashi Angelinoi*, Moscow, 1979; *Sel'skaya nov'*, 5, 1981, p. 4.

30 Sal'nikova, p. 147; *Krest'yanka*, 5, 1978, p. 1; and 1, 1976, p. 4.

31 *Krest'yanka*, 5, 1982, p. 18; 7, 1980, p. 12; and 10, 1980, p. 9; *Zhenshchiny-mekhanizatory* ..., p. 46.

32 Susan Allott, 'Soviet Rural Women: Employment and Family Life', in Barbara Holland (ed.), *Soviet Sisterhood*, London, 1985, p. 179.

33 *Krest'yanka*, 2, 1978, p. 5; 4, 1977, p. 16; and 1, 1980, p. 17.

34 *Ibid.*, 9, 1978, p. 5; 7, 1980, p. 2; 4, 1977, p. 16.

35 *Sel'skaya zhizn'*, 3 June 1980, p. 2.

36 *Krest'yanka*, 9, 1982, p. 12; and 5, 1976, pp. 7–8; *Sel'skaya zhizn'*, 1 November 1979, p. 1; Fedorova, p. 58.

37 *Sel'skaya nov'*, 5, 1981, p. 4.

38 N. P. Rusanov (ed.), *Okhrana truda zhenshchin v sel'skom khozyaistve*, Orel, 1979, p. 129.

39 *Problemy sotsial'nogo* . . ., p. 158; *Sel'skaya zhizn'*, 5 December 1979, p. 1, and 28 August 1979, p. 1.

40 R. A. Ubaidullaeva, *Zhenskii trud v sel'skom khozyaistve Uzbekistana*, Tashkent, 1969, p. 88.

41 Rusanov, p. 35; Sultanova, pp. 102–3.

42 *Krest'yanka*, 10, 1979, p. 5.

43 *Ibid.*, 2, 1981, p. 19; *Komsomol'skaya pravda*, 21 January 1981, p. 1.

44 *Krest'yanka*, 12, 1975, p. 8; 5, 1980, p. 8; and 2, 1981, p. 9.

45 *Ibid.*, 8, 1979, p. 1.

46 *Ibid.*, 10, 1979, p. 8; and 7, 1981, p. 5.

47 *Ibid.*, 7, 1975, p. 3.

48 *Ibid.*, 9, 1978, p. 5.

49 See, for example, *ibid.*, 8, 1977, p. 15; 11, 1979, pp. 12–13; and 3, 1981, p. 10.

50 Volynkina, pp. 69, 125–33.

51 *Krest'yanka*, 7, 1975, p. 3; and 8, 1977, pp. 2, 15; *Narodnoe khozyaistvo (1980)*, pp. 364–5.

52 Staroverov (1978), p. 235.

53 L. P. Lyashenko, 'Otnoshenie molodezhi k sel'skokhozyaistvennomu trudu', in T. I. Zaslavskaya and V. A. Kalmyk, *Sotsial'no-ekonomicheskoe razvitie sela i migratsiya naseleniya*, Novosibirsk, 1972, p. 146.

54 Fedorova, p. 62; S. A. Protasevich, 'Nekotorye problemy ispol'zovaniya zhenskogo truda v sel'skom khozyaistve i ikh vliyanie na sem'yu', in I. N. Lushchitskii (ed.), *Proizvodstvennaya deyatel'nost' zhenshchin i sem'ya*, Minsk, 1972, p. 165; M. Gordeeva, 'O nekotorykh osobennostyakh ispol'zovaniya zhenskogo truda v gorode i na sele', in *Lyudi v gorode i na sele. Sbornik statei*, Moscow, 1978, p. 64.

55 Volynkina, pp. 50, 69; *Sotsiologicheskie issledovaniya*, 3, 1976, p. 60; interview with officials of 'Gastello' collective farm, Minsk Region. The basic wage of dairy women on this farm was 280 roubles per month whilst machine operators received a basic wage of 250 roubles per month.

56 L. A. Erem'yan and V. N. Martynova, 'Analiz sostava zhenshchin, zanyatykh v zhivotnovodstve sovkhozov (po materialam Novosibirskoi oblasti)', in Lushchitskii, pp. 192–4; V. N. Kolbanovskii (ed.), *Kollektiv kolkhoznikov*, Moscow, 1970, p. 97.

57 *Narodnoe khozyaistvo (1980)*, p. 112; E. R. Agaev and V. V. Boldyreva, *Sel'skii vrachebnyi uchastok*, Moscow, 1975, p. 140.

58 *Krest'yanka*, 8, 1980, p. 11. For examples of the two-shift system in operation see Markova, p. 47; *Krest'yanka*, 9, 1979, p. 3; 1, 1981, p. 11; and 6, 1982, p. 2.

59 *Krest'yanka*, 1, 1981, p. 11; and 6, 1982, p. 2.

60 A. Ya. Zotov, 'Ispol'zovanie truda zhenshchin v kolkhozakh BSSR', in Lushchitskii, pp. 159–66; *Krest'yanka*, 2, 1981, p. 11; interview with officials of 'Gastello' collective farm.

61 *Sel'skaya zhizn'*, 24 October 1979, p. 2.

62 *Krest'yanka*, 11, 1982, p. 9. See also Markova, p. 47.

63 *Sel'skaya zhizn'*, 24 October 1979, p. 2.
64 *Krest'yanka*, 1, 1982, pp. 20–1.
65 *Ibid.*, 5, 1976, pp. 14–15.
66 *Ibid.*, 1, 1981, p. 11; P. S. Shelest, *Odna sel'skaya sem'ya – shtrikhi k sotsial' nomu portretu sel'skogo rabochego 70-kh gg.*, Moscow, 1972, pp. 131–2; Zotov, pp. 166–7.
67 Fedorova, p. 62; Staroverov (1978), p. 236.
68 *Krest'yanka*, 6, 1982, p. 28; Volynkina, p. 57.
69 *Sotsiologicheskie issledovaniya*, 3, 1976, p. 60.
70 *Krest'yanka*, 1, 1981, p. 3.
71 *Ibid.*, 1, 1980, p. 13.
72 *Ibid.*, 1, 1980, p. 13; 6, 1981, p. 19; and 4, 1982, p. 18.
73 *Ibid.*, 9, 1982, p. 5; 4, 1980, pp. 24–5; and 4, 1981, p. 28; *Sel'skaya zhizn'*, 15 February 1980, p. 1.
74 *Krest'yanka*, 1, 1983, p. 35.
75 Erem'yan, p. 194; Protasevich, p. 169; Rusanov, p. 92; Fedorova, p. 59.
76 Rusanov, pp. 90–1.
77 Agaev and Boldyreva, p. 140; *Krest'yanka*, 10, 1976, p. 20; and 10, 1980, p. 26.
78 Volynkina, p. 63; Staroverov (1978), p. 235; Lyashenko, p. 148; *Sel'skaya molodezh' Yakutii*, pp. 25–30; *Krest'yanka*, 3, 1976, p. 5.
79 Kolbanovskii, p. 101.
80 *Sel'skaya zhizn'*, 30 July 1980, p. 3.
81 *Ibid.*, 20 November 1979, p. 4. See also *Krest'yanka*, 8, 1980, p. 11; 2, 1978, p. 6; and 12, 1977, p. 12.
82 *Krest'yanka*, 1, 1983, p. 8; and 8, 1980, p. 11; *Sovetskaya Rossiya*, 24 August 1982, p. 2; Z. I. Monich, V. G. Izokh and I. V. Prudnik, *Rabochii klass v strukture sel'skogo naseleniya*, Minsk, 1975, p. 86.
83 *Krest'yanka*, 10, 1981, p. 7; and 8, 1982, p. 1.
84 See, for example, *Sel'skaya zhizn'*, 20 November 1979, p. 4; *Krest'yanka*, 5, 1976, pp. 14–15; and 2, 1976, pp. 10–11.
85 *Itogi … 1970*, Vol. vi, Tables 18–33.
86 *Krest'yanka*, 12, 1978, p. 4; 11, 1983, p. 5; 10, 1981, p. 7; and 3, 1981, p. 13.
87 Sultanova, pp. 82, 95.
88 *Itogi … 1970*, Vol. vi, Table 2.
89 *Ibid.*, Vol. v, Table 9, and Vol. vi, Table 18; *Chislennost' i sostav naseleniya SSSR po dannym Vsesoyuznoi perepisi naseleniya 1979 goda*, Moscow, 1984, p. 151.
90 *Sel'skoe khozyaistvo SSSR*, Moscow, 1971, p. 471.
91 Monich, Izokh and Prudnik, p. 96.
92 Zagrebel'nyi, p. 61; Anokhina and Shmeleva, pp. 59–60.
93 *Sel'skoe khozyaistvo SSSR*, p. 470.
94 Markova, p. 43; Fedorova, p. 61; Sultanova, p. 58.
95 V. D. Patrushev (ed.), *Byudzhet vremeni sel'skogo naseleniya*, Moscow, 1979, p. 108; Markova, p. 43; Zagrebel'nyi, p. 61.
96 R. V. Grebennikov, *Problemy kul'tury sovremennogo sela*, Minsk, 1973, pp. 61–3; *Sotsiologicheskie issledovaniya*, 3, 1976, p. 60.
97 Lyashenko, pp. 149–51; Volynkina, p. 69; Kolbanovskii, pp. 96–7.

98 Lyashenko, pp. 149–51; I. M. Slepenkov and B. V. Knyazev, *Rural Youth Today*, Newtonville, 1977, pp. 22–3; T. Levykin, *Sel'skaya molodezh' – sotsiologicheskii ocherk*, Moscow, 1970, p. 23; Zagrebel'nyi, p. 93.

99 *Krest'yanka*, 4, 1981, p. 19; Fedorova, p. 58.

100 Allott (1985), p. 184.

101 *Krest'yanka*, 8, 1978, p. 11.

102 *Ibid.*, 4, 1980, p. 15; 4, 1981, p. 14; *Sel'skaya zhizn'*, 3 July 1980, p. 3.

103 *Krest'yanka*, 10, 1980, p. 13; and 11, 1976, p. 20.

104 Allott (1985), p. 185.

105 *Krest'yanka*, 7, 1975, p. 5; 8, 1978, p. 11; and 10, 1980, pp. 13–14.

106 *Ibid.*, 1, 1980, p. 29.

107 *Krest'yanka*, 3, 1980, p. 10; and 1, 1983, pp. 16–18; *Sel'skaya zhizn'*, 13 October 1979, p. 4.

108 *Sel'skaya zhizn'*, 13 January 1980, p. 3.

109 M. S. Bednyi, *Prodolzhitel'nost' zhizni v gorodakh i selakh*, Moscow, 1976, p. 34; Rusanov, pp. 40, 205–11.

110 *Itogi … 1970*, Vol. v, Tables 12–27.

111 Monich, Izokh and Prudnik, p. 41.

112 *Ibid.*, pp. 44, 50–3, 82.

113 Zagrebel'nyi, p. 84; Volynkina, p. 116.

114 Perevedentsev, pp. 72, 75.

115 *Pravda*, 1 June 1975, p. 2.

116 *Ibid.*, 2 November 1982, p. 2.

117 *Nauchno-tekhnicheskii progress i sotsial'nye izmeneniya na sele*, Minsk, 1972, p. 60.

118 *Sel'skaya zhizn'*, 23 August 1979, p. 4.

119 *Ibid.*, 20 November 1979, p. 4.

120 Z. I. Monich, *Intelligentsiya v strukture sel'skogo naseleniya*, Minsk, 1971, pp. 84–5.

121 *Itogi … 1970*, Vol. vi, Table 18; *Vestnik statistiki*, 1, 1981, pp. 72–3.

122 P. A. Zhil'tsov, *Vospitatel'naya rabota v sel'skoi shkole*, Moscow, 1980, p. 58.

123 Lushchitskii, p. 144.

124 Zhil'tsov, pp. 52–5.

125 *Krest'yanka*, 6, 1980, p. 26; and 10, 1980, p. 32.

126 Monich, p. 138; *Sovetskaya Rossiya*, 5 July 1977, p. 4.

127 Lushchitskii, p. 145; L. G. Borisova 'Ustoichivost' uchitel'skikh kadrov sela', in Zaslavskaya and Kalmyk (1972), p. 185.

128 Borisova, p. 185; Monich, p. 160.

129 Michael Ryan, *The Organisation of Soviet Medical Care*, London, 1978, p. 37; 37; Monich, pp. 76–7; N. P. Frolov (ed.), *Naselenie i trudovye resursy Moldavskoi SSR*, Kishinev, 1979, p. 231; N. A. Shlapak, 'Zhiznennye plany sel'skoi molodezhi i ikh realizatsiya', candidate degree dissertation abstract, Sverdlovsk, 1967, p. 15.

130 Monich, p. 77; Ryan, pp. 70–6; *Krest'yanka*, 2, 1983, p. 16.

131 *Current Digest of the Soviet Press*, Vol. xxiv, 34, p. 8; Frolov, p. 231.

132 Monich, p. 129.

133 *Sel'skaya nov'*, 4, 1979, p. 26; Monich, pp. 78, 130–1.

134 Monich, p. 130.

135 *Sel'skaya nov'*, 4, 1979, p. 26.
136 *Ibid.*, 4, 1979, p. 26.
137 Borisova, p. 183; A. Shenderetska, 'Uchitel'skaya sem'ya (sotsial'no-demograficheskii analiz)', in *Sem'ya segodnya*, Moscow, 1979, p. 76.
138 Shenderetska, p. 76.
139 *Sel'skaya intelligentsiya i ee rol' v usloviyakh razvitogo sotsializma*, Moscow, 1979, p. 112.
140 *Narodnoe khozyaistvo (1980)*, pp. 285, 287.
141 *Ibid.*
142 *Itogi ... 1970*, Vol. VI, Tables 18-33.
143 *Sel'skaya intelligentsiya ...*, p. 48; *Current Digest of the Soviet Press*, Vol. XXVI, 22, p. 21.
144 Sh. M. Muradov, 'Zhenskii trud i voprosy ego ratsional'nogo ispol'zovaniya v sel'skom khozyaistve Azerbaidzhanskoi SSR', candidate degree dissertation abstract, Baku, 1965, p. 19.
145 Staroverov (1978), p. 264.
146 Monich, p. 87.
147 *Itogi ... 1970*, Vol. VI, Tables 19-33.
148 *Krest'yanka*, 11, 1982, p. 3; Monich, p. 86.
149 *Krest'yanka*, 11, 1981, p. 25; Monich, p. 89.
150 Monich, pp. 88-9.
151 *Krest'yanka*, 11, 1981, p. 24.
152 *Ibid.*, 11, 1981, p. 25.
153 *Ibid.*, 11, 1982, p. 3.
154 See Hedlund, pp. 97, 112; Gail Warshofsky Lapidus, *Women in Soviet Society: Equality, Development and Social Change*, London 1978, p. 227, and Chapter 3 below, 'Politics'.
155 *Krest'yanka*, 1, 1977, p. 11; 1, 1981, p. 5; and 11, 1981, p. 24.
156 *Izvestiya*, 26 December 1961, p. 4.
157 *Krest'yanka*, 11, 1981, p. 25.
158 Yu. N. Tarasov (ed.), *Professional'naya orientatsiya sel'skoi molodezhi*, Moscow, 1973, pp. 66, 69.
159 *Current Digest of the Soviet Press*, Vol. XXVIII, 49, p. 5. See also T. I. Zaslavskaya and V. A. Kalmyk (eds.), *Sovremennaya sibirskaya derevnya: nekotorye problemy sotsial'nogo razvitiya*, Novosibirsk, 1975, Vol. I, pp. 49, 59-60.
160 Kolbanovskii, p. 189; Levykin, p. 134.
161 E. V. Chekotovskii, 'Statistiko-ekonomicheskoe izuchenie zhenskikh trudovykh resursov kolkhozov', candidate degree dissertation abstract, Kiev, 1973, p. 10. See also Zagrebel'nyi, pp. 93-4.
162 N. P. Demyakh, G. M. Grinberg and N. M. Sapozhnikov, 'Proizvodstvennaya deyatel'nost' zhenshchin v sel'skom khozyaistve i sem'ya', in Lushchitskii, p. 178; L. V. Ostapenko, 'The Effect of Woman's New Production Role on her Position in the Family', *Soviet Sociology*, 12, no. 4, Spring 1974, p. 93.
163 Zagrebel'nyi, p. 100.
164 *Krest'yanka*, 8, 1979, p. 20.
165 *Ibid.*, 2, 1980, p. 27.

166 *Sel'skaya zhizn'*, 2 August 1979, p. 3.
167 *Krest'yanka*, 1, 1980, p. 14.
168 See, for example, *ibid.*, 2, 1983, p. 11.
169 *Ibid.*, 10, 1982. p. 21.

2. WOMEN IN THE RURAL FAMILY

1 *Narodnoe khozyaistvo (1980)*, pp. 32–3.
2 Perevedentsev, p. 15.
3 V. T. Kolokol'nikov, 'Marital and Family Relations among the Collective Farm Peasantry (Brest and Grodno Oblasts, Belorussia)', *Soviet Sociology*, Winter 1977–8, pp. 22–3; N. R. Kas'yanov, 'Nravstvenno-psikhologicheskie osobennosti brachno-semeinykh otnoshenii krest'-yanstva', *Uchenye zapiski Kurskogo pedagogicheskogo instituta*, 75, no. 1, 1971, p. 128.
4 Allott (1985), p. 190.
5 *Krest'yanka*, 9, 1981, pp. 28–9; 1, 1982, p. 28; and 10, 1982, p. 27.
6 Allott (1985), pp. 190–1.
7 *Krest'yanka*, 10, 1982, p. 27; 1, 1983, p. 28; and 8, 1981, p. 32.
8 Zhil'tsov, p. 50.
9 *Krest'yanka*, 7, 1981, p. 27.
10 Yu. G. Serebryakov, *Kul'tura i byt sovremennoi derevni*, Cheboksary, 1977, p. 61.
11 *Krest'yanka*, 11, 1980, p. 34; *Sel'skaya zhizn'*, 16 April 1980, p. 4.
12 *Sel'skaya zhizn'*, 16 April 1980, p. 4.
13 N. Bairamsakhatov, 'Preodolenie perezhitkov islama v protsesse sotsialisticheskogo preobrazovaniya byta sel'skogo naseleniya', candidate degree dissertation abstract, Moscow, 1968, pp. 11–12; *Pravda*, 15 October 1975, p. 4.
14 *Literaturnaya gazeta*, 28 May 1975, p. 12; *Pravda*, 14 March 1975, p. 3.
15 M. G. Pankratova, *Sel'skaya sem'ya v SSSR i nekotorye problemy planirovaniya*, Moscow, 1970, p. 2.
16 *Literaturnaya gazeta*, 28 June 1978, p. 10; *Nauchno-tekhnicheskii ...*, p. 186.
17 *Itogi ... 1970*, Vol. vii, Table 27; *Vestnik statistiki*, 12, 1980, p. 59.
18 *Sem'ya segodnya*, p. 47; *Itogi ... 1970*, Vol. vii, Table 34.
19 Arutyunyan and Kakhk, pp. 50, 119; Serebryakov, p. 61.
20 Anokhina and Shmeleva, pp. 187, 195; *Krest'yanka*, 6, 1982, p. 1 (supplement).
21 *Krest'yanka*, 9, 1982, p. 24; and 11, 1982, p. 34.
22 *Sel'skaya zhizn'*, 21 December 1979, p. 4.
23 Grebennikov, pp. 73–4.
24 *Sel'skaya nov'*, 5, 1981, p. 33.
25 A. G. Kharchev and Z. A. Yankova (eds.), *Sotsial'nye issledovaniya*, Moscow, 1971, Vol. vii, pp. 38–9, 42. See also R. M. Gorbacheva, 'Formirovanie novykh chert byta kolkhoznogo krest'yanstva', candidate degree dissertation abstract, Moscow, 1967, p. 19, and V. I. Bondarchik (ed.), *Izmeneniya v bytu i kul'ture sel'skogo naseleniya Belorussii*, Minsk, 1976, p. 52.

26 Anokhina and Shmeleva, pp. 189–90.
27 Kas'yanov (1971), p. 127; *Itogi ... 1970*, Vol. VII, Table 24.
28 See, for example, Bondarchik, pp. 50–3.
29 M. G. Pankratova, *Sel'skaya sem'ya v SSSR – problemy i perspektivy*, Moscow, 1974, p. 22; Bondarchik, pp. 48–9; *Sem'ya segodnya*, p. 18. See also Chapter 3 below, 'Education'.
30 *Current Digest of the Soviet Press*, Vol. XXIX, 26, p. 10.
31 Lushchitskii, p. 6.
32 Perevedentsev, p. 31; *Zhurnalist*, 1, 1977, pp. 54–6.
33 *Literaturnaya gazeta*, 17 January 1979, p. 12.
34 *Krest'yanka*, 8, 1977, p. 11; Ivanova, p. 70; N. A. Medvedev, *Razvitie obshchestvennykh otnoshenii v sovetskoi derevne na sovremennom etape*, Moscow, 1976, p. 129.
35 *Pravda*, 9 January 1975, p. 3.
36 *Krest'yanka*, 2, 1981, p. 9; *Sel'skaya zhizn'*, 31 August 1979, p. 3.
37 Perevedentsev, pp. 76–8; *Literaturnaya gazeta*, 17 January 1979, p. 12.
38 Guzel Amalrik, *Memories of a Tatar Childhood*, London, 1979, p. 146.
39 *Vestnik statistiki*, 5, 1983, p. 80.
40 Alix Holt, 'Domestic Labour and Soviet Society', in Jenny Brine, Maureen Perrie, Andrew Sutton (eds.), *Home, School and Leisure in the Soviet Union*, London, 1980, pp. 27–8.
41 A. M. Krylov, A. I. Slutskii and A. A. Khagurov, 'Analiz byudzheta vremeni kolkhoznikov i rabochikh sovkhoza kak sposob izucheniya sotsial'nykh problem upravleniya kolkhoznym kollektivom', *Nauchnye trudy Kubanskogo universiteta*, 205, 1976, p. 155; Patrushev, p. 134; Markova, pp. 52, 62.
42 *Krest'yanka*, 3, 1977, p. 25; and 10, 1980, p. 26.
43 Krylov, Slutskii and Khagurov, pp. 150–3; Markova, p. 62.
44 *Vestnik statistiki*, 5, 1983, p. 80.
45 Kolbanovskii, p. 203; *Vestnik statistiki*, 5, 1983, p. 80.
46 *Nauchno-tekhnicheskii ...*, p. 200; *Pravda*, 9 January 1975, p. 3.
47 Markova, p. 52; V. M. Zhelezovskaya, 'Nekotorye izmeneniya v polozhenii zhenshchin-kolkhoznits v protsesse preodoleniya kul'turno-bytovykh razlichii mezhdu gorodom i derevnei', *Nauchnye trudy Kubanskogo universiteta*, 167, 1973, p. 149.
48 Patrushev, p. 130.
49 *Krest'yanka*, 7, 1980, p. 26; 2, 1982, p. 27; and 6, 1981, p. 20; *Pravda*, 16 January 1975, p. 2; *Nauchno-tekhnicheskii ...*, p. 201.
50 Ivanova, p. 63.
51 Zhelezovskaya, pp. 148–9; *Krest'yanka*, 2, 1980, p. 28; and 4, 1980, p. 29.
52 A. D. Afonin, 'Vliyanie lichnogo podsobnogo khozyaistva kolkhoznikov na razvitie nekotorye sotsial'nykh protsessov v derevne', *Trudy Gor'kogo politekhnicheskogo instituta*, 28, no. 4, 1972, p. 51; *Literaturnaya gazeta*, 24 August 1977, p. 11.
53 V. A. Belyanov, *Lichnoe podsobnoe khozyaistvo pri sotsializme*, Moscow, 1970, p. 3; *Narodnoe khozyaistvo SSSR v 1975 g.*, Moscow, 1984, p. 258.
54 M. Makeenko, 'Ekonomicheskaya rol' lichnogo podsobnogo khozyaistva', *Voprosy ekonomiki*, 10, 1966, pp. 63–4.
55 Makeenko, pp. 63–4.

56 See, for example, *Sel'skaya zhizn'*, 28 October 1979, p. 3; *Krest'yanka*, 2, 1981, p. 9.

57 *Krest'yanka*, 5, 1981, p. 14; *Literaturnaya gazeta*, 28 June 1978, p. 10.

58 *Krest'yanka*, 5, 1981, p. 14; Patrushev, p. 122.

59 Zagrebel'nyi, p. 90; *Ekonomika sel'skogo khozyaistva*, 2, 1978, p. 77; *Problemy derevni* ..., Vol. II, p. 105.

60 Makeenko, p. 63; V. Ya. Churakov, *Aktual'nye problemy ispol'zovaniya trudovykh resursov sela*, Moscow, 1972, p. 223; Fedorova, p. 63; *Problemy derevni* ..., Vol. II, p. 105.

61 Patrushev, pp. 129, 132–3. See also Markova, p. 62.

62 Patrushev, pp. 129–30.

63 Yu. V. Arutyunyan, *Sotsial'naya struktura sel'skogo naseleniya SSSR*, Moscow, 1971, p. 216.

64 Volynkina, p. 79.

65 *Itogi ... 1970*, Vol. II, Table 3; *Narodnoe obrazovanie, nauka i kul'tura v SSSR*, Moscow, 1977, pp. 120–1; *Sel'skaya zhizn'*, 28 May 1980, p. 3.

66 *Sel'skaya zhizn'*, 28 April 1977, p. 2, and 28 May 1980, p. 3; *Sel'skoe khozyaistvo SSSR*, p. 676.

67 Grebennikov, p. 79.

68 *Sel'skaya zhizn'*, 28 May 1980, p. 3; interview with editorial board of *Rabotnitsa i syalyanka*, Minsk, 20 January 1981.

69 *Krest'yanka*, 6, 1980, p. 26; 4, 1980, p. 26; and 12, 1980, p. 27.

70 *Ibid.*, 12, 1980, p. 27; 2, 1979, p. 27; and 12, 1979, p. 19; N. S. Tonaevskaya, *Rabochie sovkhozov Zapadnoi Sibiri*, Novosibirsk, 1978, p. 86.

71 G. G. Belyaeva, 'K voprosu vliyaniya nekotorykh semeinykh faktorov na sostoyanie zdorov'ya detei i podrostkov v sel'skoi mestnosti', *Zdravookhranenie Rossiiskoi Federatsii*, 7, 1978, p. 20; *Sem'ya segodnya*, p. 23.

72 *Krest'yanka*, 7, 1977, p. 27.

73 *Ibid.*, 2, 1983, p. 12; and 8, 1979, p. 22; *Sel'skaya zhizn'*, 28 May 1980, p. 3; Zagrebel'nyi, p. 121.

74 *Sel'skaya zhizn'*, 28 May 1980, p. 3; *Izvestiya*, 25 February 1975, p. 5; *Krest'yanka*, 8, 1975, p. 14; and 4, 1980, p. 25.

75 Interview with editorial board of *Rabotnitsa i syalyanka*, Minsk, 1981.

76 Markova, p. 68; *Zdravookhranenie Rossiiskoi Federatsii*, 2, 1980, pp. 36–7; interview with Maya Grigorevna Pankratova, Moscow, 28 November 1980.

77 Z. A. Yankova and V. D. Shapiro (eds.), *Vzaimootnoshenie pokolenii v sem'e*, Moscow, 1977, p. 159.

78 Markova, p. 11; Yankova and Shapiro, p. 159; Zagrebel'nyi, p. 167.

79 Allott (1985), p. 193.

80 Serebryakov, p. 68.

81 *Current Digest of the Soviet Press*, Vol. XXVII, 30, p. 21.

82 T. D. Ermolenkova, 'Izmenenie sotsial'nogo polozheniya zhenschiny-krest'yanki v protsesse stroitel'stva sotsializma', *Vestnik Belorusskogo Gosudarstvennogo universiteta imeni V. I. Lenina*, 3, no. 1, 1973, p. 56.

83 Serebryakov, p. 68.

84 Kas'yanov (1971), p. 128; Anokhina and Shmeleva, pp. 196–7; Serebryakov, p. 68.

85 *Current Digest of the Soviet Press*, Vol. XXIX, 29, p. 9.

86   *Programma KPSS*, Moscow, 1974, p. 97; *Krest'yanka*, 10, 1980, p. 26.
87   Yankova and Shapiro, p. 157.
88   Lynne Attwood, 'The New Soviet Man and Woman – Soviet Views on Psychological Sex Differences', in Holland, pp. 54–77.
89   Larisa Kuznetsova, *Zhenshchina na rabote i doma*, Moscow, 1980, p. 179.
90   *Krest'yanka*, 2, 1980, p. 6; *Soviet Union*, 9, 1978, p. 46.
91   *Krest'yanka*, 3, 1983, pp. 5, 1 (supplement).
92   *Ibid.*, p. 1 (supplement); *Current Digest of the Soviet Press*, Vol. xxx, 8, pp. 14–15; *Krest'yanka*, 9, 1982, p. 6 (supplement).
93   V. L. Bilshai, *Reshenie zhenskogo voprosa v SSSR*, Moscow, 1956, p. 3.
94   Mary Buckley, 'Soviet Interpretations of the Woman Question', in Holland, pp. 24–53.
95   Yankova and Shapiro, p. 157.
96   Zagrebel'nyi, p. 167.
97   Compare, for example, the views expressed by N. M. Shishkan in her unpublished doctoral dissertation abstract, 'Sotsial'no-ekonomicheskie problemy zhenskogo truda v usloviyakh razvitogo sotsializma', Moscow, 1978, with those in her subsequently published book, *Sotsial'no-ekonomicheskie problemy zhenskogo truda*, Moscow, 1980.
98   V. V. Boiko, *Malodetnaya sem'ya*, Moscow, 1980, p. 204. See also Lushchitskii, p. 47.
99   See Elisabeth Croll, *Socialist Development Experience: Women in Rural Production and Reproduction in the Soviet Union, China, Cuba and Tanzania*, IDS Discussion Paper, Brighton, September 1979, pp. 31–2.
100 Perevedentsev, p. 11.
101 Interviews with Vladimir Olegovich Rukavishnikov, Minsk, 31 October 1980, and Yuri Vartanovich Arutyunyan, Moscow, 25 November 1980.
102 *Pravda*, 31 March 1981, p. 1.
103 *Krest'yanka*, 2, 1981, p. 9. See also *ibid.* 6, 1981, p. 3; *Sel'skaya zhizn'*, 25 November 1979, p. 1.
104 Ermolenkova (1973, 'Izmenenie'), p. 54.
105 T. E. Chumakova, *Trud i byt zhenshchin*, Minsk, 1978, pp. 40–6, 75–6; *Krest'yanka*, 4, 1976, p. 27; and 9, 1981, p. 25.
106 V. A. Belova, *Chislo detei v sem'e*, Moscow, 1975, pp. 127, 133; *Sotsial'no-demograficheskie issledovaniya sem'i v respublikakh Sovetskoi Pribaltiki*, Riga, 1980, p. 88; O. Ata-Mirzaev, 'Mnogodetnaya zhenshchina: sotsial'no-demograficheskii analiz', in *Zhenshchiny na rabote i doma*, Moscow, 1978, p. 29.
107 *Molodaya sem'ya*, Moscow, 1977, pp. 93–5.
108 V. L. Krasnenkov, 'Nekotorye sotsial'no-gigienicheskie aspekty aborta sredi zhenshchin Kalininskoi oblasti', *Sovetskoe zdravookhranenie*, 5, 1973, p. 22; Lushchitskii, p. 111.
109 *Krest'yanka*, 4, 1983, p. 30.
110 L. F. Filyukova, *Sel'skaya sem'ya*, Minsk, 1976, p. 137; Krasnenkov, p. 21.
111 Sadvokasova, p. 118.
112 *Krest'yanka*, 1, 1978, p. 31; 4, 1983, p. 30; 2, 1982, p. 27; and 8 1981, p. 26.
113 *Ibid.*, 1, 1978, p. 31.
114 *Zdravookhranenie Rossiiskoi Federatsii*, 2, 1980, pp. 36–7; V. A. Belova and

L. E. Darskii, *Statistika mnenii v izuchenii rozhdaemosti*, Moscow, 1972, p. 137; C. D. Davies and M. S. Feshbach, *Rising Infant Mortality in the USSR in the 1970s*, United States Department of Commerce, Bureau of the Census, P–95, no. 74, Washington DC, 1980, p. 17; Sadvokasova, p. 222.

115 *Krest'yanka*, 1, 1978, p. 31.

116 Lushchitskii, p. 109; A. I. Markov, 'Sotsial'no-gigienicheskie aspekty aborta zhenshchin v Tambovskom raione Amurskoi oblasti', *Sovetskoe zdravookhranenie*, 7, 1973, pp. 44–5; Krasnenkov, p. 23.

117 Jo Peers, 'Workers by Hand and Womb – Soviet Women and the Demographic Crisis', in Holland, p. 139.

118 *Sel'skaya zhizn'*, 15 August 1979, p. 4. See also *ibid.*, 3 November 1979, p. 4, and 14 September 1979, p. 4.

119 *Sel'skaya nov'*, 1, 1980, p. 34; *Sel'skaya zhizn'*, 3 November 1979, p. 4.

120 *Sel'skaya zhizn'*, 14 October 1979, p. 1.

121 *Ibid.*, 7 March 1980, p. 3. See also *ibid.*, 8 March 1980, p. 2; *Krest'yanka*, 3, 1983, p. 5.

122 *Krest'yanka*, 4, 1982, p. 30.

123 Allott (1985), p. 195. See also *Krest'yanka*, 1, 1983, p. 32, for the Chursina interview.

124 Allott (1985), p. 195.

125 *Sel'skaya zhizn'*, 21 September 1979, p. 4; *Krest'yanka*, 1, 1983, p. 1 (supplement).

126 Allott (1985), pp. 195–6.

127 *Krest'yanka*, 1, 1983, p. 1 (supplement).

128 *Sel'skaya zhizn'*, 6 December 1979, p. 4.

129 Allott (1985), p. 196.

130 *Ibid.*, p. 197.

131 *Krest'yanka*, 1, 1983, p. 1 (supplement).

132 Rusanov, pp. 72–3; Zagrebel'nyi, p. 101.

133 Shishkan (1978), p. 19; Yu. A. Korolev, *Brak i razvod: sovremennye tendentsii*, Moscow, 1978, p. 121; Perevedentsev, p. 32.

134 See, for example, A. I. Stupko and S. V. Sokoleva, *Tebe-mal'chik, yunosha*, Kiev, 1981, pp. 46–7.

135 Allott (1985), p. 196.

136 *Krest'yanka*, 3, 1982, p. 26.

137 P. Sedugin, *New Soviet Legislation on Marriage and the Family*, Moscow, 1973, pp. 53–6.

138 A. G. Volkov, 'Sem'ya kak faktor izmeneniya demograficheskoi situatsii', *Sotsiologicheskie issledovaniya*, 1, 1981, p. 38.

139 *Ibid.*, p. 38; Korolev, p. 187; *Narodnoe khozyaistvo (1980)*, p. 7.

140 Volkov (1981), p. 38.

141 *Vestnik statistiki*, 12, 1980, p. 58.

142 Korolev, p. 121; Kolbanovskii, pp. 215–16; Serebryakov, p. 62; Kolokol'-nikov, p. 27; Zagrebel'nyi, p. 171.

143 Korolev, p. 121.

144 Serebryakov, p. 69.

145 Pankratova (1974), pp. 14, 58; *Sel'skaya zhizn'*, 27 March 1980, p. 3, and 15 July 1980, p. 4.

146 *Sel'skaya zhizn'*, 15 July 1980, p. 4, 3 August 1979, p. 3, 10 January 1980, p. 3, and 8 January 1980, p. 4.
147 *Ibid.*, 16 April 1980, p. 4, and 18 June 1980, p. 4.
148 Arutyunyan and Kakhk, p. 56; Lushchitskii, p. 109.
149 Amalrik, pp. 147–8.
150 *Krest'yanka*, 12, 1979, p. 20; *Sel'skaya zhizn'*, 8 January 1980, p. 4.
151 *Krest'yanka*, 11, 1981, p. 11.
152 A. G. Kharchev, 'O putyakh dal'neishego ukrepleniya sem'i v SSSR', in *Sotsial'nye issledovaniya. Sbornik statei*, Moscow, 1965, p. 168.
153 *Krest'yanka*, 8, 1980, p. 24; and 12, 1979, pp. 19–21.
154 *Ibid.*, 7, 1975, p. 28; and 12, 1976, p. 21; *Sel'skaya zhizn'*, 8 January 1980, p. 4. The figures on wage rates given in the footnote are taken from *Narodnoe khozyaistvo (1980)*, pp. 254, 364.
155 *Krest'yanka*, 7, 1975, p. 28; *Current Digest of the Soviet Press*, Vol. xxvii, 34, p. 19.
156 See, for example, *Krest'yanka*, 7, 1975, p. 28.
157 *Ibid.*, 5, 1980, p. 29. See also *ibid.*, 6, 1980, p. 26.
158 *Ibid.*, 6, 1981, p. 28.
159 *Ibid.*, 9, 1981, p. 28.
160 *Ibid.*, 9, 1981, p. 28.
161 *Ibid.*, 4, 1980, p. 26; Pankratova (1974), p. 14.
162 *Krest'yanka*, 10, 1981, p. 27.
163 *Ibid.*, 1, 1982, p. 29.
164 Allott (1985), p. 199.
165 *Krest'yanka*, 3, 1982, pp. 27–8.
166 *Ibid.*, 11, 1982, p. 29.
167 Bernice Madison, 'Social Services for Women: Problems and Priorities', in Dorothy Atkinson, Alexander Dallin and Gail Lapidus (eds.), *Women in Russia*, Hassocks, Sussex, 1978, p. 134; *Krest'yanka*, 9, 1982, p. 34; *Sel'skaya zhizn'*, 15 September 1979, p. 4.
168 Kolokol'nikov, p. 30; L. V. Chuiko, *Braki i razvody*, Moscow, 1975, p. 135; Frolov, p. 35.
169 Arutyunyan and Kakhk, p. 51.
170 *Krest'yanka*, 1, 1982, p. 29.

3. WOMEN'S ROLES IN RURAL CULTURE

1 *Vestnik statistiki*, 6, 1980, p. 51.
2 See Elisabeth Koutaissoff, 'Secondary Education for All in a Forward-Looking Society', in Brine, Perrie and Sutton, pp. 75–6; Susan Jacoby, *Inside Soviet Schools*, New York, 1974, p. 101.
3 Borisova, p. 180; Zhil'tsov, p. 35; *Sel'skaya zhizn'*, 2 November 1979, p. 3.
4 Zaslavskaya and Kalmyk (1975), Vol. ii, p. 43.
5 Monich, p. 73; Borisova, p. 181; Jacoby, p. 150; *Current Digest of the Soviet Press*, Vol. xxv, 48, p. 17.
6 *Pravda*, 4 December 1981, p. 3.
7 *Ibid.*, 6 July 1973, p. 1.
8 R. V. Ryvkina, *Obraz zhizni sel'skogo naseleniya*, Novosibirsk, 1979, pp.

169–70, 205; Zaslavskaya and Kalmyk (1975), Vol. 1, p. 92; Markova, p. 39; Volynkina, p. 68.

9 Tarasov, pp. 16, 40; Frolov, p. 236; Kolbanovskii, pp. 184–5.

10 Tarasov, pp. 24, 31, 37, 39; Belikova, pp. 81–2; Argunov and Isakova, p. 58.

11 F. P. Filippov, 'Rol' vysshei shkoly v izmenenii sotsial'noi struktury sovetskogo obshchestva (Itogi vsesoyuznogo issledovaniya)', *Sotsiologicheskie issledovaniya*, 2, 1977, pp. 49–50; *Sel'skaya intelligentsia* ..., pp. 110–11.

12 *Sel'skaya intelligentsiya* ..., pp. 110–11.

13 *Krest'yanka*, 3, 1982, p. 5.

14 Levykin, pp. 131–2.

15 Pankratova (1974), p. 57; Markova, p. 13; Zaslavskaya and Kalmyk (1975), Vol. 11, pp. 55–8.

16 See Jenny Brine, 'Reading as a Leisure Pursuit in the USSR', in Brine, Perrie and Sutton, pp. 241–2.

17 L. A. Gordon and E. V. Klopov, *Chelovek posle raboty; sotsial'nye problemy byta*, Moscow, 1972, p. 115; Bondarchik, p. 101; Shelest, p. 15; Patrushev, pp. 156–7.

18 T. D. Ermolenkova, 'Preodolenie ostatkov bytovogo neravenstva zhenshchiny-kolkhoznitsy v protsesse stroitel'stva kommunizma', candidate degree dissertation abstract, Minsk, 1973, p. 13; Patrushev, p. 155.

19 Markova, p. 7.

20 *Ibid.*, p. 7; Patrushev, p. 156.

21 Markova, p. 8.

22 *Literaturnaya gazeta*, 17 January 1979, p. 12.

23 B. Grushin, *Svobodnoe vremya: aktual'nye problemy*, Moscow, 1967, pp. 57–61.

24 Patrushev, p. 183.

25 E. Mikhailova, 'Sel'skii telezritel'': shtrikhi k sotsiologicheskomu portretu', *Sovetskoe radio i televidenie*, 8, 1970, pp. 8–11.

26 Ivanova, p. 76; *Sel'skaya zhizn'*, 9 January 1980, p. 3; *Krest'yanka*, 9, 1976, pp. 26–7.

27 L. P. Zinchenko, 'Rol' komsomola, sovetskoi molodezhi v formirovanii novogo byta na sele', candidate degree dissertation abstract, Minsk, 1978, p. 14; interview with editorial board of *Rabotnitsa i syalyanka*, Minsk,1981. See also, Markova p. 123; *Krest'yanka*, 2, 1983, p. 17.

28 *Krest'yanka*, 1, 1983, p. 14.

29 *Ibid.*, 11, 1976, p. 30. See also *Narodnoe khozyaistvo (1975)*, p. 691; V. E. Poletaev (ed.), *Sotsial'nyi oblik kolkhoznoi molodezhi*, Moscow, 1976, p. 108.

30 Markova, p. 121; Kolbanovskii, pp. 165–75.

31 Serebryakov, p. 51; Kolbanovskii, p. 172; M. D. Kartofyanu, *Novyi byt moldavskogo sela*, Kishinev, 1973, p. 112; Patrushev, p. 151.

32 Levykin, pp. 107–8.

33 *Krest'yanka*, 7, 1978, p. 27.

34 Patrushev, p. 163.

35 *Krest'yanka*, 1, 1981, p. 19.

36 *Ibid.*, 2, 1982, pp. 36–7; and 10, 1980, p. 30.

37 Kolokol'nikov, p. 29.
38 Markova, pp. 13–14; *Sovetskaya kul'tura*, 1 March 1977, p. 6.
39 Markova, pp. 9–10; Ermolenkova (1973, dissertation), p. 13.
40 V. N. Mikhailov, 'Dukhovnye potrebnosti sel'skoi molodezhi i problemy kul'tury dosuga', in *Sotsiologiya kul'tury*, Moscow, 1974, Vol. 1, p. 60.
41 *Krest'yanka*, 9, 1980, p. 17; Markova, p. 21.
42 Arutyunyan and Kakhk, p. 59.
43 David E. Powell, *Antireligious Propaganda in the Soviet Union: A Study of Mass Persuasion*, Cambridge, Mass., 1975, pp. 19, 40–2.
44 *Constitution (Fundamental Law) of the Union of Soviet Socialist Republics*, Moscow, 1982, p. 34.
45 Powell, p. 43; Marie Broxup, 'Recent Developments in Soviet Islam', *Religion in Communist Lands*, 11, no. 1, Spring 1983, pp. 31–3.
46 V. D. Kobetskii, *Sotsiologicheskoe izuchenie religioznosti i ateizma*, Leningrad, 1978, pp. 25, 33, 34; *Nauchno-tekhnicheskii* . . ., p. 171: A. V. Losev (ed.), *Sovetskaya derevnya na sovremennom etape*, Voronezh, 1974, p. 325.
47 Kobetskii, pp. 33–4; Kolbanovskii, p. 232; Christel Lane, *Christian Religion in the Soviet Union*, London, 1978, p. 47.
48 Lane (1978), pp. 56, 69, 74; Kolbanovskii, p. 232; Kobetskii, p. 38.
49 Lane (1978), pp. 42, 57, 79; V. G. Pivovarov, 'The Religious Group of Parishioners in the System of a Church Parish', *Soviet Sociology*, 8, no. 3–4, Winter–Spring 1970, p. 287.
50 T. P. Timchenko, *Zhenshchina, religiya, ateizm*, Kiev, 1981, pp. 5, 89.
51 V. A. Rudnev, *Preodolenie religioznykh traditsii*, Leningrad, 1974, p. 8; *Sotsialisticheskaya obryadnost' i formirovanie novogo cheloveka*, Kiev, 1979, p. 67.
52 Kolbanovskii, pp. 244–5; L. A. Anokhina and M. N. Shmeleva, 'Religiozno-bytovye perezhitki u kolkoznogo krest'yanstva i puti ikh preodoleniya', in N. P. Krasnikov (ed.), *Voprosy preodoleniya religioznykh perezhitkov v SSSR*, Moscow–Leningrad, 1966, pp. 118–19; *Nauchno-tekhnicheskii* . . ., p. 171.
53 Kolbanovskii, p. 235; Lane (1978), p. 57.
54 *Sel'skaya zhizn'*, 14 April 1980, p. 4, and 17 June 1980, p. 3.
55 Timchenko, pp. 5, 140.
56 Karl Marx, 'Contribution to the Critique of Hegel's Philosophy of Law. Introduction', in Karl Marx, Frederick Engels, *Collected Works*, London, 1975, Vol. III, p. 175; Timchenko, p. 136; *Current Digest of the Soviet Press*, Vol. XXXIV, 52, p. 14.
57 Losev, p. 337.
58 *Krest'yanka*, 4, 1983, p. 23; Timchenko, p. 84; *Current Digest of the Soviet Press*, Vol. XXXIV, 52, p. 14.
59 M. V. Vagabov, 'Perezhitki islama v otnoshenii k zhenshchine i puti ikh preodoleniya', in Krasnikov, pp. 133–40.
60 *Krest'yanka*, 8, 1980, p. 27.
61 Timchenko, p. 65.
62 *Sel'skaya zhizn'*, 16 July 1980, p. 3; *Krest'yanka*, 6, 1976, p. 23.
63 Powell, pp. 123–6; Timchenko, p. 86.
64 *Current Digest of the Soviet Press*, Vol. XXXIV, 52, pp. 14–15.

65 Zagrebel'nyi, pp. 103–4, 111–12; Ermolenkova (1973, 'Izmenenie'), p. 56; Levykin, p. 65; Slepenkov and Knyazev, p. 67; Pankratova, p. 57.

66 Markova, pp. 85–6; Zagrebel'nyi, pp. 103–4, 112; Patrushev, p. 169.

67 *Pravda*, 21 June 1975, p. 1; *Partiinaya zhizn'*, 14 July 1981, p. 18; *Zhenshchiny v SSSR*, Moscow, 1975, p. 51; Zagrebel'nyi, p. 106.

68 Mervyn Matthews, *Class and Society in Soviet Russia*, London, 1972, P. 220.

69 Zagrebel'nyi, pp. 107, 111, 114–15; interviews with Zinaida Ivanovna Monich, Minsk, 30 October 1980, and M. G. Pankratova, Moscow, 1980.

70 *Bol'shaya sovetskaya entsiklopediya*, 3rd edn, Vol. ix, Moscow, 1972, p. 518; *Krest'yanka*, 10, 1978, p. 23; and 6, 1976, p. 23; *Rabotnitsa*, 11, 1980, pp. 7–8.

71 Vagabov, p. 132; G. P. Vasileva, *Etnograficheskii ocherk uzbekskogo sel'skogo naseleniya*, Moscow, 1969, pp. 210–11.

72 *Krest'yanka*, 2, 1976, p. 24; and 9, 1980, pp. 26–7; *Sel'skaya zhizn'*, 15 February 1980, p. 3, and 8 March 1980, p. 4.

73 *Krest'yanka*, 6, 1976, p. 23.

74 *Ibid.*, 10, 1978, p. 23; 4, 1977, p. 20; 3, 1981, p. 14; 6, 1982, p. 19; and 6, 1976, p. 22.

75 *Ibid.*, 9, 1981, p. 32; 2, 1981, p. 8; 12, 1976, pp. 20, 23; and 9, 1979, p. 21.

76 *Ibid.*, 12, 1976, p. 23; 6, 1976, p. 23; 11, 1980, p. 35; 1, 1981, p. 24; 6, 1982, p. 19; 11, 1977, p. 26; and 12, 1980, p. 29.

77 *Ibid.*, 6, 1982, p. 19; 9, 1976, p. 24; and 12, 1979, p. 20.

78 *Ibid.*, 3, 1976, p. 30; 12, 1979, p. 20; and 8, 1980, p. 24; Zagrebel'nyi, p. 172.

79 *Krest'yanka*, 1, 1976, p. 23; 9, 1976, p. 24; and 11, 1980, p. 35.

80 Bondarchik, p. 85; *Krest'yanka*, 6, 1976, p. 23; and 10, 1978, p. 24; *Sel'skaya zhizn'*, 8 March 1980, p. 4.

81 Interviews with Lidya Frantsevna Filyukova, Minsk, 30 October 1980, and M. G. Pankratova, Moscow, 1980.

82 Bondarchik, p. 85; interview with L. F. Filynkova, Minsk, 1980; *Krest'yanka*, 12, 1986, pp. 8–9.

83 *XXV s"ezd Kommunisticheskoi partii Sovetskogo Soyuza. Stenograficheskii otchet*, Moscow, 1976, Vol. ii, pp. 329–596; *Partiinaya zhizn'*, 14 July 1981, p. 18.

84 Maggie McAndrew, 'The Extent of the Participation of Women in the Soviet Political System', unpublished MA dissertation, University of Essex, 1977, Table vii.

85 *Pravda*, 4 March 1981, p. 2; *XXVI s"ezd Kommunisticheskoi partii Sovetskogo Soyuza. Stenograficheskii otchet*, Moscow, 1981, Vol. iii, pp. 289–523.

86 *Krest'yanka*, 10, 1980, p. 21.

87 Barbara Wolfe Jancar, *Women under Communism*, Baltimore, 1978, p. 212; Yuliya Voznesenskaya, 'The Independent Women's Movement in Russia', *Religion in Communist Lands*, 10, no. 3, Winter 1982, p. 336. See also Alix Holt, 'The First Soviet Feminists', in Holland, pp. 237–65.

88 See, for example, Arutyunyan and Kakhk, p. 55; *Nedelya*, 22, 1977, p. 6.

89 *Krest'yanka*, 6, 1982, pp. 11–12; and 1, 1978, p. 28.

90 *Ibid.*, 6, 1982, p. 12.

91 *Ibid.*, 6, 1982, p. 11.

92 Belova, p. 117.
93 *Current Digest of the Soviet Press*, Vol. XXIX, 29, p. 8.
94 *Literaturnaya gazeta*, 23 July 1966, p. 12; *Ekonomika sel'skogo khozyaistva*, 6, 1978, pp. 85–95; Frolov, p. 172.
95 *Sel'skaya zhizn'*, 20 November 1979, p. 4; Volynkina, p. 45.
96 Volynkina, pp. 99, 108.
97 *Sovetskaya Rossiya*, 24 August 1982, p. 2.
98 V. I. Bovsh and V. D. Laptenok (eds.), *Sotsial'nye izmeneniya v sovremennom sele*, Minsk, 1978, pp. 99–100; Zaslavskaya and Kalmyk (1972), p. 91; Monich, Izokh and Prudnik, p. 177.
99 *Krest'yanka*, 4, 1983, p. 14.
100 *Literaturnaya gazeta*, 12 March 1975, p. 5.
101 *Ibid.*
102 *Molodoi kommunist*, 9, 1977, p. 86.
103 *Krest'yanka*, 4, 1983, p. 15.
104 T. I. Zaslavskaya and I. B. Muchnik, *Sotsial'no-demograficheskoe razvitie sela. Regional'nyi analiz*, Moscow, 1980, pp. 109–11; Volynkina, p. 34.
105 *Literaturnaya gazeta*, 17 January 1979, p. 12; Zaslavskaya and Muchnik, p. 110; *Sel'skaya zhizn'*, 20 November 1979, p. 4.
106 *Krest'yanka*, 12, 1978, p. 5.
107 See, for example, *Sovetskaya Rossiya*, 24 August 1982, p. 2.
108 *Krest'yanka*, 6, 1982, p. 14; *Sovetskaya Rossiya*, 25 August 1982, p. 2.
109 *Krest'yanka*, 1, 1981, p. 29; and 6, 1981, p. 3.
110 *Ibid.*, 8, 1981, p. 18; 12, 1979, p. 15; and 10, 1979, p. 24; *Yunost'* 12, 1977, pp. 13–14; *Sovetskaya Rossiya*, 24 August 1982, p. 2.
111 A. I. Arkhippov, *Osnovnye problemy ratsional'nogo ispol'zovaniya trudovykh resursov v SSSR*, Moscow, 1971, p. 102; *Planovoe khozyaistvo*, 11, 1976, pp. 37–46; Volynkina, p. 34; V. D. Shurygina, *Sotsial'no-ekonomicheskie problemy zhenskogo truda v sel'skom khozyaistve SSSR*, candidate degree dissertation abstract, Leningrad, 1973, p. 12.
112 *Krest'yanka*, 11, 1982, p. 5.
113 Zagrebel'nyi, p. 81.

CONCLUSIONS

1 See, for example, Zagrebel'nyi, p. 4; Chekotovskii, p. 3.
2 Shishkan (1978), p. 20.
3 *Nedelya*, 7–13 June 1982, p. 19.
4 Zagrebel'nyi, pp. 91–2; Arutyunyan and Kakhk, p. 54; Arutyunyan (1971), p. 214; Pankratova (1974), p. 10; Lushchitskii, p. 61; *Literaturnoe obozrenie*, 5 May 1977, p. 51.

Bibliography

SOVIET SOURCES

Agaev, E. R. and Boldyreva, V. V., *Sel'skii vrachebnyi uchastok*, Moscow 1975.
Ambrosov, A. A. and Staroverov, V. I., 'Sotsial'nyi oblik sovremennogo kolkhoznogo krest'yanstva', *Sotsiologicheskie issledovaniya*, 2, 1974, pp. 21–30.
Anokhina, L. A., and Shmeleva, M. N., *Kul'tura i byt kolkhoznikov Kalininskoi oblasti*, Moscow, 1964.
Argunov, I. A. and Isakova, N. V., 'O professional'noi orientatsii vypusknikov sel'skikh srednikh shkol', in *Sel'skaya molodezh' Yakutii*, Yakutsk, 1979, pp. 51–66.
Arutyunyan, Yu. V., *Mekhanizatory sel'skogo khozyaistva SSSR v 1929–1957gg.*, Moscow, 1960.
Opyt sotsiologicheskogo izucheniya sela, Moscow, 1968.
Sovetskoe krest'yanstvo v gody Velikoi Otechestvennoi voiny, Moscow, 1970.
Sotsial'naya struktura sel'skogo naseleniya SSSR, Moscow, 1971.
Arutyunyan, Yu. V. and Drobizheva, L. M., *Sel'skaya sotsiologiya i istoriografiya sovetskoi derevni*, Moscow, 1970.
Arutyunyan, Yu. V. and Kakhk, Yu., *Sotsiologicheskie ocherki o Sovetskoi Estonii*, Tallin, 1979.
Bairamsakhatov, N., 'Preodolenie perezhitkov islama v protsesse sotsialistich-eskogo preobrazovaniya byta sel'skogo naseleniya', candidate degree dissertation abstract, Moscow, 1968.
Bednyi, M. S., *Prodolzhitel'nost' zhizni v gorodakh i selakh*, Moscow, 1976.
Belikova, Z. F., 'Kharakter i usloviya agrarnogo truda i zakreplenie kadrov v sel'skom khozyaistve', in *Problemy derevni i goroda*, Tallin, 1979, Vol. II, pp. 78–82.
Belova, V. A., *Chislo detei v sem'e*, Moscow, 1975.
Belova, V. A. and Darskii, L. E., *Statistika mnenii v izuchenii rozhdaemosti*, Moscow, 1972.
Bilshai, V. L., *Reshenie zhenskogo voprosa v SSSR*, Moscow, 1956.
Boiko, V. V., *Malodetnaya sem'ya (sotsial'no-psikhologicheskoe issledovanie)*, Moscow, 1980.
Boikov, N. N., *Razlichiya mezhdu gorodom i derevnei*, Novosibirsk, 1969.

Bondarchik, V. I. (ed.), *Izmeneniya v bytu i kul'ture sel'skogo naseleniya Belorussii*, Minsk, 1976.

Borisova, L. G., 'Ustoichivost' uchitel' skikh kadrov sela', in T. I. Zaslavskaya and V. A. Kalmyk, *Sotsial'no-ekonomicheskoe razvitie sela i migratsiya naseleniya*, Novosibirsk, 1972, pp. 168–90.

Bovsh, V. I. and Laptenok, D. V. (eds.), *Sotsial'nye izmeneniya v sovremennom sele*, Minsk, 1978.

Buiko, N. A., *Novyi byt kolkhoznoi derevni*, Minsk, 1976.

Burova, S. N., *Sotsiologiya i pravo o razvode*, Minsk, 1979.

Chekotovskii, E. V., 'Statistiko-ekonomicheskoe izuchenie zhenskikh trudovykh resursov kolkhozov', candidate degree dissertation abstract, Kiev, 1973.

Chuiko, L. V., *Braki i razvody*, Moscow, 1975.

Chumakova, T. E., *Trud i byt zhenshchin*, Minsk, 1978.

Churakov, V. Ya., *Aktual'nye problemy ispol'zovaniya trudovykh resursov sela*, Moscow, 1972.

Deichman, I., *Sem'ya i semeinyi byt kolkhoznikov Pribaltiki*, Moscow, 1962.

Demograficheskie aspekty zanyatosti, Moscow, 1975.

Demograficheskie problemy sem'i, Moscow, 1978.

Demyakh, N. P., Grinberg, G. M. and Sapozhnikov, N. M., 'Proizvodstvennaya deyatel'nost' zhenshchin v sel'skom khozyaistve i sem'ya', in I. N. Lushchitskii (ed.), *Proizvodstvennaya deyatel'nost' zhenshchin i sem'ya*, Minsk, 1972, pp. 172–8.

Deputaty Verkhovnogo Soveta SSSR. Devyatyi sozyv, Moscow, 1974.

Deputaty Verkhovnogo Soveta SSSR. Desyatyi sozyv, Moscow, 1979.

Deshkov, S. I., *Sotsial'nye problemy sovetskoi derevni*, Moscow, 1972.

Dovnar-Zapol'skii, M. V., *Issledovaniya i stat'i*, Kiev, 1909, Vol. I.

Dulebo, A., *Izmenenie polozheniya belorusskoi zhenshchiny-krest'yanki za gody Sovetskoi vlasti*, Minsk, 1969.

XXV s'ezd Kommunisticheskoi partii Sovetskogo Soyuza. Stenograficheskii otchet, Moscow, 1976, Vol. II.

XXVI s'ezd Kommunisticheskoi partii Sovetskogo Soyuza. Stenograficheskii otchet, Moscow, 1981, Vol. III.

Erem'yan, L. A. and Martynova, V. N., 'Analiz sostava zhenshchin, zanyatykh v zhivotnovodstve sovkhozov (po materialam Novosibirskoi oblasti)', in Lushchitskii, pp. 192–5.

Ermolenkova, T. D., 'O 'zhenskikh' professiyakh', *Sel'skoe khozyaistvo Belorussii*, 6, 1972, pp. 42–3.

'Izmenenie sotsial'nogo polozheniya zhenshchiny-krest'yanki v protsesse stroitel'stva sotsializma', *Vestnik Belorusskogo Gosudarstvennogo universiteta imeni V. I. Lenina*, 3, no. 1, 1973, pp. 51–7.

'Preodolenie ostatkov bytovogo neravenstva zhenshchiny-kolkhoznitsy v protsesse stroitel'stva kommunizma', candidate degree dissertation abstract, Minsk, 1973.

Fedorova, M., 'Ispol'zovanie zhenskogo truda v sel'skom khozyaistve', *Voprosy ekonomiki*, 12, 1975, pp. 55–64.

Fenomenov, M. Ya., *Sovremennaya derevnya: opyt kraevedcheskogo obsledovaniya odnoi derevni*, Moscow–Leningrad, 1925.

Filyukova, L. F., *Sel'skaya sem'ya*, Minsk, 1976.

Frolov, N. P. (ed.), *Naselenie i trudovye resursy Moldavskoi SSR*, Kishinev, 1979.

Gadzhieva, S. Sh., *Sem'ya i semeinyi byt narodov Dagestana*, Makhachkala, 1967.

Gorbacheva, R. M., 'Formirovanie novykh chert byta kolkhoznogo krest'-yanstva', candidate degree dissertation abstract, Moscow, 1967.

Gordeeva, M., 'O nekotorykh osobennostyakh ispol'zovaniya zhenskogo truda v gorode i na sele', in *Lyudi v gorode i na sele*. *Sbornik statei*, Moscow, 1978, pp. 59–65.

Grebennikov, R. V., *Problemy kul'tury sovremennogo sela*, Minsk, 1973.

Grigorov, G. and Shkotov, S., *Staryi i novyi byt*, Moscow, 1927.

Ignatov, V. I. (ed.), *Opyt sotsial'no-ekonomicheskogo izucheniya professional'noi orientatsii sel'skoi molodezhi*, Rostov on Don, 1974.

Ivanova, R. K., *Sblizhenie sotsial'no-ekonomicheskikh uslovii zhizni trudyashchikhsya goroda i sela*, Moscow, 1980.

Izmenenie polozheniya zhenshchin i sem'ya, Moscow, 1977.

Kalygina, A. S., *Krest'yanka v brake i sem'e*, Moscow–Leningrad, 1926.

Zadachi partii v rabote sredi krest'yanok, Moscow–Leningrad, 1926.

Sovetskii sud i krest'yanka, Moscow–Leningrad, 1928.

Kartofyanu, M. D., *Novyi byt moldavskogo sela*, Kishinev, 1973.

Kas'yanov, N. R., 'Nravstvenno-psikhologicheskie osobennosti brachno-semeinykh otnoshenii krest'yanstva', *Uchenye zapiski Kurskogo pedagogicheskogo instituta*, 75, no. 1, 1971, pp. 122–34.

'Izmenenie semeino-brachnykh otnoshenii sovetskogo krest'yanstva', in Lushchitskii, pp. 179–84.

Kharchev, A. G., *Brak i sem'ya v SSSR*, 2nd edn, Moscow, 1979.

Kharchev, A. G. and Matskovskii, M. S., *Sovremennaya sem'ya i ee problemy*, Moscow, 1978.

Khomirzaev, Z., 'Razvitie sotsialisticheskogo obraza zhizni na sele v usloviyakh sovremennoi nauchno-tekhnicheskoi revolyutsii', candidate degree dissertation abstract, Tashkent, 1979.

Khorev, B. S. and Chapek V. N., *Problemy izucheniya migratsii naseleniya*, Moscow, 1978.

Kobetskii, V. D., *Sotsiologicheskoe izuchenie religioznosti i ateizma*, Leningrad, 1978.

Kolbanovskii, V. N. (ed.), *Kollektiv kolkhoznikov*, Moscow, 1970.

Kolokol'nikov, V. T. 'Marital and Family Relations among the Collective Farm Peasantry (Brest and Grodno Oblasts, Belorussia)', *Soviet Sociology*, Winter 1977–8, pp. 18–34.

Konstantinovskii, D. L., *Dinamika professional'nykh orientatsii molodezhi Sibiri*, Novosibirsk, 1977.

Korolev, Yu. A., *Brak i razvod: sovremennye tendentsii*, Moscow, 1978.

Krasnenkov, V. L., 'Nekotorye sotsial'no-gigienicheskie aspekty aborta sredi zhenshchin Kalininskoi oblasti', *Sovetskoe zdravookhranenie*, 5, 1973, pp. 20–4.

Krasnikov, N. R. (ed.), *Voprosy preodoleniya religioznykh perezhitkov v SSSR*, Moscow–Leningrad, 1966.

Krylov, A. M., Slutskii, A. I. and Khagurov, A. A., 'Analiz byudzheta vremeni kolkhoznikov i rabochikh sovkhoza kak sposob izucheniya sotsial'nykh problem upravleniya kolkhoznym kollektivom', *Nauchnye trudy Kubanskogo universiteta*, 205, 1976, pp. 141–66.

Kuda i zachem edut lyudi, Moscow, 1979.

Kudrina, T. A.,*Kul'tura sovremennoi derevni*, Moscow, 1980.

Kushner, P. I. (ed.), *Selo Viryatino v proshlom i nastoyashchem*, Moscow, 1958.

Kuznetsov, G. Ya., *Sotsial'no-ekonomicheskie problemy sovetskoi derevni*, Moscow, 1977.

Lagutin, N. S., *Sotsial'no-ekonomicheskoe polozhenie zhenshchin v SSSR*, Moscow, 1975.

Lakomova, N., 'Dolya ty zhenskaya', *Sel'skaya nov'*, 4, 1982, pp. 12–15.

Levykin, T., *Sel'skaya molodezh' – sotsiologicheskii ocherk*, Moscow, 1970.

Litvyakov, P. P. (ed.), *Demograficheskie problemy zanyatosti*, Moscow, 1969.

Logvinova, T. F., 'Sotsial'nye i sotsial'no-psikhologicheskie faktory razvitiya professional'noi orientatsii sel'skoi molodezhi', candidate degree dissertation, Moscow, 1976.

Losev, A. V. (ed.), *Sovetskaya derevnya na sovremennom etape*, Voronezh, 1974.

Lushchitskii, I. N. (ed.), *Proizvodstvennaya deyatel'nost' zhenshchin i sem'ya*, Minsk, 1972.

Lyashenko, L. P., 'Otnoshenie molodezhi k sel'skokhozyaistvennomu trudu', in Zaslavskaya and Kalmyk (1972), pp. 133–53.

Lyudi v gorode i na sele. Sbornik statei, Moscow, 1978.

Markov, A. I., 'Sotsial'no-gigienicheskie aspekty aborta zhenshchin v Tambovskom raione Amurskoi oblasti', *Sovetskoe zdravookhranenie*, 7, 1973, pp. 43–6.

Markova, G. G., 'Svobodnoe vremya i razvitie lichnosti zhenshchin-kolkhoznits na sovremennom etape stroitel'stva kommunizma', candidate degree dissertation, Rostov on Don, 1977.

Martynov, S. V., *Sovremennoe polozhenie russkoi derevni*, Saratov, 1903.

Molodaya sem'ya, Moscow, 1977.

Monich, Z. I., *Intelligentsiya v strukture sel'skogo naseleniya*, Minsk, 1971.

Monich, Z. I., Izokh, V. G. and Prudnik, I. V., *Rabochii klass v strukture sel'skogo naseleniya*, Minsk, 1975.

Muradov, Sh. M., 'Zhenskii trud i voprosy ego ratsional'nogo ispol'zovaniya v sel'skom khozyaistve Azerbaidzhanskoi SSR', candidate degree dissertation abstract, Baku, 1965.

Murin, V. A., *Byt i nravy derevenskoi molodezhi*, Moscow, 1926.

Murmantseva, V. S., *Sovetskie zhenshchiny v Velikoi Otechestvennoi voine*, Moscow, 1979.

Myl'nikova, M. A., *Zhenskie brigady na kolkhoznykh polyakh*, Moscow, 1932.

Nauchno-tekhnicheskii progress i sotsial'nye izmeneniya na sele, Minsk, 1972.

Novikov, G., *Zhenskii trud v kolkhozakh*, Leningrad, 1934.

Novikova, E. E., *Zhenshchina, trud, sem'ya*, Moscow, 1978.

Osipov, G. V. (ed.), *Town, Country and People*, London, 1969.

Ostapenko, L. V., 'The Effect of Woman's New Production Role on her Position in the Family', *Soviet Sociology*, 12, no. 4, Spring 1974, pp. 87–96.

Pankratova, M. G., *Sel'skaya sem'ya v SSSR i nekotorye problemy planirovaniya*, Moscow, 1970.

'Funktsii sem'i v ponimanii sovremennogo sel'skogo zhitelya', in Lushchitskii, pp. 185–91.

Sel'skaya sem'ya v SSSR – problemy i perspektivy, Moscow, 1974.

Patrushev, V. D. (ed.), *Byudzhet vremeni sel'skogo naseleniya*, Moscow, 1979.

Perevedentsev, V., *270 millionov*, Moscow, 1982.

Poletaev, V. E. (ed.), *Sotsial'nyi oblik kolkhoznoi molodezhi*, Moscow, 1976.

Problemy derevni i goroda, Tallin, 1979.

Problemy sotsial'nogo razvitiya derevni Sovetskoi Sibiri, Novosibirsk, 1979.

Protasevich, S. A., 'Nekotorye problemy ispol'zovaniya zhenskogo truda v sel'skom khozyaistve i ikh vliyanie na sem'yu', in Lushchitskii, pp. 167–71.

Rosnitskii, N., *Litso derevni*, Moscow–Leningrad, 1926.

Rusanov, N. P. (ed.), *Okhrana truda zhenshchin v sel'skom khozyaistve*, Orel, 1979.

Rybakovskii, L. L. and Churakov, V. Ya. (eds.), *Sotsial'nye faktory i osobennosti migratsii naseleniya SSSR*, Moscow, 1978.

Ryvkina, R. V., *Obraz zhizni sel'skogo naseleniya*, Novosibirsk, 1979.

Ryvkina, R. V. and Koryakina, I. M., 'Spetsifka trudovoi mobil'nosti i trudovoi kar'ery zhenshchin derevni (na primere Sibiri)', in T. I. Zaslavskaya and V. A. Kalmyk (eds.), *Sovremennaya sibirskaya derevnya: nekotorye problemy sotsial'nogo razvitiya*, Novosibirsk, 1975, pp. 77–92.

Sadvokasova, E. A., *Sotsial'no-gigienicheskie aspekty regulirovaniya razmerov sem'i*, Moscow, 1969.

Sal'nikova, I. M., 'Sel'skie zhenshchiny kak sotsial'no-demograficheskaya gruppa', in *Sotsial'naya struktura sel'skogo naseleniya*, Moscow, 1976, pp. 143–54.

Sapozhnikov, N. M., 'Selo segodnya: demograficheskie protsessy, resursy truda, kadry', unpublished typescript, Saratov, 1978.

Sel'skaya intelligentsiya i ee rol' v usloviyakh razvitogo sotsializma, Moscow, 1979.

Sel'skaya molodezh' Yakutii, Yakutsk, 1979.

Semenova-Tyan-Shanskaya, O. P., *Zhizn' 'Ivana', Zapiski Imperskogo RGO po otdeleniyu etnografii*, St Petersburg, 1914, Vol. xxxix.

Sem'ya segodnya, Moscow, 1979.

Serebryakov, Yu. G., *Kul'tura i byt sovremennoi derevni*, Cheboksary, 1977.

Shelest, P. S., *Odna sel'skaya sem'ya – shtrikhi k sotsial'nomu portretu sel'skogo rabochego 70-kh gg.*, Moscow, 1972.

Shenderetska, A., 'Uchitel'skaya sem'ya (sotsial'no-demograficheskii analiz)', in *Sem'ya segodnya*, pp. 74–84.

Sheptulina, N. N., *Pravovoe regulirovanie uslovii truda zhenshchin*, Moscow, 1978.

Shishkan, N. M., 'Sotsial'no-ekonomicheskie problemy zhenskogo truda v usloviyakh razvitogo sotsializma', doctoral degree dissertation abstract, Moscow, 1978.

Sotsial'no-ekonomicheskie problemy zhenskogo truda, Moscow, 1980.

Shlapak, N. A., 'Zhiznennye plany sel'skoi molodezhi i ikh realizatsiya', candidate degree dissertation abstract, Sverdlovsk, 1967.

Shtyuka, V. G., *Sotsial'nye problemy sel'skogo byta v Moldavii*, Kishinev, 1971.

Shukurova, Khudzhume, *Sotsializm i zhenshchina Uzbekistana*, Tashkent, 1970.

Shurygina, V. D., 'Sotsial'no-ekonomicheskie problemy zhenskogo truda v sel'skom khozyaistve SSSR', candidate degree dissertation abstract, Leningrad, 1973.

Shuvaev, K. M., *Staraya i novaya derevnya*, Moscow, 1937.

Slepenkov, I. M., *Nauchno-tekhnicheskii progress i osobennosti truda sel'skoi molodezhi*, Moscow, 1974.

Slepenkov, I. M. and Knyazev, B. V., *Rural Youth Today*, Newtonville, 1977.

Snesarev, G. P. (ed.), *Sem'ya i semeinye obryady u narodov srednei Azii i Kazakhstana*, Moscow, 1978.

Sotsial'naya struktura sel'skogo naseleniya, Moscow, 1976.

Sotsial'no-demograficheskie issledovaniya sem'i v respublikakh Sovetskoi Pribaltiki, Riga, 1980.

Sovetskaya derevnya v pervye poslevoennye gody 1946–50gg., Moscow, 1978.

Sovremennaya kul'tura i byt narodov Dagestana, Moscow, 1971.

Sputnik organizatora krest'yanok, 2nd edn, Moscow, 1927.

Staroverov, V. I., *Gorod ili derevnya*, Moscow, 1972.

Sotsial'naya struktura sel'skogo naseleniya SSSR na etape razvitogo sotsializma, Moscow, 1978.

Staroverov, V. I., Timush, A. I. and Tsurkanu, N. V., *Derevnya v usloviyakh integratsii. Sotsial'nye problemy*, Moscow, 1979.

Strumilin, S. G., *Problemy ekonomiki truda*, Moscow, 1957.

Sultanova, B. S., 'Voprosy uluchsheniya ispol'zovaniya zhenskogo truda v kolkhozakh Yuga Kirgizii', candidate degree dissertation, Tashkent, 1972.

Taborisskaya, I. M., *Mayatnikovaya migratsiya naseleniya*, Moscow, 1979.

Tan-Bogoraz, V. G. (ed.), *Revolyutsiya v derevne*, Moscow–Leningrad, 1924.

Staryi i novyi byt, Leningrad, 1924.

Tarasov, Yu. N. (ed.), *Professional'naya orientatsiya sel'skoi molodezhi*, Moscow, 1973.

Tatybekova, Zh. S., *Raskreposhchenie zhenshchiny-kirgizki Velikoi Oktyabrskoi sotsialisticheskoi revolyutsiei (1917–1936gg.)*, Frunze, 1963.

Uchastie zhenshchin Kirgizii v stroitel'stve sotsializma (1938–1958gg.). Sbornik dokumentov i materialov, Frunze, 1976.

Timchenko, I. P., *Zhenshchina, religiya, ateizm*, Kiev, 1981.

Tomskii, I. E., *Sotsial'no-ekonomicheskie problemy zhenskogo truda*, Novosibirsk, 1979.

Tonaevskaya, N. S., *Rabochie sovkhozov Zapadnoi Sibiri*, Novosibirsk, 1978.

Trud zhenshchin i sem'ya, Tallin, 1978.

Ubaidullaeva, R. A., *Zhenskii trud v sel'skom khozyaistve Uzbekistana*, Tashkent, 1969.

Ugryumov, B., *Kolkhoznyi byt*, Voronezh, 1934.

Vagabov, M. V., 'Perezhitki islama v otnoshenii k zhenshchine i puti ikh preodoleniya', in Krasnikov, pp. 129–41.

Vasileva, G. P., *Etnograficheskii ocherk uzbekskogo sel'skogo naseleniya*, Moscow, 1969.

Vinnikov, Ya. P., *Khozyaistvo, kul'tura i byt sel'skogo·naseleniya Turkmenskoi SSR*, Moscow, 1969.

Vishnevskii, A. G. (ed.), *Brachnost', rozhdaemost', smertnost' v Rossii i v SSSR*, Moscow, 1977.

Volfson, S. Ya., *Sotsiologiya braka i sem'i*, Minsk, 1929.

Volkov, A. G., 'Sem'ya kak faktor izmeneniya demograficheskoi situatsii', *Sotsiologicheskie issledovaniya*, 1, 1981, pp. 34–42.

(ed.), *Demograficheskoe razvitie sem'i*, Moscow, 1979.

Volynkina, L. M., 'Ispol'zovanie zhenskogo truda v kolkhozakh Kostromskoi oblasti', candidate degree dissertation, Moscow, 1976.

Yankova, Z. A. and Shapiro, V. D. (eds.), *Vzaimootnoshenie pokolenii v sem'e*, Moscow, 1977.

Yurkevich, N. G., *Sovetskaya sem'ya*, Minsk, 1970.

Zagrebel'nyi, V. P., 'Formirovanie otnoshenii sotsial'nogo ravenstva zhenshchin i muzhchin-kolkoznikov v usloviyakh razvitogo sotsializma', candidate degree dissertation, Kiev, 1977.

Zaslavskaya, T. I. and Kalmyk, V. A., *Sotsial'no-ekonomicheskoe razvitie sela i migratsiya naseleniya*, Novosibirsk, 1972.

(eds.), *Sovremennaya sibirskaya derevnya: nekotorye problemy sotsial'nogo razvitiya*, Novosibirsk, 1975.

(eds.), *Sibirskaya derevnya v usloviyakh urbanizatsii*, Novosibirsk, 1976.

Zaslavskaya, T. I. and Khakhulina, L. A. (eds.), *Puti sotsial'nogo razvitiya derevni*, Novosibirsk, 1978.

Zaslavskaya, T. I. and Muchnik, I. B., *Sotsial'no-demograficheskoe razvitie sela. Regional'nyi analiz*, Moscow, 1980.

Zhelezovskaya, V. M., 'Nekotorye izmeneniya v polozhenii zhenshchin-kolkhoznits v protsesse preodoleniya kul'turno-bytovykh razlichii mezhdu gorodom i derevnei', *Nauchnye trudy Kubanskogo universiteta*, 167, 1973, pp. 141–53.

Zhenshchiny-mekhanizatory (ocherki o zhenshchinakh udostoennykh v 1977 godu priza imeni Pashi Angelinoi), Moscow, 1979.

Zhenshchiny na rabote i doma, Moscow, 1978.

Zhilkin, E. S., *Bor'ba perezhitkami starogo v soznanii lyudei*, Yaroslavl', 1973.

Zhil'tsov, P. A., *Vospitatel'naya rabota v sel'skoi shkole*, Moscow, 1980.

Zinchenko, L. P., 'Rol' komsomola, sovetskoi molodezhi v formirovanii novogo byta na sele', candidate degree dissertation abstract, Minsk, 1978.

Zorin, V. I., *Sel'skokhozyaistvennyi rabochii klass Kazakhstana*, Alma–Ata, 1972.

Zotov, A. Ya., 'Ispol'zovanie truda zhenshchin v kolkhozakh BSSR', in Lushchitskii, pp. 159–66.

STATISTICAL SOURCES

Chislennost' i sostav naseleniya SSSR po dannym Vsesoyuznoi perepisi naseleniya 1979 goda, Moscow, 1984.

Itogi vsesoyuznoi perepisi naseleniya 1959 goda. SSSR (svodnyi tom), Moscow, 1962.

Itogi vsesoyuznoi perepisi naseleniya 1970 goda, Moscow, 1972–4.

Narodnoe khozyaistvo SSSR (statisticheskii ezhegodnik), Moscow, various years.

Narodnoe obrazovanie, nauka i kul'tura v SSSR, Moscow, 1977.

Sel'skoe khozyaistvo SSSR, Moscow, 1971.

Vestnik statistiki (Vsesoyuznaya perepis' naseleniya), 1980–2, various issues.

Zhenshchina v SSSR, Moscow, 1937, 1980.

Zhenshchiny i deti v SSSR, Moscow, 1963.

Zhenshchiny v SSSR, Moscow, 1975.

SOVIET NEWSPAPERS AND JOURNALS

Krest'yanka
Literaturnaya gazeta
Rabotnitsa i syalyanka
Sel'skaya nov'
Sel'skaya zhizn'
Sotsiologicheskie issledovaniya

WESTERN WORKS ON THE SOVIET UNION

Allott, Susan, 'Soviet Rural Women: Employment and Family Life', in Barbara Holland (ed.), *Soviet Sisterhood*, London, 1985, pp. 179–206.

'Women in the Soviet Countryside', unpublished PhD thesis, University of Bradford, 1984.

Amalrik, Guzel, *Memories of a Tatar Childhood*, London, 1979.

Atkinson, Dorothy, Dallin, Alexander and Lapidus, Gail (eds.), *Women in Russia*, Hassocks, Sussex, 1978.

Brine, Jenny, Perrie, Maureen and Sutton, Andrew (eds.), *Home, School and Leisure in the Soviet Union*, London, 1980.

Conquest, Robert (ed.), *Agricultural Workers in the USSR*, London, 1968.

Cox, Terence M., *Rural Sociology in the Soviet Union: Its History and Basic Concepts*, London, 1979.

Dewdney, John C., *A Geography of the Soviet Union*, Oxford, 1979.

Dodge, Norton T., *Women in the Soviet Economy: Their Role in Economic, Scientific and Technical Development*, Baltimore, 1966.

Dodge, Norton T. and Feshbach, Murray, 'The Role of Women in Soviet Agriculture', in J. F. Karcz, *Soviet and East European Agriculture*, Berkeley and Los Angeles, 1967, pp. 265–98.

Dunn, Stephen P. and Dunn, Ethel, *The Peasants of Central Russia*, New York, 1967.

The Study of the Soviet Family in the USSR and the West, Slavic Studies Working Paper 1, Columbus, 1977.

Elnett, Elaine, *Historic Origin and Social Development of Family Life in Russia*, New York, 1926.

Fainsod, Merle, *Smolensk under Soviet Rule*, London, 1958.

Fitzpatrick, Sheila, *Education and Social Mobility in the Soviet Union 1921–1934*, Cambridge, 1979.

Geiger, H. Kent, *The Family in Soviet Russia*, Cambridge, Mass., 1970.

Gill, Graeme J., *Peasants and Government in the Russian Revolution*, London, 1979.

Hedlund, Stefan, *Crisis in Soviet Agriculture*, Beckenham, 1984.

Heitlinger, Alena, *Women and State Socialism: Sex Inequality in the Soviet Union and Czechoslovakia*, London, 1979.

Holland, Barbara (ed.), *Soviet Sisterhood*, London, 1985.

Jacoby, Susan, *Inside Soviet Schools*, New York, 1974.

Khan, Azizur Rahman and Ghai, Dharam, *Collective Agriculture and Rural Development in Soviet Central Asia*, London, 1979.

Laird, Roy D. (ed.), *Soviet Agricultural and Peasant Affairs*, Lawrence, 1963.

Lane, Christel, *Christian Religion in the Soviet Union*, London, 1978.

The Rites of Rulers, Cambridge, 1981.

Lapidus, Gail Warshofsky, *Women in Soviet Society: Equality, Development and Social Change*, London, 1978.

Lewin, M., *Russian Peasants and Soviet Power*, London 1968.

McAndrew, Maggie and Peers, Jo, *The New Soviet Woman: Model or Myth?*, London, 1981.

McAuley, Alastair, *Women's Work and Wages in the Soviet Union*, London, 1981.

Male, D. J., *Russian Peasant Organisation before Collectivisation: A Study of Commune and Gathering 1925–1930*, Cambridge, 1971.

Massell, Gregory J., *The Surrogate Proletariat: Moslem Women and Revolutionary Strategies in Central Asia 1919–1929*, Princeton, 1974.

Matthew, Mervyn, *Class and Society in Soviet Russia*, London, 1972.

Maynard, John, *The Russian Peasant and Other Studies*, London, 1942.

Millar, James R. (ed.), *The Soviet Rural Community*, Urbana, 1971.

Powell, David E., *Antireligious Propaganda in the Soviet Union: A Study of Mass Persuasion*, Cambridge, Mass., 1975.

Ransel, David L. (ed.), *The Family in Imperial Russia*, Urbana, 1978.

Robinson, G. T., *Rural Russia under the Old Regime*, New York, 1932.

Ryan, Michael, *The Organisation of Soviet Medical Care*, London, 1978.

Sacks, Michael Paul, *Women's Work in Soviet Russia*, New York, 1976.

Schlesinger, Rudolf, *Changing Attitudes in Soviet Russia: The Family in the USSR*, London, 1949.

The Nationalities Problem and Soviet Administration, London, 1956.

Shanin, Teodor, *The Awkward Class: Political Sociology of Peasantry in a Developing Society, Russia, 1910–1925*, Oxford, 1972.

Smith, Jessica, *Women in Soviet Russia*, New York, 1928.

Smith, R. E. F. (ed.), *The Russian Peasant 1920 and 1984*, London, 1977.

Stites, Richard, *The Women's Liberation Movement in Russia: Feminism, Nihilism and Bolshevism, 1860–1930*, Princeton, 1978.

Strauss, Erich, *Soviet Agriculture in Perspective*, London, 1969.

Vucinich, Wayne S. (ed.), *The Peasant in Nineteenth-Century Russia*, Stanford, 1968.

Wadekin, Karl-Eugen, *The Private Sector in Soviet Agriculture*, Berkeley, 1973.

Wheeler, Geoffrey, *The Peoples of Soviet Central Asia*, London, 1966.

Index